2206

Human Well-being

CHALLENGES FOR THE 1980s
SOCIAL, ECONOMIC, AND
POLITICAL ACTION

Proceedings of the XIXth International
Conference on Social Welfare
Jerusalem, Israel
August 18–24, 1978

Published 1979
for the International Council on Social Welfare
by Columbia University Press
NEW YORK AND LONDON

Library of Congress Cataloging in Publication Data

International Conference on Social Welfare, 19th, Jerusalem, 1978.
Human well-being.

Includes bibliographical references.
1. Social service—Congresses. I. International
Council on Social Welfare. II. Title.
HV8.I56   1978   361   79-16655
ISBN 0-231-04854-8

Columbia University Press
New York   Guildford, Surrey

Preface

THE JUBILEE Conference of the ICSW, in celebrating fifty years of work and achievement, inevitably sought to strengthen the capacity of the organization to function and contribute yet more effectively in the decade to come. The biennial ICSW conference has facilitated the meeting of professional workers of different disciplines in the social field. They range from top governmental and agency planners to village community workers from every corner of the world. The opportunity afforded for mutual exchange of know-how and experience has invariably proved both stimulating and constructive.

The pre-conference evaluation and study of the conference themes, on both national and regional levels, provided background material for conference discussions. Consideration of national and regional reports at pre-conference working parties was, on this occasion, replaced by the nomination of a world rapporteur, Robert A. B. Leaper, C.B.E., who wrote a "world report" based on this material, which also included answers to a comprehensive questionnaire prepared by K. E. de Graft-Johnson.

The experience of previous years had also indicated the need to broaden the base of participation at the conference. A new organizational structure was, therefore, introduced based on four identical miniconferences or sections, with delegates joining round-table discussion groups, generally on subjects related to their own professional competence and experience.

The theme of the conference—"Human Well-being—Challenges for the 80's—Social, Economic, and Political Action"—was broad and all-encompassing to enable, on this occasion, more general evaluation of past experience projected to the needs of the future. For many years the importance of integration throughout the policy-making process had been emphasized, the inevitable interrelationship of social, political, and economic factors. Furthermore, there was reiterated concern for the difficulties encountered in implementation and in the delivery of comprehensive services, which could not be attained at a satisfactory level. The tremendous changes that had occurred and were taking place in the economic and social realities of most societies also indicated an urgent need for innovative approaches.

It was felt, therefore, that rather than rely primarily on papers presented by distinguished authorities, this special Jubilee conference, in addition to hearing from experts, should take more advantage of the accumulated experience of the working members of the many disciplines represented, in a more intense and concentrated exchange of views. It was important to achieve greater understanding of the trends of change and the many constraints influencing the policy-making processes as viewed from as many different angles as possible. Maximum input of experience and know-how was also desirable in the search for ways to provide more adequate services with limited and scarce resources.

The breakdown of the subjects along horizontal and vertical lines (see chart), the daily speakers, and the input of both section and focus rapporteurs were expected to bring together the main direction of thinking and recommendations. The appointment of the conference rapporteur, David Scott, ensured a comprehensive conference round-up which, in addition to dealing with substance, highlighted the advantages and problems of this new organizational set-up. On-the-spot evaluations and the comments of the ombudsman, James Dumpson, who monitored the meetings, have been invaluable.

The general consensus favors the new scheme precisely because it enables all participants to be more actively involved. It represents a process of democratization and more interchange among the various aspects and levels of work both in administration and in the field which too frequently remain mutually exclusive in practice. However, modifications will be needed as a result of the conference experience, particularly with regard to more movement between the different discussion groups, better utilization and preparation of expert papers, and more plenaries of the whole at which outstanding authorities can be heard. It will be necessary to ensure the preparation of na-

All Sections

	MONDAY	TUESDAY	WEDNESDAY	THURSDAY
SUGGESTED FOCUS	PHYSIOLOG-ICAL AND MATERIAL NEEDS	ECONOMIC AND SECURITY NEEDS	EDUCATION, CULTURE, VALUES, AND COMMUNI-CATION	HUMAN RELATION-SHIPS: INDIVIDUAL, FAMILY, COMMUNITY
	(HEALTH, FOOD, SHELTER, WATER, ECOLOGY)	(WORK, INCOME, SOCIAL SECURITY, TAXATION, ECONOMIC GROWTH COSTS)	(COGNITIVE AND SKILLS DEVEL-OPMENT, AESTHETICS, RECREATION, THE MEDIA)	(COMMUNITY DEVELOPMENT, SEX ROLES, PLANNED PARENT-HOOD)

Policy Development and Planning

Targets
Approaches and tech-
   niques
Administration and fi-
   nance
Individual and collec-
   tive well-being

| The Child | Youth | The Middle Years | The Older Years | The Disabled (Physical and Mental) | Social Deviants (Drugs and Crime) | Dis-placed Persons (Refu-gees and Mi-grants) | Volun-teer Roles |

Implementation and Serv-ice Delivery

Manpower competence
   and deployment
Organizations
Bureaucracy
Selective and universal
   services

| The Child | Youth | The Middle Years | The Older Years | The Disabled (Physical and Mental) | Social Deviants (Drugs and Crime) | Dis-placed Persons (Refu-gees and Mi-grants) | Volun-teer Roles |

Research and Evaluation

Fact-finding and fore-
   casting
Social indicators
Uses and abuses of
   evaluation

Research   Research   Research

Regional and International Action

Treaties and agree-
   ments
Multi- and bilateral aid
Role of NGOs
Exchange of informa-
   tion

International Cooperation   International Cooperation   International Cooperation

tional and regional reports according to strict time schedules to enable the compilation of the world report in time to serve the needs of prospective conference key persons. In preparation for their respective roles they may well require more guidance and orientation, particularly with regard to the conference theme.

Large international conferences are rarely able to achieve consideration of the subject matter in depth, since they are generally of short duration and, by their nature, unwieldy. Their greatest value lies in their capacity to assemble persons of like professional pursuits who, as a result of new contacts, are stimulated to improve their own performance and increase the scope of their knowledge. Learned papers are valuable even though much of their content is usually available in the professional literature, but it is the give-and-take of debate, the personal interchange with persons of diverse backgrounds, cultures, political, economic, and social realities, which provides the most profound experience and has the most lasting impact.

It is hoped that by facilitating more dialogue in smaller units, this conference may have introduced a more effective technique and methodology for increasing individual satisfaction, which can only redound to the benefit of social welfare goals and achievements on both the national and the international scene.

Thanks are due to members of the Program Committee for their contributions, which led to the development of the new conference format, and to the cooperation of the secretariat and regional offices for their encouragement and assistance.

ZENA HARMAN
Chairman, International
Program Committee

Foreword

THE THEME of the XIXth International Conference on Social Welfare, "Human Well-being—Challenges for the 80's—Social, Economic, and Political Action," is of special significance not only for the International Council on Social Welfare, but also for all those concerned with human well-being who are involved in activities aiming toward an amelioration of the human condition.

This world-wide gathering was being held while ICSW celebrated its fiftieth anniversary. Fifty years of endeavor toward the improvement of conditions of those who have not been able to benefit from and enjoy the things in life that are due them. Fifty years of earnest, though not always successful, attempts to discover ways and means to penetrate the jungle of poverty, ill-health, lack of education and housing, and other deprivations. Fifty years of world-wide gatherings of men and women of good will with considerable knowledge and experience.

In 1928, in concert with a number of other international organizations that shared an interest in social work, a "Social Work Fortnight" was held in Paris. The first ICSW president was Alice Masarykova, and the first secretary-general was René Sand. In 1932 the theme of the IId Conference was "Social Science and the Family."

As it should be in an ever-changing world, the focus of concern has changed as the years have gone by. Not so many conferences ago, the discussions were centered on topics like "rural development," "urbanization," and so on. Single, concrete issues were reviewed, mainly by social work professionals. Eventually, the conference papers and the participants dealt with "social welfare" and "social development" and ceased to concentrate on the involvement of one specific profession.

"New Strategies for Social Development" was the theme of

the XVth International Conference, 1970 (Philippines). The theme of the XVIth International Conference, 1972 (Netherlands) was the natural next step: "Developing Social Policy in Conditions of Rapid Change." No more static concepts; recognition was given to the need to develop and adjust policy to rapid changes.

The XVIIth Conference, 1974 (Kenya) represented a milestone: "Development and Participation—Operational Implications for Social Welfare." For the first time, the theme and, of course, the discussions reflected the recognition of the necessity to have people participate in development, to involve them actively in the shaping of their own destiny. Reuben C. Baetz, then president of ICSW, wrote in the foreword of the proceedings: "Development, as we were reminded again and again at the Conference, is an unfolding of the future—it is dynamic, not static."

In 1976, the XVIIIth Conference (Puerto Rico) went a step further, when it recognized that people may have to struggle for their opportunities and that social welfare may become much more active than in the past. The theme, "The Struggle for Equal Opportunity—Strategies for Social Welfare Action," left no doubt that strategies and programs have to be geared toward equal opportunity and that social welfare needs to develop strategies for action if it is intended to remain involved in the welfare of people.

No better choice could have been made by the conference planners when it was decided to treat "Human Well-being" at the XIXth International Conference, 1978 (Israel) and to envisage the social, economic, and political action needed for the 1980s to enable humanity to live in a better world. President Lucien Mehl wrote in his preamble to the Conference Program: "The subject is especially acute because of the growing concern with the human environment, the protection of nature, a more beneficial distribution of activities in space and time, greater self-fulfillment for the individual and the development of a new international economic order."

The sequence of topics treated during the conference shows clearly the first concern with physical and material needs, then economic and security needs, followed by education, culture, values, and communication, and, finally, human relationships, individual—family—community. Underlying these progressive steps, however, is the well-accepted fact that people themselves must participate in shaping their destiny, in attaining their aims. If this, our Fiftieth Anniversary Conference has contributed ideas and ways toward these goals, ICSW has acquitted itself nobly of the task it has set for itself.

Those of us who were involved in this conference believe that this event crowned our fifty-year history aptly and constitutes a challenging beginning of the next half century of ICSW.

KATE KATZKI
Outgoing Secretary-General

Contents

Preface   *Zena Harman*   v

Foreword   *Kate Katzki*   ix

Basic Working Document for the Conference   *Robert A. B.*
Leaper, C.B.E.   1

Well-being: a Concept of Social Science and an Objective of
Social Policy   *Lucien Mehl*   28

Physiological and Material Needs

Part	I.	*Robert A. Derzon*	45
Part	II.	*Charles A. Egger*	53
Part	III.	*Antonio Garcia Lizana*	62
Part	IV.	*Kim Hak Mook*	73
Part	V.	*Bruce Rawson*	79
Part	VI.	*Gunter Witzsch*	87

Economic and Security Needs

Part	I.	*Victor I. A. Barrett*	94
Part	II.	*Ahmed Fattahipour*	97
Part	III.	*Melvin A. Glasser*	105
Part	IV.	*David S. Hurwitz*	112
Part	V.	*Philip A. Idenburg*	121
Part	VI.	*Moacyr Velloso Caraoso de Oliveira*	129
Part	VII.	*Robert Verger*	131

Education, Culture, Values, and Communication

Part	I.	*Werner W. Boehm*	138
Part	II.	*Otto H. Driedger*	143
Part	III.	*K. E. de Graft-Johnson*	154
Part	IV.	*Olavi Riihinen*	164

Human Relationships: Individual, Family, and Community

Part	I.	*Anne Kohn-Feuermann*	169
Part	II.	*Sanford Kravitz*	177
Part	III.	*Peter Kuenstler*	194
Part	IV.	*Catherine McGuinness*	199
Part	V.	*Rosa Perla Resnick*	204
Part	VI.	*Georgette St-Arnaud*	207

The René Sand Award

Presentation to the United Nations Children's Fund   *Lucien*
Mehl   216

Acceptance   *Charles A. Egger*   218
The UNICEF Experience from Programs for Children—and
   Needs for the Future   223
Remarks by the Outgoing Secretary-General   *Kate Katzki*   241
Remarks by the Incoming Secretary-General   *Ingrid Gelinek*   245
Summary and Review of the XIXth International Conference
   on Social Welfare   *David H. F. Scott*   247

APPENDIX

Executive Committee   265
Israel Organizing Committee   266
Program Committee   267
Section Chairmen and Rapporteurs   268
International Staff   268

Human Well-being

Challenges for the 1980s
Social, Economic, and Political Action

Basic Working Document for the Conference

ROBERT A. B. LEAPER, C.B.E.

PROFESSOR, UNIVERSITY OF EXETER, UNITED KINGDOM; VICE-
PRESIDENT, INTERNATIONAL COUNCIL ON SOCIAL WELFARE

THE PROGRAM Committee for the 1978 conference, under the chairmanship of Zena Harman, resolved on new methods of working, one of which was to be the production of a "world report" based on responses to a questionnaire and guidelines sent out through regional offices to all national committees of the ICSW. The committees were thus invited not just to respond to a program prepared for them by a small group, but to participate from the outset in setting the framework of their own agenda. K. E. de Graft-Johnson, of Ghana, prepared a questionnaire to obtain basic social statistical data and general information from each national committee. The timetable for the whole operation was accepted by the Executive Committee of the ICSW in Frascati in 1977, and the questionnaires were sent out as agreed. Each region was to appoint a regional rapporteur who would synthesize the replies from each committee and forward them to me as world rapporteur.

Unfortunately, the agreed timetable has not been adhered to, and both the quality and the quantity of responses from national committees have varied considerably. With the exception of those from Europe, all regional reports have arrived very much later than the deadline and from the African region there has been no response at all. Of necessity, therefore, this basic document was compiled from material whose coverage is incomplete and the quality of whose data varies. Inevitably, there are more questions than conclusions in this document.

We are all grateful to the regional rapporteurs for their careful preparatory work: Hans F. Zacher, of the Federal Republic of Germany, for Europe and the Mediterranean; John F. Jones, of Hong Kong, for Asia and the Pacific; James R. Dumpson, of the United States, for North America; and Felicidad R. Catala, of Puerto Rico, for Latin America and the Caribbean.

I have drawn upon the substance of their work and have also referred to the social and economic reports of such bodies as the United Nations, the Organization for Economic Cooperation and Development (OECD), the European Community, the Council of Europe, the Food and Agriculture Organization, as well as the international and regional reports and publications of the ICSW itself, and of the International Association of Schools of Social Work (IASSW).

The national committees that responded to the invitation to help in the compilation of regional reports are:

1. Europe and the Mediterranean: Austria, Belgium, the Federal Republic of Germany, Finland, France, Israel, Italy, the Netherlands, and the United Kingdom
2. Asia and the Pacific: synthesis prepared from reports from committees in the region
3. North America: Canada and the United States
4. Latin America and the Caribbean: Chile, Jamaica, Mexico, Panama, Peru, and Puerto Rico.

This working document projects its assumptions and its information into the 1980s, cooperating with others in outlining your preferences and aspirations for the 1980s, and indicating where individuals, groups, governments—and the ICSW itself—should place their priorities in the years immediately ahead.

HUMAN WELL-BEING

The tendency to choose global themes for international conferences is excusable, perhaps inevitable. It has advantages: it enables an all-around exploration from which people of different regions, cultures, and philosophies can derive some benefit both in reassessment and in further development of thought and action. It has disadvantages: real variations both in thought and practice can be masked by noble rhetoric, by the assertion of aspirations and grand declarations to which no one can take exception and from which little of practical use can be drawn in the face of hard practical daily work after one's return from the heady experience of international meetings.

To consider seriously what forms of social, economic, and political action contribute most to human well-being demands a clarity and unanimity of ultimate and of short-term objectives, and a choice of priorities, about which a general consensus is not yet evident. It is not surprising, therefore, that few national committee responses attempt to analyze the elements of "well-being" and that there is little explicit reference in them to recent writings which have called in question the general direction of human societies of various ideological positions, which place high priority on the increase and wider distribution of material goods of all kinds.

The Asian and Pacific report does refer to such fundamental questions in a brief consideration of Ivan D. Illich's well-known arguments. This regional report also comments:

> The concept of well-being in Asia and the Pacific differs not at all from the idea of social progress shared by the rest of the world in that it is based on the common needs of people for food, shelter and liberty. . . . but it has a conscious emphasis on social development—the integration of social, economic, and political progress.

The Latin American report makes a brief reference to the deeply felt need to balance material progress with the more real achievement of personal and political freedom and self-determination, while the North American report refers to the as yet unmet aspirations for equality of opportunity and for "the acceptance of difference in life styles as well as the concept of human equality." In the European regional report two ideological emphases are implicit: a commitment, at least in name, to a more equal distribution of wealth and income and a concern for a greater democratization of decision-making and of real participation in social and economic action.

It may, of course, be argued that the tendency to philosophize about the ultimate end of human well-being was always more attractive to Greek aristocrats than to Greek slaves and that today the cult of simplicity is more appealing to those in, for example, Northern Europe and North America who have access to high material standards than to masses in Asia and Latin America who struggle to achieve minimum health, food, and shelter. However, it would be wise for any conference participant who is invited to commit himself to human well-being, and to action to achieve it in the 1980s, to pause to discuss the real concepts behind the rhetoric before passing on to the complex questions of instrumentality. In what consists "human well-being?" If it is a social and not an individual concept (unlike human "happiness"?) can we reach sufficient general consensus about its components to ensure that the "social, economic, and political action" we take is tending toward a common goal?

THE DEMOGRAPHIC BASE

Let us start with birth and with death. The European regional report is cautious about making generalizations or discerning trends since the evidence varies from one country to another, but it is clear that the birth rate generally has declined, and certainly the average family size has been reduced, but "attitudes in regard to family planning and natural population growth are as equally varied as the extent of emigration and immigration." Longevity has increased, more markedly among females, with the inevitable problems of dependency. Clearly, trends in migration affect population density and distribution within a nation-state and between nation-states to an increasing extent.

In North America we have a not dissimilar picture with notably wide disparities in population densities between regions. Canada is a classic example of high concentration in, proportionately, a very small total land surface, due to reasons of both climate and economic development. The projections for North American life expectancy in the 1980s are higher than elsewhere, except for a few European countries, and the regional rapporteur comments that "the challenges for the requisites for human well-being for populations that are predominately very young and progressively aging must be apparent."

A different picture emerged from the Asian and Latin American reports. In the latter there is concern at the consequences of very rapid population growth, the decline in the birth rate being insignificant compared with the reduction in the death rate. There is great contrast in population distribution between urban and rural areas, with the rural exodus being followed by poverty belts around the cities. There is very high population concentration in islands like Jamaica and Puerto Rico which, though not more so than the Netherlands, for example, lack the advanced technological development to sustain the population. Faced with inexorable population growth, and currently a reduction in possibilities of out-migration programs of birth control (and of care for the aged) have taken on a new urgency. The Asian report is even more minatory on this topic: "uncontrolled population growth unmatched by production increase spells inevitable poverty." Indonesia, Iran, Pakistan, the Philippines, and Thailand expect their population to double in the next twenty-five years, and almost the same growth may be expected, if present trends continue, in eight other countries of the region. This means that only the countries with the highest income per capita have stable or moderately increasing populations—a trend shared with similar countries in Europe and North America.

It is, of course, necessary to make a more sophisticated analysis of population data than is possible here. Moreover, there can be quite sudden changes in trends, which confound demographic projections. The changes in social mores evident in some regions, the legalization or greater prevalence of abortion as well as birth prevention—all these social trends are noted in national reports, as in the UN and other world reports—and their precise outcomes are not yet clear. But the relationship of people to living space, of dependent humans to productive workers, is certainly not yet in balance, either within countries or between regions of the world. Moreover, there are wide variations within nation-states, both regionally and between ethnic and religious groups. The consequences are seen not only in terms of family planning and manpower distribution, for example, but in terms of family relationships, the comparative status of women and men, the responsibility for, and the provision of, care of children and elderly people. These will be spelled out in relation to services and provisions, but fundamental ethical and human relationship questions must be discussed: medical care has intervened universally to change the balance of life and death—what further social interventions must follow?

FAMILY AND SOCIETY

The family and its evolution in modern industrial society have been the subject of many sociological studies in the past ten years, and the diagnoses of its situation have ranged from the "death of the family" school to those who point to its apparent resilience in greatly changed social, moral, and economic environments. Alternative models of basic structure have also been the subject of study—communes, extended family networks, kibbutzim. Traditional roles of men and women have been called in question not merely in long-established industrial societies, but in others that are evolving new patterns of economic and political development. A speaker at the ICSW regional conference for Asia and the Pacific in 1977 is quoted in that region's report as urging the need for "a thorough reorientation of the parental attitude toward girls from one of preparing them solely for marriage as a career to one of useful citizenship with fully developed faculties." Several national reports from Europe note that the nuclear family was legally the basic unit for the procreation and rearing of children and for the computation, for example, of taxation and social security obligations and benefits. A strong emphasis on family policy continues in many countries, despite the increase in divorce rates and the greater acceptance of transient sexual relationships and of children born outside formal marriage. The Latin American report speaks of the family as "the principal agent for the transmission of the cultural values and patterns of the people" and mentions that the national constitutions of several countries contain clauses giving protection to the family unit by the state. Reports from two Nordic countries note changing roles within the family, and the increase in the number of married women working outside the home, but assert that the nuclear family remains the accepted basic unit of society.

The North American report, on the other hand, speaks of "emerging new life styles with people living in and out of various household arrangements" and delineates work and family as "separate enterprises." Public education is said to have removed an important function from the family unit, and care of the elderly is increasingly assured by societal units outside the family. In the two North American countries "there is a growing increase in divorces, separations, and abandonments by partners in marriage, and a dramatic increase of out-of-wedlock births among all economic and social classes in the region."

In this context we may have to separate aspiration from reality; there is often a time lag between legislation and social practice. Alternately, the frequent assertion of attitudinal change by innovators, magnified by powerful media for the dissemination of ideas, may bring about the very change in behavior patterns which are claimed merely to be objectively reported. The self-fulfilling prophecy is commonplace, and new conventions are apparently as binding as those they shatter in the name of freedom.

What, then, will be the patterns of social behavior in the 1980s? Where will reponsibility, both in law and in common practice, really lie for the raising of children, for the transmission or questioning of value systems, for the care of the elderly, the disabled, the dependent? Will "the community" replace "the family," and if so, in precisely what way? The development of social policy, and the possibility of much economic development, must depend on answers to these questions.

MIGRANTS AND MINORITIES

Major migrations within regions of the world seem to continue for a wide variety of causes—the desire for experience and even as a sort of rites of passage, the compulsion to seek work and income even at the cost of hardship and separation, the obligation to flee violence or persecution and settle in a new home. The phenomenon of migration has been studied in both generalized and personal service terms at several ICSW regional meetings, and mention of it is made in regional reports. The major migration movements between the Caribbean and Europe, between the Indian subcontinent and Europe, between Europe and Australasia, seem to be slowing down, as have the earlier massive immigrations to the United States and Canada. But substantial migrations continue, and concern for migrants is still a major preoccupation.

Moreover, both previous and recent population movements have meant the presence of minorities within a majority culture, which has opened the wide debate about pluralism, assimilation, and ethnic identity. Many national reports from Europe mention special and additional provisions for recent migrants or for cultural or ethnic minorities, and many also speak of conflict or a strong sense of grievance at instances of discrimination or inequality in societies officially committed to equality of treatment and opportunity. The North American report is preoccupied with such issues and focuses on the situation of minority racial groups in the United States, and also on the claims and demands in Canada of the French-speaking Québeçois. Plainly, the position of minorities within nation-states and the situation of migrants—of whatever class or category, and for whatever motive or cause—raise questions for international cooperation as well as for national action. Can anything further be done between national committees of the ICSW or by the ICSW itself, regionally and at world level?

THE USE OF LAND AND NATURAL RESOURCES

The two technologically advanced countries of North America report concern for the "balanced integration of the social and economic sectors." The exploitation of natural resources has produced a higher standard of living than elsewhere, although there remain large discrepancies between regions and between groups of people. There is now an increased emphasis in publicly declared policies on conservation of the environment and on husbanding the region's natural resources which are being consumed at a rate which bodes ill for the future. The use of urban land in a comparatively unplanned way seems all too often to have produced areas of crowded and poor-quality housing where the quality of life appears to sink lower despite a rise in the total control over rich resources.

The same concern is to be found in some European reports, where the problems surrounding the exploitation of newly discovered mineral and fossil deposits and the protection of the environment in the face of increased leisure and the demands of tourism continue to exercise planners and environmentalists. Some European countries have also mounted programs to improve conditions in their inner cities and seek a coordinated attack upon problem areas by planners, builders, industry, and social welfare agencies, moderated by a variety of government sponsorship or overseeing.

In a discussion of indicators of well-being the Asian and Pacific report comments that "a country's agriculture in relation to its share of the gross domestic product (GDP) serves as an indicator of its wealth." It concludes that on this basis only six countries in the region (two of them very small and densely populated) might be considered rich, while the rest have a long program of diversification of the economy to undertake before the use of land and resources can result in a rise in the standard of living. Its more equitable distribution, however, depends on several other factors. If the mechanization of agriculture proceeds apace in order to increase food productivity, what of the inevitable increase in the rural exodus and the crammed city slums?

The extent of arable land and its efficient use to provide resources for feeding a still rapidly increasing population, though centered predominantly in the Asian and Latin American regions, clearly has implications for the whole world. The demands upon land usage and the supply of food and raw materials determine the likelihood of an increase or a decline in human well-being and of any resources available for social action. The Asian and Pacific report comments: "The benefits of the Green Revolution have remained confined to a few already developed areas which have irrigation facilities or assured rainfall . . . it nonetheless continues to offer substantial hope, and agricultural surpluses are on the horizon in some countries." Those cut off from the mainstream of such changes and apparently trapped in rural poverty will not remain passive for long. Land reform has been only partially successful, and greater efforts in this direction are urgently required. Soil is so often used to produce cash crops for export, while the least productive acreage may be used inefficiently for food production. A coordinated program of land tenure reform, food production, international trade, family planning, nutrition, and education is needed "to ensure that the food system operates for the benefit of the poor and hungry."

It is a sobering reflection that in the Latin American report and in the Asian and Pacific report the basic problems of food production and population are major preoccupations, while in the other regions problems of longevity, personal and social problems, and maximum use of existing resources for social welfare predominate. Would the wealthier regions be prepared to accept a (temporary?) drop in their standards of material living in order to emphasize human solidarity in relieving suffering? Or is that question an irrelevance, and is our system of distribution and control of resources at fault? If so, what is to be done in the 1980s at the national and international levels?

ECONOMIC AND POLITICAL CHANGES

Many references throughout the reports emphasize the increase in world economic interdependency, and in some cases political changes have come about because of that realization. The price rise demanded by oil producers in countries which have now become the newly rich (in total national terms, at any rate) and the monopoly of other basic essentials for economic development have changed the political balance between countries dramatically over the past few years. The social consequences have been equally dramatic in many instances, and social welfare bodies have to deal with consequences, but often merely offer palliatives in situations beyond their control or even their influence.

The Latin American report states: "Unemployment is becoming more serious in all of the countries for the age group 14 to 25 years, reaching very high levels in Jamaica and Puerto Rico, while wages below the legal minimum are reported from Peru and Mexico." In the same region, accelerated development programs seek to deal not only with endemic economic and allied social problems, but also with the new situation of international commodity prices and the apparent substitution in some cases of a new economic dependence for the former political dependence.

Comparatively high levels of unemployment have been an unwelcome recent feature of many European countries, too, and have had a disproportionate effect upon school-leavers without qualifications. The demand for unskilled labor has dropped, a development which might be welcomed if there were any real substitute in more skilled work evenly spread through the working population. Often this is not the case, and special programs of temporary employment have been launched by some governments. Elsewhere, longer-term plans in retraining for new types of work have been formulated, and some national committees (Austria, for example) report special efforts "to find an apprenticeship for every school-leaver."

The struggle to control inflation has taken on a new urgency as inflation's effects on employment and upon low wage earners and those on fixed incomes have become painfully apparent. (Some instances of special measures to favor the latter disadvantaged groups are reported.) Wage indexing to prices has been adopted fairly widely in Europe, but many countries report the connected need to control both prices and wages and to obtain consent to a national wages and prices policy. In countries traditionally wedded to a system of free collective bargaining for at least a substantial part of the working population, this is a painful process.

The North American report also speaks of high rates of unemployment, describing the general economic situation in pessimistic terms: "It is a region where double-digit inflation rates exacerbate the economic deprivation of so many and where the malfunctioning of systems tends to create a permanent underclass where upward economic mobility is virtually impossible." The Asian and Pacific report mentions unemployment as a negative indicator of living standards, but has difficulty in quoting accurate statistics, or in assessing the extent of underemployment in that region. This is clearly linked to the high percentage of the population engaged in agriculture, many at subsistence level.

The economic crisis through which so much of the world is at present passing has compelled a reassessment of expenditure patterns, especially those connected with health, education, and social security. In general terms, health expenditure as a percentage of the gross national product (GNP) has expanded in all regions, but the upward curve of potential health and social services expenditure has been temporarily slowed down in many countries where harsh choices of priorities have been forced upon governments and independent social agencies alike. The Asian report, which devotes much space to the need for better coordinated economic and social planning, speaks of between one third and one half of central government expenditure being devoted to social services, with education taking by far the largest share. This priority is maintained, with health, social security, and social welfare services following in that order (though there are wide national variations).

Clearly, the existence of a genuinely operational system of planning, which sets priorities for social expenditure and states how these are to be paid for, depends upon a consensus of the people in a democratic society or a compulsion upon citizens to accept what is planned for them with or without their genuine choice. The North American report speaks of the absence of social planning mechanisms in the United States and Canada, with resulting fragmentation and lack of coherence in social provision. This may be due to an ingrained belief in individiual freedom and self-reliance; "until quite recently little help from the state was expected, and when personal social services were needed, there existed a preference for the provision of services by voluntary rather than governmental agencies."

The Asian and Pacific report refers to a 1969 Economic Commission for Asia and the Far East (ECAFE) study in which different mechanisms for plan implementation are set out. Clearly, plans are promulgated and targets set by central and by more local autonomous units aimed at a systematic use of resources for greater human well-being. It is not quite so clear that the rhetoric of much of this planning is followed through in practice and results in a more equitable distribution of the results of increased resource production. Perhaps for this reason the Asian report devotes much space to the need for more systematic research and evaluation of the results of planning strategies and the mechanisms whereby priorities are set—and by whom—in a changing economic situation.

For the European region the British report sets out starkly some of the choices before them:

Demands for social provision are insatiable. However real our wish to do more to promote human well-being we have to deal with scarcity and we have to determine priorities . . . . we may have to abandon some long-held beliefs and withdraw some benefits that have already been given . . . . this can only be achieved by a greater public understanding of real, alternative choices.

In turn, the French report speaks of the need to continue planning machinery, to subject proposals from planners to wide and free debate, but reminds us that the slowing down of economic growth does not imply that such growth was in itself misguided. Another way of defining priorities is to set down what are seen to be the most intractable social problems; here the Dutch report mentions three priorities which figure to some extent in most reports from the European region: unemployment, the integration of minority groups, and the increase in criminality. To deal with these social problems and to agree on priorities for expenditure of public funds, to which each citizen contributes to some degree, a system of democratic participation has to be assured which will operate more frequently than at election time. Many political formulas are being tried in the region in an effort to assume some agreed central formulation of objectives combined with a devolution of operational decisions.

"Political freedom," states the Asian report, "is one form of social progress and more likely than not a prerequisite of other types of development." The relationship of political freedom and social progress is variable, and widely differing forms of political systems are to be found in Asia and the Pacific, "each claiming to be acting in the interest of the masses." The theme is also taken up in the Latin American and Caribbean report, where various countries have gone through drastic political changes in the past decade which are closely bound up with their economic systems and the choice of priorities in public revenue raising and expenditure. It is one of the national committees of this region, too, which asks that conclusions reached at ICSW conferences "cease to be generalized abstractions and are converted instead into 'power and action' formulas to be applied according to each country's situation." What is our response to this challenge for the 1980s?

SOCIAL POLICY

The evolution of social services of all kinds has followed a general pattern, starting with piecemeal provision by voluntary and philanthropic bodies to a greater assumption of responsibility for intervention by governments and public bodies. While regional reports commonly trace this road, there is great variation in the distance traveled along it by the countries whose national committees have reported. Nor is it clear that everywhere the road leads to what would seem to be the final destination—the assumption by the state or publicly financed bodies of all the major functions designed to ensure human well-being: economic planning and resource distribution; health, education, social work, housing, and environmental plans; social security, labor, and income distribution.

The attempts to work out a more or less consistent series of measures and general provisions in these functions have also varied in the extent to which general principles have been explicitly laid down in national constitutions or general public declarations of policy. Some countries, in fact, have eschewed generalized statements of social principles, perhaps doubting the value of what appears to be rhetorical assertion only loosely allied to practice.

Commenting on the comparatively recent arrival of social security programs in Asian-Pacific countries, the regional report observes that there was an early recognition of the need for measures to help the weaker sections of the population, measures now publicly financed but originally provided through various networks. These provisions persist, supplemented and aided by more formal public bodies. Social security was only introduced to cover the limited number of industrial workers in countries with a high proportion of rural population, in contrast to economically advanced countries in the region where formal social security and social services have been more firmly established and mutually integrated for a long time. A recent study and analysis of social welfare literature by Sharad Gokhale shows that many governments have made conscious attempts "to formulate a coherent and consolidated social policy statement in terms of long-range goals, immediate objectives and strategic measures to obtain it." The fifth five-year plan of India is quoted as an example.

Within the limitations of economic feasibility and the setting of priorities in national expenditure previously referred to, certain choices are apparent within the range of social services—and also between various agencies that provide services. The role of local (as opposed to central) government bodies in social provisions seems to receive increasing recognition. The role of voluntary bodies (aided often by statutory funds) seems more generally established in societies with an advanced network of social provision than in others with more modest provisions, which may appear paradoxical. For a variety of motives and based on different religious and ideological assumptions, self-help and mutual-aid activities are lauded as having a vital part to play in the advancement of human well-being in all the very different regions here reported on. Such terms as "innovative," "pioneering," "experimental," and "assuring independence" occur frequently to describe the role which societies ascribe to voluntary initiative in social policy and social provisions.

Some reports from the European region mention the critical self-examination currently being undertaken by many private social welfare and community work bodies. Indeed, several ICSW national committees have been instrumental in helping this process of reassessment of role and function by nonstatutory social agencies. It is clear, however, that in the European region, at any rate, almost the entire provision of health care, social security, and education is assured through government or public bodies sustained by the law; there is no major political influence urging a return to main-line provision by voluntary action in the three areas mentioned. It follows that a better system of coordination of voluntary and statutory effort is demanded if the best use is to be made of limited resources, and several provisions for ensuring this are currently in operation or under discussion—notably in the Netherlands and in Britain.

A similar picture emerges from Latin America and the Caribbean, where two additional elements are mentioned—the limited geographical coverage of voluntary and charitable services and the governments' fear of losing political power—which have caused an increase in public social services, with a continuing, though altered, role for voluntary initiative. The need for coordination seems even more strongly felt than in Europe: "Practically none of the countries has properly integrated similar and complementary services in a general organism." What are the national committees affiliated to ICSW doing about this? Do they have the required stature, influence, and grass-roots support to take an initiative in this direction?

It is clear that there is a good deal of public debate about the role of social workers and allied professionals in all regions. Without giving a detailed prescription, the North

American report asserts the need for "the knowledge and skills of trained social work manpower," adding that government financing must ensure the supply of trained professionals. Latin America reports that in the training and establishment in society of professional social workers, many countries first followed European traditions; North American influences predominated later. In recent years there have been attempts to work out patterns of training for social workers and their distribution in the social services generally which have a distinct indigenous identity. Social workers became intensely politicized in many instances and more involved with political and economic struggles than with individual rehabilitation or readjustment on the casework model.

"The crises with which Asian social workers must deal have accounted for their identification with the goals of social development," says the Asian report. There follows an analysis of Asian social problems, which is taken from a 1977 report of the IASSW. The social worker confronted with the most urgent problems of the masses in rural areas will, in fact, be a social development officer, encouraging self-diagnosis of their problems by village groups and acting as a catalyst in self-help and mutual-aid schemes, establishing social centers and ensuring their continued servicing by emergent leadership. All this will require a different orientation and training from that relevant to the needs of other regions, and a quite different concept of relationships between "professional" and "volunteer" from that prevalent in most parts of Europe and North America.

The 1977 ICSW regional conference for Asia and the Pacific had as its theme "Assessment of Manpower Needs and Identification of Manpower Strategies." The regional report quotes its conclusions about professional social workers, in particular commenting on the frequent lack of clear task delineation for trained workers and others engaged in social welfare. The problems of Japanese social workers are examined, including recent reports aimed at establishing a basic plan for training all personnel related to social welfare. The regional report, quoting Ivan D. Illich's *Deschooling Society* [1] reminds us "not to downgrade in the name of professionalism the value of rural social workers and professionals with rudimentary training. . . . Community-based programmes and participation in service on a volunteer basis is a standing requirement of development." New forms of social work training are now growing up in many parts of the region, taking into account indigenous need and relying less on imported models than happened in the past.

The question of professional social workers' role within the complex of social provisions appears less acutely in the European report, although the Dutch, German, and British reports speak of the need to forge closer patterns of cooperation among professional social workers, neighborhood groups, and volunteers and "not to regard those less formal networks merely as supports for the statutory services."

In this whole area of the formulation of social policy and the realization in practice of accepted general objectives we surely have an opportunity and a need for close and frank consultation between national social welfare committees and associations of professional social workers. At the international level much better integration of our conferences and of our ongoing work is clearly called for. The ICSW, the IASSW, and the International Federation of Social Workers need to work out programs and strategies to reduce their isolation and undertake common programs to the benefit of all, and in fear of none. How can this best be done?

EMPLOYMENT AND INCOME DISTRIBUTION

The effects upon employment of world economic recessions and of price vagaries have been discussed. Here we refer to the permanent questions that affect employment policies and the resulting distribution of the fruits of our work. Plainly, the regional reports express dissatisfaction with the present situation, but the degree of antipathy is a function of ideological

[1] Ivan D. Illich, *Deschooling Society* (New York: Harper & Row, 1971).

standpoints, particularly concerning equality in society and income differentiation.

Minimum wage scales are found in all the Latin American and Caribbean countries covered in the report, but they were found to be neither adjusted sufficiently to account for cost-of-living increases nor universally respected in practice. In the Asia-Pacific region it is the dramatic variations in per capita income both between countries and, to a lesser extent, within them which is most striking. "Poverty" in this context means deprivation of basic needs such as food, good shelter, and basic medical care. In other regions, such as North America and Europe, absolute poverty in the Asian sense is almost eradicated, and poverty becomes a comparative concept. The United States reports that ethnicity closely overlaps with its "social and economic underclass" who are "the core population of the urban areas of the United States as well as being scattered in the rural and suburban areas of the country." Both economic growth and specific measures like the antipoverty program have contributed to the reduction of comparative poverty, but not to its elimination. Where the work ethic remains strong the implicit disapproval of dependency among the able-bodied will also be powerful.

The European report contains a careful review of incomes policies, distinguishing minimum *wages,* related specifically to the labor market, from minimum *income,* denoting a social provision incorporating a redistributive device. There is thus a close connection between the wage and social security/assistance systems, and a good deal of social action is concerned with the relationship between the two. Most European countries have minimum wage legislation, and almost all have a definition and guarantee of a minimum income per capita. The definition of "minimum income" and its relationship to average wages varies considerably between countries, and any judgment on its adequacy would be impossible. Governments have had to turn their attention increasingly to the interrelatedness of taxation, social security contributions, and wages, despite protests that the three must be considered separately. Incomes policies for the self-employed present special problems, particularly for farmers. Redistributive income policies appear less sure in their effects than is sometimes claimed, but it is clear that taxation does more than social security to redistribute income, except in countries that have comparatively high family allowances. The latter clearly redistributes between parents with dependent children and the rest of the population, but its redistributive effect between income groups is less sure.

The extent to which countries have energetic programs to bridge or narrow the gap between high and low incomes is to a large extent politically determined. The tolerance by the majority of workers of taxes and other devices to transfer income to poorer people in society is variable and seems to some extent to be a function of the general economic situation. A buoyant economy breeds tolerance of transfers; a stagnant or depressed one causes intolerance between the mass of better-off workers and the poorest minority. To what extent, and by what means, should we aim at a restructuring of incomes and rewards for work? How far should the results of bargaining between unions and employers be modified by government intervention to protect or improve the lot of the poorest? Are our taxation and our material rewards systems fair and honestly observed? If not, what new policies should we adopt?

HEALTH

Health is a basic need and requires a range of services. The provisions for health are fundamental to any society that aims to sustain life and postpone death. The emphasis on preventive care evident in all reports remains an aspiration rather than a reality in many countries where the actual emphasis and professional kudos lie with curative provisions. The two basic health indicators are infant mortality rates and the number of physicians per person; the wide variations are startling, even if well-known by now. We find so commonly in the reports the plaint that medical care is concentrated in the big cities and that rural areas are lacking in facilities. Positive countermeasures are reported in some instances. Another common development with the reduction or eradication of the major communicable or parasitic illnesses is the increase in the frequency of degenerative, metabolic, and hypertensive illness.

There are interesting variations in the method of providing health care—from the universal national health service financed almost entirely from taxation, through the various schemes linking social security with health care and providing it free of charge only to those in the lowest income group or to patients suffering from specified illnesses. "The challenge of the 1980s" writes the Latin American reporter, "in reference to health will be to find the equilibrium between costs and adequate services."

A different dilemma mentioned in the European report (which also deals with costs) is that between emphasizing hospital and clinical treatment and giving a major role to general practitioners, leaving hospital care to chronic cases. The German report is among those preoccupied with this question, which of course has implications for many related social services.

The medical problems of this region include those connected with drug abuse, alcoholism, and nicotine abuse, and subjection to these conditions can to some extent be imitative; hence the mounting of public health campaigns against the hazards of these three behavior patterns. Coupled with such campaigns are those connected with road safety since road accidents account for an ever increasing proportion of medical care needs—a situation even further deteriorating in North America. Thus the etiology of disease is altered with the economic and environmental situation: contrast the Asian report generally with some sections of the North American or European where obesity and lack of exercise are mentioned as health problems.

The status and role of doctors remain powerful in all regions. Their training, supply, and allocation in society are keys to the well-being of most people, and the question of their international mobility is one which has exercised many minds throughout the preceding decades. Since the link between medical and social provisions is strong in most countries the organization and distribution of health services are inter-connected with social work, social security, and personal social services of all kinds. The various systems for ensuring their better integration deserve more attention than they receive in the reports.

HOUSING

The European report states, somewhat optimistically, per-haps, that with the exception of Israel, the national commit-tees reported that the current rate of building was judged ade-quate to meet the growing needs of their populations both in quantity and quality. This, however, may disguise the fact that populations are very mobile and most housing is not. More-over, the backlog of poor and old housing in the center of the older European cities is still unsatisfactory, even if the over-all national picture is reasonably good. Changes in demography produce special problems: Norway, for example, mentioned the lack of adequate provision for young families with chil-dren, the large number of single persons who have to share housing, and the unsatisfied demand for special housing for elderly people—a trinity of problems echoed in the Dutch report. A variety of devices is used to subsidize house building or to help with the cost of rented housing or home ownership. Rent control is a fairly widespread but controversial measure whose effects on housing supply are sometimes unanticipated. Everywhere the amount of home ownership shows an in-crease, but there are considerable national variations.

The Latin American report speaks of a decline in housing construction since the economic crisis of 1974 with only Chile optimistic about meeting its housing needs in the 1980s. Peru reports that 78 percent of its housing units lack drinking water, electricity, and indoor sanitation; other countries supply less precise data, but express concern at their inability to build housing of a reasonable standard to provide for an in-creasing population, let alone raise the standard of existing houses. Many shantytowns have had to be recognized rather than forcibly cleared, and provided with basic facilities by gov-ernments unable to find alternatives.

"In the United States, by and large, housing is considered a market-place endeavor and is not classified as social welfare." The North American report makes clear that low-rent housing for the needy and special housing for the elderly and the handicapped is afforded government assistance.' The federal government's housing acts are quoted as examples of forays into the market economy to modernize, reconstruct, and repair houses as well as promote construction of new ones.

The rather sketchy information on this issue in the Asian and Pacific report shows fewer disparities between countries in the region than might have been expected, although housing conditions in crowded Asian cities (Calcutta, for example) are notoriously bad compared with conditions elsewhere. Indeed, one almost has the impression that the pressure of population in Asian cities has simply overwhelmed the housing and environmental services, and planners and social service personnel alike can only be concerned with remedial efforts for the most deprived. The influx of refugees periodically presents a dramatic housing crisis as does the incidence of natural disasters in the region.

Is housing a social service? If so, how should it be dealt with? What can be left to market forces and what forms of social intervention are justified as priorities?

EDUCATION

The largest proportion of social expenditure in all countries goes to education: schools, technical training, university and higher education, and mass education programs. Of course a high proportion of the cost is devoted to teachers' salaries, and an increase in these (as with medical and dental fees) may give a false impression that there has been an extension of the service.

Illiteracy remains a severe problem in parts of Asia and the Pacific, with dramatic contrasts between, for example, Iran and Nepal and Japan, Australia, and New Zealand. In the former countries—and elsewhere—literacy campaigns have been part of the national development plans. Expenditure in less developed countries in the region not only remains low in absolute terms but represents a lower percentage of the GNP than in richer countries. In these poor countries the dilemma over whether to train an elite to serve as key persons in the country's development or to concentrate first on a minimum standard of education for all is especially acute. The report for the region adds: "A particular problem has been the lack of technical education and training. Even in countries where educational systems are extensive, there are still young people too poor to take advantage of schooling. Girls and young women are frequently barred from education by culture and male-oriented tradition."

Latin America also has grave illiteracy problems, to which the report from Mexico makes special reference. School education has a high priority everywhere, but the population explosion has forced many schools to work in shifts to ensure a minimum education for all children. Jamaica and Peru are among the countries that mention the educational needs of preschool children:

Several of the concerns inferred from the reports are: (1) the decrease in quality because of the emphasis on quantity; (2) the inequality of education between urban and rural areas; (3) the decline in the ability to stay in school; and (4) the impact of all these problems on the acquisition of skills and qualifications for employment.

The general trend of education in Europe is to provide a minimum guarantee of compulsory schooling for everyone and a system of education running from primary school to university. The provisions are state-financed, either locally or centrally, and the education of only a very small proportion of the children is directly paid for by their parents. There have been moves generally, but surrounded with much controversy, to eliminate explicit differentiation in secondary schooling and integrate all into comprehensive schools. The school-leaving age has been pushed up everywhere, but a number of the least academically inclined children either do not respond or do not choose extended schooling, thought to be a pancacea for underachievement. The patterns of financing education vary considerably, but no one is now debarred from education solely by inability to pay for it. The assessment of ability to benefit from forms of further educational provision is made in ways which are sometimes contested, and there is concern that more children of manual workers are not found in higher education. The latter is particularly the worry of those concerned with creating a more egalitarian society.

According to the North American report:

In the United States education is not considered as a social service as in most other parts of the world . . . . two major issues remain as barriers to ensuring education's full contribution to human well-being: (a) the uneven quality of education; and (b) racial segregation and the nation's inability to achieve acceptance of multiracial public education.

In Canada elementary and secondary education are provincial responsibilities (compare the states' responsibilities in the United States), but the federal government pays half the cost of postsecondary education. Language questions allied to education occur in the systems of many countries, but they have recently become acute in the Province of Quebec.

One senses that though education is still highly prized, and though it is certain that there is a very long way to go before even minimum provisions are universal in Asia, the Pacific, and Latin America, formal education is not *in itself* the panacea for all social evils and personal shortcomings that it was once thought to be. Why not? How much more needs to be done in programs of mass literacy, retraining in technologically advanced countries, preschool provisions, extended availability of university education? What should be our priorities?

SOCIAL SECURITY

Everywhere there is a clear division in income-maintenance provisions between those based on the insurance principle and those based on a belief in social solidarity to provide assistance to people in need, according to certain defined rules. "Social security" in many countries refers exclusively to the first category, and its coverage in economically less developed countries is limited to those in regular industrial or commercial employment under wage contracts. European countries mostly started with these limited categories and have progressed to virtually universal coverage, though often with variable provisions for the self-employed.

Social security provisions in Europe are the core of social policy, many of them—notably in the Federal Republic of Germany—going back to the nineteenth century. Most developed quickly immediately after World War II and now cover all the major risks which bring interruption or cessation of earnings. Definitions of risks covered, provisions and procedures, organization, and financing are the subjects of widespread public debate and eventual governmental decision and promulgation. The bodies actually responsible for the administration of social security vary from one country to another. Britain and Ireland, for instance, have a total state monopoly of social security (except for optional extra life insurance, for example). Most continental European countries favor a different formula, that of making public bodies responsible for the actual operation of the schemes. A new common objective for retirement pensions is emerging: to pay more in contributions during the working life and so raise the amount of the pension compared with average working wages. Only in Britain is there an administrative integration of both forms of income maintenance, but here as elsewhere different criteria are exacted for the award of social assistance compared with the allocation of social security benefits.

Since 1935 the federal government of the United States has administered contributory social insurance—unemployment insurance, old age, survivors, dependents, and health. The federal government also subsidizes state governments for their public assistance programs for needy families and individuals. Canada has had since 1966 an assistance plan, under which the federal and provincial governments share the cost of assistance programs for the needy. The federal government also carries responsibility for social security for old age, family allowances, unemployment and sickness benefits. In both North American countries the present social security systems—

especially the assistance part—are under discussion, and reforms may soon come about.

The six countries reported on in Latin America and the Caribbean have social security systems, but the highest coverage of the population reaches 80 percent. There is a concentration on health care and the coverage of medical expenses. Pension schemes are best developed among certain professional groups and government employees, but they tend to be separate from the insurance schemes. Other fringe benefits for employed workers mentioned in the Latin American report are: paid holidays, sick leave, gratuities on certain feast days, free day care for children. Those who are not covered by social security must rely on private charitable bodies or local municipalities. One special program was the Puerto Rico food stamp program which benefited 46 percent of the population and extended their purchasing power at a time of galloping inflation.

A basic policy question about social security concerns its ultimate objective. Is it intended to provide for temporary interruption or cessation of earnings and to redistribute income over a life span, or is it intended to be used as a corrective mechanism in society, redistributing income more equitably than the market system allows, compensating for "social diswelfares," and engineering a more egalitarian society? What should be the relationship between social security and health services and between social security and social work?

Well-being: a Concept of Social Science and an Objective of Social Policy

LUCIEN MEHL

CONSEILLER D'ETAT, FRANCE; PRESIDENT, INTERNATIONAL COUNCIL ON SOCIAL WELFARE

THE ACTUALITY of the theme of well-being is significant of the image that we create for ourselves of our condition and of our destiny.

By "actuality" should be understood to mean not what this word can sometimes evoke, that is, something fleeting and futile, but on the contrary, as all that it can express of presence and reality—the true meaning, moreover, that the word has in English. What is necessary, then, is to question what is the state of well-being for those who have obtained it, and which is only a hope or a demand for others. But hopes and demands are part of social reality.

Throughout time, of course, man has been searching for a state of well-being. But for a long time, the notion of well-being had scarcely been the subject of philosophic or scientific interest. This is no longer true. Work in this field has been multiplied considerably at the same time that well-being has become an implicit or stated objective of social policy.

WELL-BEING: A RECENT CONCEPT IN SOCIAL SCIENCE

A SUBJECT OF STUDY AND REFLECTION LONG NEGLECTED, IF NOT IGNORED

A brief glance at the history of religion, philosophy, and political ideas shows that well-being is not a favorite theme of prophets and great thinkers. Happiness is the theme they prefer.

This is because, for an appreciation of the state of happiness, spiritual considerations have the upper hand over material preoccupations, though these are essential where well-being is concerned. This approach to the human condition, where ethics predominates, is undoubtedly admirable, but it is not without a certain superficiality. One thereby avoids having to deal with contingencies that are multiple, complex, sometimes also awkward, indeed disturbing.

These contingencies, however, certainly cannot be ignored, and thus opinions expressed about the human condition are generally pessimistic. The possibility of happiness in this world is most often denied;[1] the material and moral misery of man is pointed out. Happiness may even be rejected as a value: Friedrich Nietzsche saw in it only the derisory satisfaction of the "last men."

One is scarcely more successful in turning toward the founders of the ideal state, the creators of Utopias, be they Plato, Thomas More, or Tommaso Campanella; whether they conceive of a society that is more free, more united, as did Goethe in *Faust,* second part. In these works, there is very little consideration of the well-being of members of the social organization advocated by one and all. What is here exalted are, with community organization, virtue and austerity. One important exception is Fourier's *phalanstère,* where work is done with joy, indeed, with enthusiasm.

This inventory is undoubtedly not comprehensive. An exploration of the works of Rabelais or Montaigne might perhaps offer some views on well-being. We must not, moreover, limit ourselves to Western culture. A perusal of Arab, Persian, Indian, Chinese, and Japanese authors of past centuries, as well as the contemporary ones, should be fruitful. But a first

---

[1] The myths of the lost paradise, or the Golden Age, where man lived in abundance and peace, without worry and ignorant of aging, confirm this pessimism through contrast. These myths are numerous: Adam and Eve, chased out of the earthly paradise; Ulysses and the gardens of Alkinoos; Plato and Atlantis; cf. also Ovid, in the *Metamorphoses,* and so on. The utopias of the future are also generally pessimistic: Aldous Huxley, *Brave New World;* George Orwell, *Nineteen Eighty-four.* One exception (are there any others?) is H. G. Wells, *Mr. Barnstaple in the Land of the Demigods.*

glance, certainly brief and subject to revision, would seem to establish that no doctrine of well-being is to be found in these works either, nor is there a doctrine of well-being for all. Whenever well-being is mentioned, it is usually from an elitist or aristocratic point of view. This is so in Japan during the period of the Fujiwara regents, from the ninth to the twelfth centuries A.D. At the same time, in China, more precisely, in the eleventh century, that is during the Song dynasty, a current of ideas favorable to social welfare is observed, leading to the state creation of hospitals, homes, clinics, and nursery schools. Nevertheless, this was not to assure general well-being, but only to relieve the misery of the poorest.

The notion of pleasure, on the other hand, is better analyzed. For a number of moralists, the spirituality of happiness, felicity, and beatitude is contrasted with the materiality of pleasure, which is related to certain components of well-being. On this notion of pleasure, interesting treatments are found in the works of philosophers of antiquity, notably Epicurus, and also some hedonistic philosophers such as Bentham, who set out an "arithmetic of pleasures."

Epicurus, however, creator of an abstract and austere philosophical system, had a static, almost negative conception of the state of satisfaction. For this philosopher, even if there is a certain pleasure in quenching one's thirst, the real pleasure is in no longer being thirsty. The reality of pleasure exists only in a stabilized pleasure and not in a moving pleasure. Thus the perfect and complete pleasure is the absence of pain.[2]

If pleasure or, in a more neutral fashion, the state of satisfaction is a state of nondesire, of serenity, of ataraxia, there is an austere but effective means of arriving at it; that is, by the elimination of desire. This is what Buddha recommended: an annihilation, or even an individual repression of desire.

This repression, however, may be social. If Freud contested a purely static concept of pleasure (which was that of neither Plato nor Aristotle), he is no less a pessimist. According to

---

[2] On this Epicurean concept see Leon Robin, *La Pensée grecque et les origines de l'esprit scientifique* (Greek Thought and the Origins of the Scientific Spirit) (Paris: Albin Michel; republished 1973), p. 377.

him, civilization cannot accommodate an uncontrolled putting into practice of the pleasure principle. Desires are thus held in check. At the best, and not without suffering, our hedonistic tendencies can be sublimated in socially accepted activity. And if our superego, the social order's deputy, is not vigilant enough, the repressive machinery of Leviathan (the name by which Hobbes designated the power of the state) is set in motion.

It is known that Herbert Marcuse has attempted to offer a revised and more optimistic version of the Freudian thesis. As Alastair MacIntyre, a commentator on Marcuse, has brought out, Marcuse "recognizes that a certain basic repression and a certain asceticism were necessary for the construction of civilization, because of economic scarcity and the work needed to surmount this scarcity." But nowadays, according to Marcuse, repression of the libido has become, in part, unnecessary.

The thought of Marcuse, even if his analyses have been contested, is interesting for our purposes on two accounts. On the one hand, he gives credit to the idea that it is possible to go less against our hedonistic tendencies: on the other hand, and more important, he introduces the economic dimension into the debate. This is a complex notion, certainly, including components of a nature which is either material or "spiritual" (or nonmaterial; that is, affective, aesthetic, or intellectual).

Well-being, however, is distinguished from pleasure, joy, and happiness on the one hand and from welfare, on the other; welfare having taken on a different meaning, closer to action regarding well-being rather than the state of well-being itself. This state of well-being is that of the person who is capable of dealing with his material needs and satisfying his spiritual aspirations. It is, then, a state subjectively evaluated by the person; and from a certain point of view, its study comes under psychology or even psychoanalysis.

It is also, however, a social concept, a concept of social science, of a general, noncompartmentalized social science, integrating the data and the methods of sociology, anthropology, economics, and ecology. In fact, our needs and aspirations, even the most material, are socially governed. Certain needs and certain aspirations are even, in all or in part, created by society or by the components of society, particularly by the system of production. It follows that needs and aspirations are, according to the case, broadly enough common to all human beings or to large numbers or groups. They may, then, be subjected to objective definition, affected certainly by averages and approximations, notably toward the ends of social policy. Works on well-being are analyses of real situations and plunge into the realm of contingency; they are not limited to abstract speculations.

It is true that before the coming of the "affluent society," which is, moreover, geographically limited and today menaced, wide currents of economic thought were marked by pessimism. Even in the work of those writers who escaped from this tendency, considerations of production or reason, order, and effort could be exalted, and were more developed than those concerning consumption. In fact, consumption assumes not only the need, but also that which often accompanies it: egoism, covetousness, and envy, just that which should be repressed in the name of morality and religion. Furthermore, we have long been marked by what John Kenneth Galbraith calls in *The Affluent Society* the "tradition of despair in economic theories." Think about famines, recessions, the restraints of the primary investment phase, whatever the political system considered about the conditions of the workers described by Villerme and Malthus. Nothing of that leads to holding forth on well-being.

RECENT DEVELOPMENTS IN STUDIES ON WELL-BEING

During these last few years one has seen the multiplication of studies on this theme. The precursors who wrote on the subject of welfare economics must not be forgotten. One thinks of Vilfredo Pareto and his theory of the optimum concerning the repartition of incomes; of Paul Samuelson and his social, well-being function; of A. C. Pigou, who wrote *The Economics of Welfare,* and of many others. However, it is more recently that well-being has been studied in a more precise and more specific manner. This development is noticeable for more than one reason.

In the first place, well-being is, in these works, regarded as a notion that has its own importance. It concerns, on the one hand, methodical surveys (by polling) on the various components of well-being, its relative importance attributed by different people, the degree of satisfaction, and its relationship to income level and other elements, with various comparisons, particularly on the international level. These surveys have been made principally in the Nordic countries, the European Community, and North America, but also in the developing countries.

On the other hand, a great number of works emanating from authors in the developed countries, as from the developing countries, set out views on the future of the economy and social welfare and wonder, directly or indirectly, about well-being. The ecology movement made a particularly important contribution in this field. This is not the place to give an inventory of these works; this was done, partially at least, in the Fiftieth Anniversary publication of the ICSW.[3]

It is necessary to inquire about the motives for this present interest in well-being. The reason, it seems, is that well-being, at first thought unfeasible inasmuch as it involves the well-being of all, everywhere in the world, now appears to be possible. At the same time, however, an awareness has developed that the path to universal well-being is lined with ambushes.

The absence of discussion on well-being can be understood when it is seen as impossible of achievement for the large majority of mankind. Whenever a perspective of the evolution of production asserts itself, a vague future of an era of abundance "to each according to his needs" is at first envisaged. More carefully considered has been the hope that rapid economic growth accompanied by setting up redistribution mechanisms would be the generator of well-being. However, what this well-being consisted in, or what it was confusedly represented as, was hardly worried about.

But in the last few years, the facts and ideas have changed. First, there is the reality of the economic recession, or at least the slowing down of growth, and for the moment we are in-

---

[3] *Human Well-Being* (New York: International Council on Social Welfare, 1978).

capable of remedying this situation, at least with sufficient efficacy. The perspective of an abundance easily created, growing endlessly, has disappeared. Besides, it is known that if
important decisions in the field of international cooperation
are not taken, and effectively put into practice, the gap between living standards in rich and poor countries will continue
to widen. In any case, the possibility of arriving, even in the
absence of recession, at a universal consumers' society that
would be the West on a larger scale is contested by many authors, not only by those of the Third World, but also by those
of the developed countries, as one can see in the Fiftieth Anniversary publication of the ICSW.

A number of economists and sociologists of the Third
World reject the Western world's growth model—as they do,
moreover, the Communist one as well. Aside from the efficacy
of these models in their region, they contest the possibility of
arriving by this road at the well-being of the whole population.
A certain development can be attained by these models, but
they are creators of new inequalities. Certain Western authors
do not think otherwise, even in respect to their own region.
But not all are pessimistic; many believe that well-being for all
is quite possible.

What is also noticeable is the similarity in the ways and
means suggested—with variations, of course, imposed by the
diversity in the demographic, political, economic, social, and
cultural orders. It concerns arriving at a social state in which
institutions are more decentralized; in which individuals and
intermediary groups have more autonomy and are more interdependent; in which inequalities, if not eliminated, are
largely attenuated. Western authors also preach the elimination of waste and useless consumption, as well as the production of longer-lasting consumer goods. For their part, Third
World writers insist on the need to conceive of a development
model that does not lead to dependency, that has its roots in
agriculture, that includes the local handling of primary products and an industrial development that proceeds, at least
partly, from the treatment of local resources without creating
a disequilibrium between cities and countryside. Writers on all

sides support the bringing into question of needs and desires, some of which have been artificially created.

There are some interesting suggestions here for future social policies.

WELL-BEING: OBJECTIVE OF SOCIAL POLICY?

Well-being is in fact, or at least in principle, an objective, and one could even say *the* objective of social policy. Certainly, it cannot be asserted for a fact that social policies always and everywhere have well-being as their unique objective. Considerations of technical efficacy, economic importance, and political equilibrium may influence social policy; not that that should, however, be necessarily open to criticism. It does remain, however, that the objective of well-being is tending to become preponderant, and in any case, that is as it should be.

The very meaning of this well-being, however, the nature of its various elements, presents difficult problems in the determination of priorities, the fixing of levels, and, more seriously, the compatibility between certain of these elements. These difficulties are increased whenever well-being is to be for all human beings that make up the nation, and even larger aggregates, and not that for a privileged minority, even though differences among individuals concerning income and power, undoubtedly legitimate, are accepted.

As for making the choice of ways and means which could lead to well-being for all, it is at least as difficult as the definition and analysis of well-being itself.

HARMONY AND CONFLICT AMONG THE COMPONENTS OF WELL-BEING

On the subject of well-being, as for all questions relating to ethics and politics, it is necessary (without falling into skepticism) to avoid idealism. The notion of well-being is partly made up of an apt synthesis of various satisfactions, but it also includes internal contradictions.

This is not the place to undertake a rigorous analysis of the notion of well-being; that would be to anticipate ambitiously the results of the conference's work. However, for the convenience of the demonstration, the following components will be provisionally distinguished:

1. Physiological and material well-being in its widest sense, which includes, therefore, that which concerns not only food, but also clothing, housing, and so forth
2. Security, not only to face natural catastrophes, but also in dealing with health, employment, and so on
3. The benefits of knowledge, also in its widest sense (professional abilities and general knowledge)

The benefits of knowledge are partly a spiritual (in the nonmaterial sense) and nonutilitarian element of well-being; but knowledge and, even more so, know-how are also generators of well-being. Then we have the elements that are essentially spiritual:

a) The possibility of human communication (love, friendship, adjustment to the group and to the community)
b) Freedom, not only freedom of movement and expression, but also autonomous freedom in various activities
c) The satisfaction that any human being has in being treated with respect and dignity by others and by administrations; and when powers are applied, with equality or, in any case, with equity—a concept that concerns more generally the role of justice agencies in the establishment of a state of well-being.

It is clear—and that is certainly satisfying—that certain elements of well-being are not only compatible but are also mutually reinforcing. Without pretending to exhaust all possible combinations of these elements, one can think through several significant examples.

Thus a high level of physiological well-being (which excludes, of course, any excesses of consumption) increases security (of health notably) and the ability for the growth of knowledge. Inversely, security and knowledge increase physiological well-being. This is notably why security is a real socioeconomic value, a good that can, moreover, be acquired by owning an insurance policy, for example. It is also evident that knowledge, in its widest sense, increases the possibilities of communication and the exercise of true liberty.

Not enough light, however, is shed; certain elements of well-being are incompatible among themselves. The most remarkable example is that of the competition between material well-being and security.

Maximum security "costs the earth," as they say. Consider the case of people who live in places that are below sea level. They protect themselves from the fury of the floods with dikes. But they are not beyond the danger of an exceptional tidal wave since the very high cost of protection against so unlikely a calamity is prohibitive. In this case, the insecurity arising from an eventuality with a very small probability is preferred to a major reduction of consumption.

There is also a certain degree of contradiction between security and freedom. Men are tied by contractual clauses, or else they agree to receive a certain status including rights and obligations, especially toward the goal of security. It can furthermore be observed that a rigorous equality in individual incomes, assuming that it should be recommended, would require an undertaking, on the part of the public authorities, of constraints and controls incompatible with freedom.

It may even happen that incompatibilities exist within a particular component. Freedom is such a case. One may accept the institution of a constraint such as the highway code that creates a freedom of a higher order than the freedom that was cancelled. The code, a set of minor regulated constraints, particularly by means of the signals which have resulted, makes automobile traffic possible and reduces the risks of driving. The highway code, although by definition a constraint, has thus created the freedom of being able to travel by automobile, which is, as an element of autonomous freedom, far superior to the fanciful freedom of driving without any traffic rules.

From the preceding considerations, however, comes the possibility that there are alternatives more cruel than those presented by traffic regulation. The difficulties and contradictions in the notion of well-being are manifested, moreover, on turning to practice. Any individual choice related to well-being plays the part of compromise. One comes to terms with oneself. A fortiori this is a compromise in the political realm. Political decision-makers are led, most often in an approximate and implicit manner, to making choices that are held to be acceptable.

It is seen, then, that an analysis of the notion of well-being, if it does not lead to abandoning all hope, does not leave a place for illusions. This is so too for policies of well-being whose road is narrow and uncertain, which does not at all, however, prevent following it with resolution.

If it can be held as evident that the objective of well-being is manifested in social policy, it is a question of social policy in its widest sense. In fact, the epithet "social" is not used only in its technical sense here. It is, therefore, not sufficient, when well-being is concerned, to consider only measures taken, and actions executed, concerning social security, and more generally concerning social protection and social transfers. By "social" must also be understood that which deals with the desirable finality of economic activity and which ought to be the reason for the existence of institutions and government. This legitimate finality and this legitimate reason for existence are precisely human well-being.

Social policy thus understood in a wide sense in which the social objective has a sense of finality and is not only technical, exercises its influence on economic policy. The reverse, moreover, is true. It would be absurd to fix objectives of well-being without consideration of available resources. But if one admits that the purpose is no longer to produce for reasons of power, or even domination, but to build an economy oriented toward well-being and offering also the conditions of well-being in the very foundation of the activities implied, it follows that social policy must influence economic choices.

Social policy interferes with educational and training policies as well, since one of the components of well-being is the autonomous freedom which is asserted through knowledge; another is the satisfaction that comes through cultural activities. Social policy cannot be unrelated either to political-administrative institutions or to the organization and functioning of systems of production that have the same aims in the evolution of freedom, notably through decentralization and participation.

In other words, just as there is an economic relationship in social welfare, inversely economics is also social, just as are political, administrative, educational, and cultural institutions—not only in the commonplace meaning of the word "social" (that is to say, that which relates to society), not only in a technical sense, but also, and especially, in its meaning of an end in itself.

This over-all, systematic conception of social policy is, moreover, often implicitly admitted. It is this that is retained, notably, in plans for economic and social development, even though the realization is not up to the level of intentions. It is expressed more and more frequently in the speeches of political leaders, whether they be in power or in the opposition, and it is symbolized by such expressions as "the new society," "the choice of society," and so on.

Principal difficulties in the undertaking of social policy in its widest sense, that is, a policy of well-being, appear, however, on the level of the consistence of well-being and putting into practice the means designed to promote it. The objective of well-being which is in question is an objective of well-being for all, without which it could not be considered worthwhile.

Now, the difficulty is not based only on a limitation of resources. It is the very significance of the notion of well-being which is in question. It is impossible to proceed, even if one had the means, to identify the components of well-being, particularly in the material order such as this well-being is conceived of in the West. To cite but one example, the nightmare that would be created by the use of an automobile by each inhabitant of the planet, if that were possible, can only be imagined. More generally, the spread of certain types of over-consumption that lead to waste, practiced by the inhabitants of the rich countries, is inconceivable.

In order to achieve well-being for all, it is not sufficient to find other technical solutions. It is necessary to accept a moderation of desires, to tend toward the state of reasonable desire, according to Spinoza's apt phrase.

Is this, however, a realistic objective? One can certainly doubt it. The announcement of a "choice of society" where the emphasis is put on at least a relative equality and austerity, certainly legitimate, can have an immobilizing effect on the economic order. There are already front-running signs in this direction. Executives are seen to refuse promotions precisely in the name of well-being, because in their eyes the marginal increase in income is not in proportion to the increase in worries and the loss of leisure. This attitude can be criticized in the name of morality, even though it may be doubted that one could properly blame it. But the essential is not here. In politics, that is to say in practice, it is the *de facto* situation that must be considered. Without going so far as to say that in an egalitarian society everyone would want to be a watchman in a museum, the road that could lead to a less inegalitarian society is made up of many detours and obstacles.

The divorce between economics and ethics, as Jean Pierre Dupuy, director of the Center of Research on Well-being in Paris, refers to it, merits consideration. In a recent article[4] he quotes some astonishing reflections from Keynes, drawn from the latter's *Economic Possibilities for Our Grandchildren*. Keynes expressed the hope here that one day everyone might be rich and that the good would be preferred over the useful. Thus the moderation of wants beyond a certain level of well-being is again found. But Keynes added, as Dupuy recalls for us: "Careful, we are not yet there. . . . and for at least a hundred years we shall have to persuade ourselves. . . . that fair is foul and foul is fair; for foul is useful and fair is not." In other words, morality is an obstacle to economic progress. In the eighteenth century, a Dutch author, Bernard Mandeville, quoted by Keynes, chose "Private Vices, Public Benefits" as the subtitle to his work *The Fable of the Bees*. And it is conversely true that attempts to create virtuous societies have failed, through economics.

[4] "L'Economie et la morale ou la morale de l'economie" (Economics and Morality, or the Morality of Economics).

Keynes thought that a hundred years were needed before everyone would be rich and would moderate his wants. Surprisingly enough, a similar idea is found in W. W. Rostow's *Stages of Economic Growth*.[5] He calls it the Buddenbrook Model, a sort of socioeconomic mechanism of libido sublimation. The name of the model is evidently borrowed from the celebrated novel *Buddenbrooks* by Thomas Mann in which the author presents three generations. The first pursues money; the second, already rich, goes after social prestige; the third turns toward artistic activities. Well, three generations account for about a hundred years. But not everyone is in accord with the Buddenbrook Model, and so Keynes, and Rostow even less so, does not leave us much hope for the next decades.

Furthermore, the undertaking that leads to well-being for all is difficult; not only from the technical standpoint, but perhaps even more so from the psychological standpoint. On the one hand, a good number of these measures, especially those through which an improvement in the sharing of national revenue is attempted, concern not a small minority of the well-off as is sometimes asserted, but a large number of the population, close to the majority in the developed countries.

For example, a redistribution of incomes by means of taxation is only effective if the payment, certainly progressive by income bracket, extends not only to high incomes but also, with suitable moderation, to those around the average. It is not the overtaxation of the richest alone that will permit a sufficient improvement in the situation of the most underprivileged. More generally, the most legitimate measures tending to promote equality are necessarily of a restrictive nature. Reducing freedom and autonomy, they are frustrating and tend to generate various resistances.

Is it possible, however, to increase well-being for all without upsetting the workings of economic activity, without creating excessive frustrations which generate disorder, without dealing a serious blow to freedom? The reply appears to be in the

[5] W. W. Rostow, *Stages of Economic Growth* (2d ed.; New York: Cambridge University Press, 1971).

affirmative; but to attain such an objective there is no solution that is simple, let alone unique and at hand.

The most that one can do here is to sketch out a model in which the various components of well-being will be situated at a minimum acceptable level for all. The principal outlines would be the following:

1. The economic system is oriented, so much as it concerns finished products, toward the production of consumer goods and durable equipment, without waste. The contributory public service has been developed.

2. Small units of autonomous production are encouraged. In large units, indispensable in certain branches of production, participative structures have been instituted.

3. A minimum income is assured to all, as well as protection against risks of existence (without prejudice to complementary and voluntary insurance). This minimum guarantee requires centralized institutions. Income taxes and capital taxes, steeply progressive, reduce inequalities and set up barriers against the accumulation of abnormally large fortunes.

Thus each one with his available minimum can, within the framework of an equitable economic game, notably if equality of opportunity is watched over, try to acquire a more favorable situation than that which provides him with the minimum. But his additional income and wealth will be contained within such limits that he may never control or dominate.

In such a system, heteronomy—regulation, centralization, the power hierarchy, as well as economic concentration—is reduced to what is strictly indispensable to economic efficiency and social justice. For the remainder, it is autonomy that is encouraged; that is, contracts, negotiation, participation, initiative, and decentralization.

This model applies, with variants, equally well to developing countries as to the developed countries. It ought to be completed by an international model rendering more equitable the new relations among the economies of rich countries and those of poor countries (by an "active scenario," in the words of Wassily Leontief) with regard to an acceleration of economic development in these countries.

A twofold criticism can undoubtedly be made of this model. First is its lack of originality: it ends up recommending improvement of systems that already exist. However, is this not only the road most acceptable to everyone but also the road that offers the greatest chance of success? In fact, the refusal to increase autonomy, the maintenance of centralized bureaucratic structures, is extremely dangerous. In any case, these are obstacles to well-being. It is thus necessary to go from an excess of heteronomy to a greater autonomy.

Conversely, in spite of the sympathy aroused by these theses which call for the widespread constitution of small economic and political units, more or less federated, the worst can be feared for productivity and justice if the whole political-administrative framework, of whatever degree, if all regulation, if all redistribution were to disappear. Just as there is a certain degree of opposition between freedom and centralization, there is also a partial antagonism between decentralization and equality or equity. It is necessary, then, to look for an acceptable compromise.

The second criticism that can be made of the model would be, in a contrary sense, its "idealism." The effective reduction of heteronomy and of inequalities will encourage strong resistance. To produce an active scenario of equitable development for everyone in the world, those who are most well off—and that includes many among us—will have to accept being less so.

On the whole, the solution is to do that which was going to be done for the last quarter century. It is possible, however, that the number of perils, partly attributable to our inaction, may lead us to a salutary reflection.

At the beginning of this discussion, well-being was distinguished from happiness—legitimately, I believe; yet there was no development of the theme "happiness," for it is of quite a different nature.

Well-being is a legitimate objective for the individual as for the community, and it is even a true individual and social value. It is not always accessible even to the most fortunate who may lack that precious good, bodily health. Happiness, however, does not depend on ourselves alone. The words of Albert Camus according to which Sisyphus is imagined to be happy may be surprising. But the reading of philosophers and daily observations show us that it is not exceptional that human beings claim to be happy while undergoing an ordeal.

An attachment to worldly goods, to the earthly realm, the will to be well, to live well, are surely the signs of good physical and moral health. It is necessary, however, to stand back from the temporal, and even more so from the daily routine. This surprising association of attachment and detachment is perhaps one of the conditions of happiness. Like Job, it is necessary to be capable of saying (though perhaps in a different form for nonbelievers): God gaveth unto me, God hath taken away; may the name of the Lord be praised.

Physiological and Material Needs

PART I

ROBERT A. DERZON

DEPARTMENT OF HEALTH, EDUCATION, AND WELFARE, UNITED STATES

ONE OF our most important challenges is to provide for the health care needs of people throughout the world—particularly in developing countries where those needs are often critical and frequently not met.

The United States recognizes its responsibility to contribute toward meeting those health care needs through a number of programs. The Agency for International Development and the Peace Corps spent over $400 million on the direct provision of health-related services in 1977, an increase of 100 percent over 1976 spending. The United States also contributes significant amounts (over $150 million in 1976) to the UN and other international agencies for health care programs. Finally, there are research and development programs within the Department of Health, Education, and Welfare and the Department of Defense, such as immunization and research into tropical disease, which concentrate on health problems of underdeveloped countries. However, an analysis of the structure and evolution of the American health care system, or, as some argue, our "nonsystem," can provide important input into other nations' thinking about their own. (The reverse, of course, is also true.)

HEALTH CARE SERVICES IN THE UNITED STATES

Almost from its birth, the United States has provided for the health care needs of society as a whole through sanitation, water purity, prevention of epidemics, and so on. This has been set up at the national level with primary authority delegated to states and then to localities. The evolution from those public concerns to a strong interest in providing personal health care services is a much more recent phenomenon. Even more current is the major role of the federal government in the financing and delivery of personal health care services through a partnership primarily with the private sector—that is, nongovernmental providers of health care services.

Today, the federal government, through tax incentives and other means, has encouraged and aided almost all individuals in one way or another to purchase personal health care services. The federal government, through construction support and training programs, has encouraged people to assume that facilities will be there to provide those services and that they will be staffed with the necessary practitioners.

In addition, the federal government since 1966 has taken upon itself to provide significant financial relief for the personal health care needs of the aged, the disabled, and the poor of our society through the Medicare and Medicaid programs. This commitment now extends to 45 million Americans— approximately one of every five of our citizens. This effort has not been totally successful; there are still unmet needs, but the goal has been set, and movement continues in that direction rather than away from it.

Personal health care services today comprise 85 percent of all health spending in the United States. They are of higher intensity than public health services and they are much more dramatic. For instance, new surgical procedures attract more attention than vital but more mundane immunization programs. Personal health care services are also extraordinarily expensive—well over $600 per year for every man, woman, and child in the United States. These costs when measured against the benefits are increasingly being questioned. Although the ratio of cost and benefit can and sometimes does fall below that of other societal expenditures, personal health expenditures are still growing very rapidly, far outstripping the over-all growth of America's gross national product (GNP).

A number of key factors help to explain the growth in health care expenditures in the United States from $12 billion in 1950 to over $160 billion in 1977, and their ability to outstrip over-all growth (per capita income grew 100 percent in the past ten years while per capita health care spending grew 200 percent).

The American public's purchasing power for health care services has increased dramatically, particularly through the acquisition of broad health insurance coverage. That coverage is especially strong in the areas of costly highly intensive health care services such as hospitalization. Government, particularly the federal government, has provided for the health care needs of most of those unable to secure private health insurance, as noted previously. Ninety percent of hospital expenditures are paid for by public or private insuring organizations; 55 percent, by government.

A second factor, characteristic of most Western nations, has been an increase in the needs of the population in the United States associated with an increase in its average age. Persons over sixty-five use six times more health care services than persons under twenty. The government pays two dollars out of every three for our senior citizens. Per capita health expenditures by persons over sixty-five are currently more than $1,600 per year.

The American health delivery system has traditionally been quite open-ended, and with the expanded need of the population and its increased ability to purchase services to satisfy that need, there has been enormous growth in the size, sophistication, and cost of the supply side of the health care equation. In fact, the peculiar characteristics of the American health care industry have allowed that supply to create its own demand for the very medical services it provides. Physicians and other health professionals who are paid on a fee-for-service basis can and do expand demand for their services, often aided by willing and frightened patients. Despite the perverse behavior of the United States health care economy, it has only recently been recognized that special public policy approaches to the peculiar economics of health are definitely required.

IMPLICATIONS OF THE GROWTH IN HEALTH EXPENDITURES

The rapid increase in expenditures for personal health care in the United States has now bumped up against our ability to pay for these services. Inflation in health care costs combined with much higher prices for food, energy, and housing is threatening the American standard of living of most of our middle class and raising clearly for the first time the need to treat public and private expenditures for personal health care as one of a number of competing claims on finite resources.

This view of health care as something that must be balanced against other needs in determining allocations of resources is difficult for Americans to accept, and, in fact, not all Americans *do* accept it. This is partly because our health delivery system has grown up without constraints. However, it is also true that part of the problem lies in the nature of all health care services. We are able and willing to recognize society's finite resources and to say, for example, that fifteen square meters are "sufficient" living space or decide what constitutes an "adequate" diet, but there is no easily defined corollary in the health care field—either in terms of dollars or in duration and scope of treatment. We are much more likely to hear that "One cannot and should not put a dollar value on human life in health care matters." The right to health care services has been a limitless right for all practical purposes.

Despite these problems of dealing with our health care needs and allocating expenditures in relation to society's other requirements, we in the United States have begun to recognize that some priority-setting in the area of human needs, even in very healthy countries, may be necessary. Health care's ever increasing share of the GNP must of necessity crowd out other needs whether they be housing, education, transportation, or energy. After all, the GNP measures our total production of goods and services. If a disproportionate amount of the GNP is devoted to health services, it will not be available to devote to other services regardless of whether they are publicly or privately produced.

Within the health sector itself, the rapid increase in personal health expenditures has in fact already severely affected our ability to devote resources to provide new initiatives in public health prevention and health education. We are at the point where the annual increase—the increment—in government spending for personal health care services through Medicare and Medicaid alone is at nearly the level of total government spending for all other health needs. This virtually destroys our ability to develop and target other important health care programs. The proposed separate federal Department of Education would bring into that organization $17 billion for public education programs—exactly the dollars that our federal health program for the aged and disabled will spend on hospital services for only twenty-five million beneficiaries in those categories.

Obviously, the strain of personal health care expenditures on the federal budget could potentially limit our ability to make public policy choices to provide health care and other assistance to developing countries.

THE UNITED STATES EXPERIENCE

The United States is now working its way through the very difficult process of coming to grips with the need to allocate resources to personal health care needs more widely and carefully. In 1966 the concentration was on providing benefits to the aged and the poor. In 1972 Congress amended the Social Security Act to provide more safeguards and tighter regulations for implementing these statutes. In 1974, Congress passed the strongest health planning legislation to date, and that law is being implemented. It requires expansion of capital and medical services as part of an over-all health services development plan in each local area and state and that it be justified on the basis of documented need.

The federal government, as part of its assistance to medical education, is now instituting requirements that more new physicians be trained to provide needed primary care services rather than more expensive, technologically based specialty services of which the United States already has more than enough. Congress is examining ways in which the federal government can control the sensible introduction of new technology in health care. Congress is also currently debating provisions that would limit the growth of hospital expenditures in relation to over-all inflation.

All of these areas—health planning, manpower policy, and expenditure limits—are sure to be discussed and debated within the United States (and in other nations) for years to come both individually and as part of the consideration of a national health insurance program. The debate itself demonstrates a new chapter in the United States effort to assure affordable health care services to each and every American.

I have presented a general review of how and why we wrote the earlier chapters in the development of our health care system. Some lessons contained in this development are worthy of discussion, which I shall suggest from my perspective as a former Health Services administrator and as the present director of federal government health care financing programs which will spend over $45 billion in 1979 on personal health care services for the aged and poor of our society.

It is inevitable that as a society increases its income and purchasing power, one of the needs it will seek to satisfy is personal health care. That is entirely understandable because many personal health care services prolong life, increase its quality, and strengthen the creative productivity of our fellow human beings. Care must be taken, however, to recognize that the production of other goods and services can also provide some of these advantages and perhaps others. Therefore a balance must be struck between health and other services, one which will be easier to achieve if society enters the debate understanding that the values of personal health care services are considerably more elusive than measuring the value and the cost of other essential human services.

It is important to avoid unilateral determinations of how much is spent on health care services or how it is spent. These decisions in the United States have been too much the province of our health care professionals and our health industry. All individuals bear some responsibility for their own and society's health care spending. It is a natural extension of the freedoms we cherish so highly. At the same time, the perverse nature of medical economics makes it impossible to rely solely on individual choice to make the system operate efficiently. There is clearly a need to construct a mechanism, or more likely a series of them, which involves both health professionals and consumers together with government in trying to resolve the questions of how much to spend, what to spend it on, and how to develop efficiency—one of the major missing links in America's third largest industry, health care.

An overemphasis on technological solutions to health care problems should be avoided. They are extremely costly and less flexible than more basic medical services or health prevention and health education programs with which they should be compared in terms of relative benefits. Technology can be an extremely beneficial tool in promoting better health, but its relative effectiveness will be so much greater if it is put to a rigorous needs and efficacy test prior to acquisition.

A great deal of effort should be spent on developing ways of paying for health care services which encourage efficiency. My agency is devoting millions of research dollars to this question, and it is clear that there are no simple answers.

Although it is critical to moderate the total that society expends on health care in relation to its total income, we must do more than merely "narrow the end" on health expenditures; we need to worry about "the middle" as well. Work on peer review and other utilization control devices is needed as well as more efforts to improve and measure the productivity of the health sector. Utilization review and control seem to be an almost uniquely American idea. As a result, the lengths of hospitalization continue to decline, and we are becoming more adept, I think, in assuring appropriate treatment.

Despite the many problems that the United States faces in attempting to provide, or at least assure, high-quality health services for all of its citizens in a reasonably efficient and affordable manner, I remain convinced that it can be done—but only with continued and more strategic governmental intervention. We can correct some of the "slack" (the waste in this rather free-form system of ours) by limiting payments. We can make the planning of services more rational and we can reform certain aspects of the delivery and reimbursement systems. Surely we can strengthen the social support systems, particularly for the aged. This last strategy is particularly crucial. We must discover ways to minimize dependence of the aged on expensive and somewhat less than perfect health services when better alternatives exist.

Heretofore, we have not searched so assiduously for cost savings alternatives. We were content to applaud the explosion in personal health care services. For perhaps two decades we have also had a compassionate and willing middle-class taxpayer. I have great fears that his compassion is being exhausted. In the state of California, our largest state, with 10 percent of the American population, we have recently witnessed a tax revolt of serious proportions. Not inconsequentially, one of every four state budget dollars goes into health services, probably at the expense of education, cash assistance, and other vital programs.

Many believe that the health of a nation is the strength of a nation. The health of our nation is indeed the sum of the composite health of all of our individuals, and is in fact largely determined in a free society by the willingness of those who share income, resources, and their hearts with the victims of poverty, bad health, and misfortune. Personal health care is but one critical element among several. We stand a danger, as do others, of harming our over-all health by unintended and misallocated events, some of which are natural; some of which are quite controllable; and some of which continue to be irascible but must be resolved.

You who share a broad perspective on the social condition of mankind must recognize in these deliberations the disjunction of unbalanced, uncontrolled public strategies in the name of good health care with the more disciplined, demarcated approaches that usually characterize public policy development in most social welfare programs. I hope I have succeeded in increasing awareness to this newer battleground—one which if unchanged and unchallenged threatens to jeopardize the delicate balance that is needed to achieve human well-being as defined in its most expanded and comprehensive meaning.

PART II

CHARLES A. EGGER
DEPUTY EXECUTIVE DIRECTOR, UNITED NATIONS
CHILDREN'S FUND

I SHALL concentrate primarily on the first four basic needs without qualifying them further because there are so many factors that can influence a definition of basic needs: climate, state of development, cultural latitude, environment, and so on. I shall do it primarily from the point of view of the developing countries with which, through my work, I am more familiar; they do represent, of course, a very large percentage of the total needs. I also want to underline that there is a certain danger to present needs on a sectoral basis, as the theme indicates, because there is a very close linkage and interrelationship between these various needs, such as the relationship between unsafe water and the disease pattern, the problem of malnutrition which can be aggravated by communicable diseases.

With regard to health, I am utilizing a definition that has been attempted by a study group of the World Bank, in order to have a foundation on which to define basic health as the public and private measures needed to prevent and cure the most common avoidable and curable diseases and other forms of bodily harm. They include, in the first place, maternal and child health care—the whole process of prenatal and postnatal periods and birth. They have to include communicable diseases which are still prevalent in the Third World—malaria, measles, tuberculosis, and so forth. They include diseases of the respiratory and gastrointestinal tracts and are of course much related to the syndrome of poverty, ignorance, and squalor. There is therefore an enormous discrepancy between the situation in developing and industrialized countries, if you think of average figures of infant mortality of 140 per 1,000 in developing countries, as compared to an average of about 27 per 1,000 in industrialized countries, if you think of the statistics on child mortality in the age group from 0 to 5, which in developing countries can be 30 percent to 50 percent higher than in industrialized countries. We also now know a lot more about discrepancies within countries, between different regions, due either to their accessibility or to the fact that they are generally underprivileged or represent a less advanced population group. There is no question that in past decades, thanks to the economic and social measures introduced, better distribution of income, and more adequate communications, considerable progress has been made in many but not all countries and for many but not all population groups. The percentage of people who have no access to regular public health services is, according to the estimates of the World Health Organization (WHO), still between 70 percent and 80 percent, and this represents, in the poorest of the population groups, still a terrible number of about 800 million people. If we look at the expenditure pattern, we see that 80 percent of all expenditures for public health purposes are still concentrated in urban-hospital-oriented approaches, and therefore 20 percent only is available for the masses of the people. This basically unsatisfactory situation is now increasingly common in all countries but also especially so in the developing countries. Better communications have contributed to that. There is an awakening taking place in many of the countries, including neglected population groups.

Governments and public opinion leaders have experienced more and more frustration with the unsatisfactory and inadequate results achieved so far. Over the last decade we have witnessed increasing pioneering and exploratory work undertaken by universities, research groups, voluntary agencies, and spirited public health officials who have been able to demonstrate that there are other more adequate public health approaches that can be pursued. They are advocating a shift in the public health emphasis from concentration on urban areas to reach out to the population at large with simple yet effective health measures, where the communities no longer are being looked upon simply as a final passive target but as a responsible and participating element. The characteristics of this new primary health care policy are to bring medical care in an effective way to the people, and for this purpose to use available human resources, multiply auxiliaries, and encourage the communities to make available members of the community who can take over responsibility for the first primary health care in the community itself. This policy will make the community the responsible guiding element that will influence priorities and the orientation of basic health care, as well as redirect the existing services to support, to guide, and to underpin this front-line approach. This has now been officially supported by the responsible international agencies, by many bilateral aids and voluntary agencies, and the World Bank. In a few weeks, in Alma Ata, U.S.S.R., an international conference will take place which will review and examine the experiences gained by many developing countries in applying in different forms this primary health policy which has met with an encouraging and positive approach among many of the developing countries.

The second basic health problem is water. The basic need for drinking water is defined as reasonable access to water that does not contain any substances that harm the consumers' health or make the water unacceptable. Reasonable access is defined as availability of public hydrants within 200 meters in urban areas; in rural areas, the source of water should be sufficiently close that no disproportionate part of the day is spent in fetching water. The population at large that is not served or that does not have access to drinking water, among the poorest groups of the population, is still estimated at one billion, 200 million people. The problem is, of course, much more difficult in rural areas where roughly three fourths of the population have no access to an easily available safe water source.

Water is not only a question of water itself, one must think in terms of the quantity of water. It has been reported, for instance, that a Masai nomad would need roughly between four and a half and five and a half liters of drinking water per day. It is also necessary that the water be of desirable quality and, as the definition has indicated, that it be accessible.

We see now that there is a great demand for available and often scarce water resources coming from different users, irrigation being by far the most important. There is need to provide water for animals, while human beings require water for drinking purposes as well as for washing and for cleaning. All of this is competing for a safe source of water. We not only have to think in terms of water as such, but see this in relationship to the need for improved sanitation, hygiene, and the disposal of fecal matter so as to avoid infections.

As part of all our wider effort of development, one has to include measures to protect the source of water. Why is it that urban areas have received so much priority attention? On the one hand, the pressure of demand that the political influence of the urban areas can exercise has a great bearing on decision-making and allocation of resources. The setting up of urban water supply systems is more attractive for technical services in terms of professional competence. In the future, a greater shift of emphasis has to be made to meet the needs of widely scattered rural populations. There are many problems involved: the search for water, different users, the setting up of systems to preserve and bring water to the people, problems of maintenance, and ways to finance their upkeep. This all will require proper planning, coordination, increased resources. It will also require a quite different and more intensive collaboration with the concerned communities in the various stages of planning, implementation, and maintenance of water systems.

At the international conferences in Vancouver, in Canada, and Mara del Plata, in Argentina, a goal has been set to make water available for all the people by 1990. These are of course important and impressive resolutions, but they will require an extraordinary effort by all concerned. There is, I think, an effort spearheaded by the WHO and the United Nations Development Programme to mobilize both international agencies and the countries concerned, and to bring donor and developing countries together to see how these resolutions that have such influence on the well-being of millions of people can gradually be put into effect.

I come to the problems of nutrition. An adequate basic diet is the daily intake of sufficient proteins, carbohydrates, fats, vitamins, and minerals to allow human beings to conduct their physical and mental activities in good health. The average daily per capita calorie requirement for such survival, calculated on a world-wide basis, is about 2,350 calories for an adult male. At the moment, it is estimated that roughly one billion people do not have access to the minimum required level of calories and other elements. It would take about 25 million tons of additional food grains to meet the present food deficit in developing countries. This represents about 5 percent of the world consumption of cereals, or 15 percent of the amount of cereals now being fed to animals. As a result of more favorable weather and other conditions, food production in 1976 and 1977 somewhat improved though at a rate which does not keep up with population growth. This improvement, if we look at the various regions and countries, is uneven and certainly not as much as would be required in many African countries and many of those in Asia. However, when we speak about food and nutrition, we cannot, of course, think only of the staple food requirements, we must consider the qualitative aspect, the food basket. We must also consider the particular requirements of the vulnerable groups.

This will have to be part of a forward-looking nutrition policy that will really consider the problems of the vulnerable age group of children from 0 to 5, as well as the special food requirements of pregnant women and nursing mothers, such as iron, calcium, and so on. There are a number of associated questions that I would list briefly. The first one relates to the need to give appropriate recognition to the first food that the young child receives, namely, milk from its mother's breast. There is now developing a campaign to give more adequate recognition to the importance of breast feeding babies which is still more prevalent on another scale in developing countries but is threatened by aggressive marketing policies, the wrong concepts of the advantages of infant food. We have to see that the child will, during a sufficiently long period, receive what it needs most, the milk from its mother, and at the appropriate time, that this is supplemented by simple, locally prepared weaning food mixtures. These can be made with a combination of cereals and vegetables grown locally, which the mother can be taught to prepare, and feed the infant in an intelligent way in addition to her own milk. Supplementary child feeding in an emergency can be justified in certain cases, based on utilization of imported or locally available surplus food. It is, however, not a long-term answer and is often very costly. Therefore, the major effort has to go into a diversification of the production of appropriate types of food at the local level, involving both changes in agricultural policy, effort in education and nutrition demonstration, as well as changes in consumers' attitudes. It will require understanding and close involvement of the communities, of important national leaders as well as of women, both of whom involve the main provision of food and are concerned with the special demands of the young child. In addition, there are the special nutritional requirements due to lack of vitamin A, of iron, the problem of goiter, and so on, which can be tackled through both immediate and long-term measures. Many nutritionists advocate the establishment of systems to draw attention to early signs of deficiencies, which again requires collaboration of families and communities, also naturally with the support of governments. While it is possible to diagnose early signs of nutrition deficiencies, it is equally important to show the mother how such deficiencies can be overcome, and where to find the local resources to do so.

Here I must also refer to an additional requirement which is very closely linked with food, and that is firewood. Firewood is essential to provide food that has to be heated. The provision of firewood and therefore the economic exploitation of available forest resources is again one of the problems when one has to find a balance between the national resources and the national demand and a rational management of these resources.

The last of the four problems, that of shelter, is probably the most difficult one. The basic need for housing is more difficult to define but can probably be brought down to the need for shelter, usually permanent, which protects human beings, their families, or other social groups, from harmful climatic influences and other dangerous factors in their natural environment. Basic housing represents the minimum socially acceptable dwelling standards among the poorest strata of the society. It is very difficult to estimate how many people are deprived of housing, but the World Bank estimates that, among the poorer groups, 800 million people are deprived of a minimum standard of housing. It is very difficult here to think of any wide-ranging measures that concern individual housing because that exceeds available resources and means. The only way in which such standards can be improved is through demonstrations, better utilization of local material, and by making simple building elements available at cost, by training people, or, in certain cases, perhaps making special building teams available. Many governments have not recognized this importance as yet.

The demand for shelter and housing is becoming very serious and excruciating where people are concentrated in large groups in urban areas, in the peri-urban belts, slum areas, and so forth. And as you know from the information that came from the Habitat Conference, the rate of growth of urban population, now also in developing countries, is assuming very disquieting proportions. In Latin America at the moment, the percentage of urban population is between 35 percent and 45 percent of the total popilation, and it is expected that by the end of the century the proportion will reach 60 percent to 70 percent if not 75 percent. Even on the Indian subcontinent, where the largest groups are still in rural areas, the percentage varies from 18 percent to 25 percent. According to the projections of urban population growth, it may reach by the end of the century 35 percent and in some countries 40 percent. That is to say, we are witnessing a clear shift of the environment in which people live from rural to semi-rural to urban or peri-urban areas, with all the implications that must be faced.

It is clear that, among the policies that are open, one can only think of either improving existing slums or at least making some facilities available to the Site and Service Programme which provides some minimal measures. There are a number of certain complicating factors to be considered. Public services, governments, provincial administrations, and municipalities usually concentrate on the physical planning only. The provision of common utility services such as roads, sewage, transport, water, and electricity is a first necessity as well as the minimum of a social infrastructure, and often leaves it to the community itself to initiate, with a minimum of public support. An important element, however, is to establish the link between the two, because populations that have migrated to urban areas do not necessarily represent homogeneous groups and have to adapt themselves to entirely different living conditions. They face tremendous difficulty in adaptation and education.

These resources, however, also can be turned into a productive process of development through a combination of such physical planning and minimum services, and the establishment of essential social services. This is being more realized now, and we see at least a beginning in many urban areas in Latin America, in East Africa, and in Asia where the possibilities of joining forces are being recognized, and where we begin to have interesting examples of joint efforts opening the way to offer beginning solutions or a process to make life at least bearable and with the hope for further development. This is also being supported by the World Bank and other agencies. It does require tremendous efforts of adjustment and coordination between different administrations. It requires, as I indicated, a process of stimulation, encouragement, and education of the communities concerned, and the development of a linkage of measures that will really help communities to develop their own self-reaction in improving their environment.

I realize that this is only an overview of these physiological problems and material needs. They are presented in a sectoral way. On the international scene a more coordinated effort is taking shape. The World Bank has been encouraging this through its integrated rural development with an emphasis on its poorest areas, through the basic-needs philosophy of the ILO, or the basic-services concept of UNICEF regarding children and together with WHO, the primary health care which we are trying to encourage. We want to bring together the answers, so there is a more common and interrelated approach which does require, on the one hand, a much greater response from the international community, and on the other, a much closer link and association with the community and those forces in the community that are aware of these problems and are willing to participate and really seek answers, mobilizing the resources of labor, financial means, and other means of participation. It is here that we see a new role for social welfare in this tremendous joint effort that has to be undertaken to meet such basic needs and to help orient, encourage, and prepare the communities to play the role to which they aspire and that they must take if there is to be progress. I hope that the International Year of the Child, with its emphasis on a national dialogue, on a critical examination of the problems, will involve both governments, voluntary agencies, autonomous bodies, and the public in a searching analysis of outstanding and further problems of children. I would hope that countries, and especially social welfare workers, will take advantage of this conference, this critical conscious-raising exercise, and thus see and examine how some of these basic needs really can be met, or, if not, that at least approaches can be found and resources mobilized so that the participation of people can move ahead in the direction of a real conscious and concerned effort to improve social conditions.

PART III

ANTONIO GARCIA LIZANA
PROFESSOR, UNIVERSITY OF MÁLAGA, SPAIN

ARTICLE 25 OF the Universal Declaration of Human Rights refers to the right that every person and his family have to enjoy a level of living sufficient to meet their health, welfare, clothing, housing, and social service needs. We know, however, that millions of people are hungry, lack housing, do not enjoy adequate medical services, and therefore their health and general well-being are of very poor quality.

This fact, which reflects a very serious situation, becomes even more serious, ironically dramatic, when we realize that other groups of mankind not only do not suffer from those problems but are beginning to worry about opposite problems which threaten the destruction of their health, well-being, and even life itself: overmedication, overeating, alcoholism, overuse of tobacco, drug abuse; the destruction of their environment due to urbanization and uncontrolled industrialization; the dehumanization of human relations within too functional and depersonalized a context—all of which force health authorities to campaign against them.

When we look at this situation, we begin to wonder what can be done.

NUTRITION

Nutrition is indispensable to maintain human life, not only from a biological point of view but also to maintain life under the best possible physical, emotional, and intellectual conditions. Nutritional deficiencies may damage health, may undermine children's performance in school, and thus they may be impaired to such an extent that they will be unable to progress in the social world and secure the necessary resources to obtain adequate nutrition. This situation, in turn, will again affect work performance, lowering earnings and preventing them from earning more, a circle that will repeat itself indefinitely in the future. Three vicious circles are interrelated:

1. A particular individual at a specific point in his life has inadequate nutrition and unsatisfactory work achievement.

2. A particular individual during his entire life has inadequate nutrition, which causes poor performance in school and brings about poor employment opportunities and work achievements, which in turn have a negative impact on the possibilities of his having good nutrition.

3. Several generations have inadequate nutrition, influencing parents' unsatisfactory work performance, inadequate nutrition of their children, and so on.

Thus, it is important to point out the following:

Nutrition and the individual and family situation. 1. Nutrition conditions the development of a full life within the perspectives mentioned.

2. The resources allocated to nutrition should be a very important item in the family budget. The smaller the income, the larger is the proportion spent on nutrition. This may put the family under financial stress.

Nutrition and community life. 1. Nutrition is closely related to the development of nations and both influences and is influenced by it. If there are insufficient resources to support a population, the nutrition problems that will emerge will negatively influence the health conditions and the school and work performance of the community.

2. The nutrition needs in a community along with the real possibilities of meeting them will influence its self-sufficiency or its dependence on outside means. The community will be more or less vulnerable according to its specific circumstances and the external conditions, pressures, and fluctuations that limit the initiatives and the real possibilities for the community's development.

3. The nutrition intake of the community will have an important effect on the total population's consumption.

4. The demands to respond to the nutrition needs of the population, along with the mobilization of resources to do so, imply that the nutrition sector has great repercussions on the productive sectors—not only on agriculture, cattle raising, and fishing but also on the continuing development of new industries that process and sell food, on the presentation and distribution of new nutrition items, and the emergence of the hotel industry.

Therefore, adequate satisfaction of the nutrition needs of the population includes:

a) An increase in the wealth, particularly for specific productive sectors, but in general, for the entire economy

b) The opening up of new employment opportunities, so much needed so many times

c) The industrial development and stimulation of business and economic activities in general.

Due to the fact that the sectors closer to nutrition are the most affected (agriculture and so forth) and are the predominant ones in the less developed countries, the foregoing comments are even more important.

Nutrition and the world community. If we agreed that mankind is a unity where the ethnic, national, and generational groups are only subgroups, we should assume that the responses to the world nutrition problem should also be world responses. This is to say that:

1. The different groups that constitute mankind are so closely interrelated that when problems have historically appeared in one of the subgroups, sooner or later they have also been transferred to the other groups. Today this interrelation is much closer.

2. It cannot be denied that except for pragmatic considerations, human solidarity is important in itself; there have been many expressions of this attitude throughout history.

3. No matter what, it is true that each day there is a clearer awareness that this should be so, and in order to reach this

goal, a lot of work is being done from multiple perspectives.

4. World nutrition is of extraordinary importance, as is the fact that many millions of people in the Third World and many thousands in other countries are hungry, while in both groups are people who are overfed. Is this reasonable?

Availability and needs—supply and demand. It is necessary to establish a difference between the nutrition needs of a population and its actual demands for food. At the same time, it is necessary to differentiate between the availability of food production and its actual supply to a specific community. Even though this difference may not appear to be too important, it certainly is. It should be kept in mind that every increase in population makes an impact on the actual food demands, and therefore on the supplies. However, this should not be so because even though an increase in population does mean an increase in its demands, what becomes visible at the economic level is not the totality of needs but a different figure, which is modified by financial factors. If this is the case, then an increase in population where the density has previously been low and has now expanded because of industry does not imply that food demands will increase, but that there will be a reduction in the median level of nutrition and, thus, an undermining of health and welfare.

It can be said that something similar occurs with supply and demand. While food supplies for a population larger than the actual world population are available, the difficulties in obtaining them cause undernutrition of large groups. The food supply that really reaches the economic circuits is highly governed by group interests and rivalries, technical organizational difficulties, lack of financial resources, and so forth.

The problem is even more serious if one considers that while the increase in the world supply of food is greater than the world population growth, when we deal with the concrete needs of many countries we see that the increase is unable to meet even the demand. This situation can only lead to a reduction in the well-being of the people, reinforced by the emerging inflationary trends.

At a qualitative level it is not proper to talk about nutrition needs, food supply, and demand in a general way. It is necessary to:

1. Adjust the situation to specific human communities and compare it to the world situation
2. Consider the implications of a balanced diet quantitatively and qualitatively, and note that it is sometimes too large or too small
3. Remember that the demand, including the balanced diet itself, is influenced by cultural, ecological, and labor considerations, as well as purely financial ones.

In this regard, the fact that modern man in changing his eating habits and technology is making new contributions to nutrition possibilities should not be overlooked.

WATER AND ITS IMPORTANCE

It has recently been recognized that drinkable water is a human right and not only a simple convenience. It is known that water, along with food, air, and energy, is one of the essential factors for human existence. This is acknowledged by mankind's history when great civilizations flourished on the shores of the Euphrates, Tigris, Indus, and Nile. However, it is possible that the relationship between cultural development and water streams has deeper origins. In this connection, Bengt Sjörgen suggests that water has always been a source of inspiration, has stirred the imagination of children and adults, and has indeed been one of the contributing factors in mankind's development.

Without supporting or dismissing these theses, the need for water, its importance for health, hygiene, and therefore life, is beyond any quantitative analysis. However, only a few data will help us present the situation.

Today mankind is facing the serious problem of assuring a water supply that is appropriate for drinking, cooking, and general usage even though three quarters of the earth's surface are covered by water. This is due to the fact that only 3 percent is sweet water and only a small amount of that is available. If we also realize that much of this minimum is contaminated and unevenly distributed around the world, we will understand that one billion, 200 million people lack drinkable water in larger or smaller quantities and therefore, no matter why, they are not enjoying one of the basic human rights.

The uneven distribution of water brings about both lack and superabundance, neither of which is more favorable than the other. There are parts of the world that suffer because of the prevalence of one of these conditions. On the other hand, climate, geography, culture, habits, sanitation, the quantity and quality of water supplies, and sewage methods may be factors related to certain diseases associated with water. These diseases can be listed in five sometimes overlapping groups:

1. The lack of sanitary facilities produces diseases *contained* in the water, such as cholera, typhus, infectious hepatitis, and so forth.

2. The lack of water, poor personal hygiene habits, and inadequate sewage systems contribute to a group of diseases *transmitted* through water.

3. The presence of aquatic animals brings about diseases *originating* in water, such as intestinal worms, urinary infections, and so on.

4. Some diseases are produced by vectorial insects: malaria, yellow fever, and others transmitted by flies and mosquitoes.

5. Some diseases are associated with the elimination of fecal residues.

In those areas where water is the cause of disease it is particularly urgent to improve the water supply systems. However, this should be accompanied by educational campaigns so that the relationship between pure water, good conditions, and lack of disease becomes clear to the community. It should be remembered that perhaps certain groups may initially resist the new quality of the water since it will have a different taste from that to which they have become accustomed.

WATER AND DEVELOPMENT

The contributions that better water supplies make to development can be considered from two points of view:

Direct contributions. 1. The elimination of disease can contribute to an improvement of health conditions in general, with implications for productivity and school performance: a greater optimism on the part of the population, clearer minds, parents who need not worry about the potential death of their children.

2. With productive gardens and farms, nutrition will improve, and the income of both the family and the community will increase.

3. At another level, improving water supplies to family homes may bring about important progress toward the liberation of women. If they are relieved from the necessity of carrying water from distant places, they will have more time to devote to other activities.

Indirect contributions. 1. Building wells and pipe systems can be an important stimulation for community work using local labor for projects of mutual interest through mutual aid and neighbors' cooperation. Not only will this experience be beneficial in terms of the material results but also from a community activity point of view. Thus, water supply projects can indeed become development projects.

2. In any case, new water supply projects, including water filtration and treatment, can be an important source of job openings if appropriate techniques are applied to the local socioeconomic and labor situation.

3. The construction of these projects by using local rather than imported materials can also help in the development of complementary industries, which can in turn contribute to local wealth.

4. New activities will also emerge, like manufacturing new pumping engines, repairing old pipes, and so forth.

5. Other productive activities will also be stimulated, such as freezing and processing fish, raising vegetables and fruits, dyeing fabrics.

6. Finally, a guarantee of clean and abundant water implies a promise of citizen solidarity, increased wealth, and concern for the people and their well-being.

HEALTH

When health is understood in a broad sense, it includes a complete state of physical, mental, and social well-being and not merely the lack of disease. On this basis two points emerge:

1. Health services should cover not only the treatment and prevention of disease, but also the promotion and maintenance of health so that higher levels can be attained according to national, regional, and local indicators, such as infant mortality; morbidity of, as well as mortality from, certain diseases; life expectancy, and so on.

2. Some factors not considered conventionally as health services can also have a very important impact on the health conditions of the population: nutrition, water, housing, ecology, and so forth. Therefore, adequate health policies should take these into consideration and include the actions taken in relation to them.

Several other problems emerge in the health field, such as: health as a citizen right and obligation and its social implications; disease; health care; and the development of nations.

Health as a citizen right and obligation. Health is a fundamental human right, but there is a need to see health not only at the individual level but also at the community and world level.

There is a need for interpersonal and international cooperation for adequate health care. Health should not only be understood as something that is not isolated, but also as something that influences other aspects of human life, such as security and peace, education, and development. In this connection we should also point out that:

1. The right to health can be seen as related to personal and to public health.

2. Due to the fact that these two aspects are so closely interrelated, as well as related to peace, security, and development, we should talk about an obligation or duty that each citizen and each community should have toward health, which would justify many campaigns against alcoholism, drugs, to-

bacco. This obligation should be demanded by governments from citizens within certain limitations, and by citizens from governments as part of their political and constitutional obligations.

3. It is sad how many inequalities are still prevalent in today's world. And it is also sad how human beings themselves are responsible for road accidents, drug and alcohol abuse, suicides, and so on.

4. From a practical point of view the right to health should be found in:

   a) The right to health care for all citizens, wherever they live, and regardless of their nationality or place of residence

   b) Effective world cooperation to face the most serious diseases of mankind or parts of it

   c) Education and preparation on health problems provided to people, governments, and citizens.

Another aspect that should be emphasized is the accessibility of health services to the population, not only from a legal point of view but also from a practical one. This implies:

   a) Hospital services, sufficient number of beds, physicians, and nurses

   b) Effective possibilities for the citizens to use these services in terms of their cost, location, degree of bureaucratization, and so forth.

Discrimination against rural populations, children, the aged, the poor, and the handicapped should not be overlooked.

Health and development. It has been stated that as long as development occurs, mortality decreases and life expectancy increases. However, this is not always so. Urbanization brings the anxieties of modern life, automatism, and an exaggerated industrial development which may cause cardiovascular and psychiatric problems and accidents on the job and on the roads, as well as other negative consequences for the health conditions which arise from contamination, alcoholism, venereal disease, and overeating, which are threatening the highly developed countries today.

Finally, dramatic questions emerge from issues such as abortion, euthanasia, capital punishment, wars (whether just or unjust), suicide, political assasination, all of which are considered rights by some and denied by others. This is not the place for polemics as to whether they are legitimate or not.

However, it should be remembered that even with the best of intentions the march of humanity does not seem able to separate itself from the shadow of death attacking human life itself.

At this point we can ask ourselves what kind of response would be most appropriate to these problems. Here are a few suggestions:

1. There is a close relationship between the different aspects analyzed here and the circular and accumulative character of the problems detected.

2. The fact that the problems studied have two basic dimensions, an individual/family one and a community one, means that the latter is not a summing up of individual and family problems but appears as a separate unit, with its own character originating in the social structure of men and the problems emerging from their life together.

3. In view of the current situation of mankind regarding the organization of social life, and in view of the magnitude of existing problems, it is necessary to respond simultaneously and complementarily at different levels: public and private, on the one hand; individual and community, on the other hand; and still also at the level of local, national, and international communities until the entire world is reached.

These aspects lend themselves to reflections about the ultimate implications they represent.

Interconnection and circularity. It is interesting to establish the following differences:

1. For the human being to attain an adequate state of health and well-being, different services should be provided simultaneously. Otherwise the positive effects of some may be lost.

2. A human being whose health and well-being are adequate will at the same time have an adequate personal, family, and social life, which will enable him to get the necessary ser-

vices from his physical and social surroundings in order to maintain and even to improve his health and welfare. A deficient situation will undermine what such a human being can get from his environment (food, water), which, in turn, will bring about difficulties in improving his situation and condemn him to remain there.

These reflections may be valid not only for individuals, but also for social groups.

Individual and community dimensions. Due to the fact that both these dimensions are so closely interrelated, any policies that attempt to be successful should deal with both of them, taking into consideration their own peculiarities. For example, national health policies should differentiate between two large goals: those common to the entire population and specific ones for individuals and groups, providing the opportunities for each one to secure the general benefits available.

Levels of action. On this basis, the following points should not be forgotten when policies are formulated:

1. Human needs should be met by the individual himself as well as by nature and society.

2. Considering the weakness of the people who are most needy and their unfavorable environment, social or natural, as well as the circular characteristics mentioned earlier, very strong actions are expected either from themselves or others in order to help them get out of their poor conditions.

If human or material resources are not sufficient, then it will be necessary to resort to outside individuals or communities to assist them. Therefore, these actions may be seen as undertaken by the people themselves, by the private sector on a profit or nonprofit basis, and by public bodies. On the other hand, actions may be taken by other communities, including the international community, both public and private.

Depending on the most serious problems prevalent in a community, priorities for action should be established by public initiative. In other cases international assistance in the health field should be used as a beginning effort for further action, for example, in the area of housing.

In any case, if the goal is to attain the good health and well-being of individual and social groups, in the end their full maturity is expressed through their own participation in the process, which then acquires the utmost importance, no matter what strategies have been used to fulfill it.

PART IV

KIM HAK MOOK

BOARD MEMBER, KOREA NATIONAL COUNCIL OF SOCIAL
WELFARE, KOREA

I AM not quite sure when and where clothing, food, and shelter were first referred to as the three basic human needs. However, man has made individual and collective efforts to meet these three needs. While science and civilization have progressed enough to conquer space, even today the fundamental questions of these needs have not been solved. Furthermore, the development of science and civilization increases the needs for health, water, and ecological suitability. Sometimes I wonder about the value of modern civilization and human knowledge. Thus, I feel that life is nothing but a process of solving problems to serve all the needs of human beings.

Korea has made organized efforts to solve such problems of physiological and material needs in recent years.

FOOD

Since 1976 Korea has maintained a surplus of rice and barley. It is said that the farmers' food crisis has been overcome thanks to land reform, the green revolution, and international cooperation. However, we should not forget to appreciate the farmers' aspirations and their self-help community efforts nourished and enhanced through the New Village Movement

(Saemaul Undong) for their better life. This movement is generally interpreted as the community development program.

To heighten the quality of food and the nutrition programs, in line with recommended dietary allowances for Koreans, voluntary agencies are also participating. The orientation on marketing must be given more emphasis.

The school luncheon service was started for poor students but now covers the other students in many communities. It was not easy to differentiate this service from the so-called "mass-feeding" program. It was found that it is good to start on a school or community base rather than a national one.

People require more protein food, and authorities encourage livestock raising and importation of foreign protein products. The consumption of processed food is increasing, and voluntary groups are involved in classes in cooking processed foods as well as in determining the quality of imported protein foodstuff. The physical condition of Korean youngsters appears to indicate a rapidly changing society.

HOUSING

The population increase, the drift of rural residents to cities, and the younger generation's eagerness to set up nuclear families intensify the general housing problem.

Public housing authorities are serving low-income groups while private housing industry groups serve the upper-middle class in general. Recently, the appeal for a rental scheme for low-income groups has become stronger, and a public housing program is being adjusted to meet the need.

In rural areas, as a project of Saemaul Undong, the farmers' housing development program is being carried out on the basis of cooperative efforts and with the financial aid of the authorities throughout the country, and farmers are enjoying improved housing.

There is a tendency to think that housing in city areas these days is almost synonymous with apartment living. However, since the planner, the architect, as well as the would-be occupants had never experienced apartment life, it was not easy to construct apartments to meet their practical daily life and social needs.

The Salary and Wage Earner's Fortune Formulation Saving Scheme, in addition to long-term low-interest loans from the housing bank, is increasing housing purchasing power.

Certainly, housing is the matrix of human growth and development. Thus, people are aware of the importance of the various social amenities, the housing resident training services, as well as the legal provisions of apartment management.

Public authorities encourage the private housing industry to construct both large and small apartment units in the same building or in the same compound for the sake of social integration.

These social aspects will work out soundly with dialogue between physical planners and social planners. Social work educators need to give attention not only to the human service delivery process, but also to such social planning processes. It is good to involve voluntary agencies in these areas, using their community work knowledge and skills.

HEALTH

It is a fact that the mortality rate and the incidence of communicable diseases are decreasing while both the numbers of senior citizens and the incidence of chronic diseases of adults are increasing. Good health is still an acute need, and at present Koreans recognize health as their fourth necessity.

Since the fourth five-year economic development plan started in 1977, some drastic measures have been taken to cope with the medical treatment problem. Under the medical protection law, the disabled poor and the outpatients of the able-bodied poor receive free treatment while the able-bodied poor are entitled to benefits from the 70 percent medical fee installment for their hospitalization. The remaining percentage is borne by the government.

The medical insurance law, enacted experimentally in 1963, was revised in 1977. Business firms which hire more than 500 employees are covered by the latter law, while government employees and private school staff are to be covered by a separate medical insurance law. Thus it is estimated that 26 percent of the total population will benefit from these three laws.

Even the smaller firms, farmers, and the self-employed will be able to organize their medical unions, on a geographical basis, separately. The formation of such unions may be hindered by the lack of cohesiveness, especially in cities, for local leadership and socioeconomic reasons.

Special efforts have been made to set up a standard medical cost-point system, contribution rate, and poverty line for medical relief and public assistance programs respectively. The means test schemes are not yet established firmly. The information services, through the mass media, play an important role in the medical insurance program, but not so much for the medical relief program. It is inevitable that there should be health workers' information and orientation services on the medical relief scheme, on a face-to-face basis.

It appears to be imperative to establish better understanding and a closer relationship between the medical community and the consumers concerned and also with the public authorities to make the health care program successful. The training needs of health care field workers are important.

The problems of imbalance between curative and preventive health services, integration of public and private sectors, and the inefficient medical referral system are not solved yet. The emphasis on training medical specialists rather than general practitioners is also a problem.

The remote rural areas face the problem of lower utilization of health care facilities, in the midst of a rather sufficient supply of health manpower trained in Western medicine. The inequitable distribution of manpower is the main cause of this problem. Therefore, the redistribution of medical manpower and the establishment of a comprehensive health care delivery system are being studied intensively. However, there are pros and cons about the latter.

There are pronounced criticisms of the underevaluation of traditional methods in curative as well as preventive fields. The herb doctors are not involved in the medical insurance schemes. It is said that the rating system of herbal medical treatment is not easy to administer.

Accessibility of health care services is being enhanced by developments of new roads and other transportation facilities.

Some health and social services are being carried out through Saemaul Undong. However, the professional collaboration for people's integrated services between public health and social services at the central and local levels and the two concerned school communities is strongly emphasized. It is my feeling that aptitude tests should be used for applicants in medical and social welfare services.

ECOLOGY AND WATER

Environmental pollution is in many ways one of Korea's most difficult problems. In 1978 the government enacted two special laws: an environmental protection law and a marine pollution prevention law.

The imbalance between water demand and supply is especially acute in urban and industrial zones. On the other hand, in rural areas, to have better-quality drinking water, people are vigorously working through Saemaul Undong for piped water supplies and rural electrification.

Human excreta, particularly when there are poor septic tanks, and industrial wastage may lead to water pollution. Air pollution is caused mainly by exhaust gas from the rapidly increasing number of motors and heavy use of anthracite as home fuel. It is of interest that anthracite causes cerebral palsy. People in the industrial and urban areas begin suffering from noise and vibration, solid wastage, and garbage, all of which intensify the problems.

It is often heard that rural farmers are suffering from producing or mishandling poor agricultural medicines. Nevertheless, there are not enough comprehensive data to evaluate the ill-effects of environmental pollution hazards. There are not enough trained human resources, adequate tools, and machines which can handle the problem efficiently.

It will be more than welcome to have a national environmental study center with assistance from the United Nations.

This center will advise the authorities, factories, and others concerned with ecological suitability. However, despite the government's intensive efforts in line with the legal provisions, private business circles, academic authorities, voluntary agencies, and student groups are fighting against solutions of the ecological and environmental needs, such as antipollution and nature protection programs being undertaken by urban Saemaul Undong.

Certain conclusions may be drawn:

1. When the top leadership and voluntary grass-roots workers are matched together simultaneously, development can be achieved.

2. Participation is a cultural assumption, but it is becoming a universal one.

3. National stability is a prerequisite of economic and social development in a given setting.

4. National unity calls for social development, but social development must be found in humanitarianism and/or humanism.

5. The development elite, that is, policy-makers, planners, and administrators (including front-line workers), should remember that all well-being, at all social levels, is everybody's business.

6. Without encouraging spiritual and moral values, it may be difficult to achieve the well-being of all.

While I appreciate such terminology as "wholesome," "balanced," and "integrated," development, how can we find a workable definition and measurement?

Despite unprecedented economic growth for more than a decade and a half, the Republic of Korea still faces resource constraints in directly improving human well-being. These constraints stem from three important sources: the import requirements for supporting a dense population without much natural resource endowment: the need for industrial and social overhead investments to absorb a more than 3 percent per annum increase in the labor force; and the defense requirements under the peculiar geopolitico-military situation. Therefore, it is inevitable for us to establish a strategy and priorities in meeting and improving the physiological and material needs.

The fourth five-year economic development plan, 1977–82, currently under implementation, recognizes the improvement of social welfare as the ultimate goal of economic development and specifies the promotion of equity and the enhancement of the quality of life as one of its guiding principles. Under the given emphasis and framework of the formal plan, a planned effort is directed to meet the physiological and material needs of low-income classes and the farm population.

PART V

BRUCE RAWSON

DEPUTY MINISTER, DEPARTMENT OF NATIONAL HEALTH AND
WELFARE, CANADA

HERE WE ARE examining the physiological and material prerequisites of human well-being, and the challenge we face in ensuring that each member of our society has access to these prerequisites. In placing this challenge in the context of the 1980s we must also take into account the popular opinion that the salad days of what has been called the "welfare state" may have run their course. If that is the case, the challenge we face will be a challenge indeed.

No one of us could fail to be aware of the growth of so-called "antigovernment" sentiment during the 1970s. These opinions are in fact not truly antigovernment, since they often call for stricter law and order, stronger national government, and more active economic stimulation; but direct government spending and, most particularly, social welfare spending have suffered sustained criticism. This may be largely a consequence of the present period of world-wide slow economic growth. In the conservative climate which slow growth seems to engender, welfare expenditures are too often seen to be dabbling in frivolous egalitarianism when stern measures are necessary to raise production. And, as we know all too well, some critics go so far as to cite past welfare spending as a primary cause of the present inflation and economic downturn.

In reaction to this apparent public disapproval of government spending, governments everywhere have turned to a self-imposed austerity. Anti-Keynesian sentiments prevail as balancing budgets and restraining monetary growth are the order of the day. However, there has been a subtle change in the nature of this criticism over the last six months or so, at least in Canada. Faced with a continuing recalcitrant economy and with the plain fact that cutting back expenditures too deeply in a time of slow growth may lead to a serious recession, even some of the harshest critics of government spending are now adopting a different line: the problem is not too much government spending, it is ineffective and inefficient government spending. This apparent change, if it is real, affords us an opportunity to rethink our approach to providing for basic human needs.

It is tempting to define material needs as those things strictly necessary to sustain life. However, we must not forget that the well-being of man requires much more than physiological maintenance, or that many people will undergo what most of us would consider to be intense physical deprivation in order to satisfy other needs which to them are more important.

Man does not live by bread alone, as the saying goes. However, a hungry person can easily define basic needs, and for the sake of this discussion I shall treat health, food, shelter, water, and a clean and safe environment as the basic elements of physiological and material needs. But I must add this precaution: we may, for the moment, turn our backs upon "higher" needs but we can never forget them for long. The question of basic social needs will present itself once people have satisfied their basic physiological and material needs.

In the very beginning, everyone was responsible for meeting his basic needs. Whether as hunters and foragers or as rudimentary agriculturalists, early men were, of necessity, self-sustaining. However, with the coming of a more complex society came the first examples of "welfare recipients." In feudal societies, for instance, those unable to sustain themselves were protected by tradition. The lord owed it to his wards to maintain them whether they contributed directly to production or not. Furthermore, the medieval church found room in it for all souls, again whether these souls were directly productive or not. The obligations of religion and tradition guaranteed that all members of the feudal community obtained the wherewithal for life.

As society grew increasingly complex, fewer and fewer people directly sustained themselves. The division of labor developed, the cities swelled, and the feudal ties evaporated. The human costs of the resulting industrial and commercial progress were very great. Many individuals were "pauperized," bereft of land and unable to find work.

Society reacted to the needs of these people. Charities continued, as did frequent individual donations to the needy, and "self-help," in the form of crime, thrived. It was at this time that the state first involved itself in aiding the disadvantaged.

As the benefits of industrialism began to be appreciated, it was seen that those who had historically suffered so much to produce it deserved a fairer share of the proceeds. Hence, the state assumed a more balanced view of its responsibility for the underprivileged.

Today, the bulk of material and physiological needs is met by the workings of the economy, largely independent of government programs. However, there remains a segment of the population which is left aside by the market economy. It is this diverse group which concerns social workers the most in their day-to-day work.

One of the major difficulties that we face is related to this evolutionary development of our programs. No one person decided that "in 1978, the Canadian social security system will be thus." Instead, individual programs were developed to meet specific problems, often a specific problem in a specific place. Today, we are called upon to justify our expenditures and rationalize our efforts. We too often find ourselves defending not a coherent approach toward meeting our clients' basic needs but a jumble of diverse and occasionally contradictory programs.

For example, no Canadian would claim that we have succeeded in ensuring the material and physiological needs of Canada's native peoples. Malnutrition, alcoholism, inadequate shelter and sanitation are continuing problems. There are many reasons for this, but among them is the way in which our programs fit together—or, more properly, often fail to do so. Canada's Department of National Health and Welfare provides health services to native peoples living on reserves. The Department of Regional Economic Expansion assists these people to establish productive enterprises and an economic infrastructure. This program should provide the long-term solution. However, yet another department, Indian Affairs and Northern Development, has the primary responsibility for the other programs provided for these people. None of us could claim to be pleased with the problems of administration arising from this mélange of departments and of programs, but rationalizing them requires the people and money that are in increasingly short supply.

To cite another example: Canada has many different income-maintenance programs, some in the form of subsidies for producers, some in the form of partially funded social insurance programs, and some as direct income transfers. Unfortunately, many potential recipients "fall between the stools" of these inadequately coordinated programs. Too often they do not receive a level of support sufficient to meet even their physiological and material needs.

Unfortunately, these examples are not isolated. The present state of social welfare provisions for basic needs in Canada tends to be somewhat haphazard and somewhat inefficient, and I would assume that every country would make a similar admission. The rectification of these problems is not easy, especially when resources are tight and there are pressures to make further cuts. However, one obvious starting place is the need to clarify, improve, and better integrate three sets of relations: first, the relations among government agencies; second, the relations between government welfare administrations and their clients; and third, the relations between the public and private sectors of the economy.

I can perhaps best illustrate the need to improve relationships among government agencies by citing an example from my own area of responsibility—health and welfare. We are now focusing upon the interrelationship between health and social problems. Our emphasis in the health care field is shifting from curing illnesses to preventing them. This has involved us in far greater efforts to improve the living conditions and styles of life of Canadians. This new direction toward the health of Canadians has involved us in the welfare and economic well-being of Canadians, and eventually in the employment opportunities of Canadians.

We are also considering a guaranteed income as the basic approach to rationalizing our income-maintenance programs and ensuring that the basic physiological and material needs are met. To this end, we are watching with great interest the progress of similar proposals in other countries. I might mention the better jobs and incomes program as a very good example of the integration of large and tangled welfare programs into one, more coherent approach.

Broadening our horizons also means reconsidering the nature of our welfare services to individuals: our goal is to develop better means of helping them gain better control over their lives and to become fully participating members of the Canadian economy. This immediately involves the relationship between our government and its clients.

Ensuring the material needs of those left behind by the modern economy is at the best of times a difficult task. In addition to the problem of providing an adequate level of support, we can too easily create other problems for the people we intend to help. In particular, the right of an individual to social assistance may entail the loss of some of his or her other rights.

A particularly vexing loss, especially from the new perspective that I have been discussing, is the loss of the right to work, at least the right to work for pay. Here I am deliberately overstating the effect of the various tax-back and benefit reduction provisions that can severely limit the incentives to work, by reducing benefits in relation to wages earned.

We are producing in Canada a large group of people extraordinarily skilled at computing the net benefits of a job. Too often these net benefits are negative.

It is not the proper function of social welfare to make people dependents of the state. It should assist them to earn a place in the modern economy, the modern society, so that they may depend upon themselves rather than upon the government. A reassessment of our relations with our clients could help to remove many of these problems and, in the process, better provide for their physiological and material needs. Such a reexamination may enable us to break the cycle of dependency, and, what is in some ways equally important in the current social climate, it may enable us to do so at a lower cost.

What I am suggesting is that, in addition to providing for basic needs, we must consider "enabling programs"—programs that will enable people to help themselves. One example is Canada's New Horizons program. New Horizons extends funds to senior citizens who are engaged in projects that help either themselves or their communities. Many of Canada's elderly are doing such things as running their own museums, publishing books and periodicals, visiting and providing meals for isolated persons. Rather than simply pensioning off our elderly, we are helping them become involved in their communities and ensuring that their time is spent in an atmosphere of productivity and enjoyment. No doubt there are similar programs in other countries.

Of course, New Horizons has its shortcomings. Many of our most isolated and lonely senior citizens do not have access to, or simply do not know about, New Horizons projects. This is a problem which proper planning will correct. On the other hand, it will not resolve a complaint made by many involved senior citizens to the effect that macrame work, publishing "golden age" periodicals, and running museums are all very well but that they are more concerned with housing and nutrition and with producing marketable goods. In other words, many of the citizens most involved in New Horizons projects want to use our funds and their initiative to treat their own material and physiological needs, something which suggests to me a very reasonable policy alternative. Unfortunately, we have met some resistance to this change from the commercial enterprises which normally provide for the physiological and material requirements of senior citizens and which are not enthusiastic about the use of tax revenues to establish competitors.

Our problems in promoting change in the New Horizons program are typical of the ambiguity surrounding public and private sector relations. This example could be multiplied in Canada, and I am sure in other countries as well. The problem stems from an uncertainty regarding the proper role of the public sector. Historically, welfare programs grew in response to diverse needs that the private sector could not or would not meet. Welfare programs "sneaked into the gaps." As a result, the jumble of programs we call welfare and the realm of economic enterprise are often thought to be antagonistic.

This is simply false. The government acts as an overseer of the economic system, and where the latter cannot serve essential physiological and material needs, the state must step in. This is the rationale behind unemployment insurance, income maintenance, social services, and so on. As the capacity of the system to provide for its members increased, so too our concept of the needs and rights of individuals expanded. Many nations now offer universal medical care coverage, and adequate welfare programs. These are not contrary to the spirit of the economic system: they support that system and in so doing, help the people who may not yet have found a place in that system to do so.

One of the most profitable courses open to us is to clarify and expand our relationships with the private sector, to enlist them in our cause, and to ensure that programs work to our mutual advantage. The Canadian Commission of Employment and Immigration has several programs designed to do just this. From employment subsidies, the developmental use of unemployment insurance funds, and assistance to apprenticeship training, these programs help employers in assisting the "unemployable" to become productive members of the modern economy. These programs are a promising start; however, I know that Canada lags behind many countries in this type of initiative.

I have presented a large task: to clarify and coordinate the relations between departments, between sectors, and with our clients, and cut costs at the same time. We must find ways to integrate, rationalize, and coordinate our programs. We must convince the critics that these programs represent an essential support of the economic system as well as a means of meeting society's basic obligations to its less fortunate members.

If this last has an old-fashioned, religious tone, so be it. All three of the world's great religions are predicated upon social justice and, in its largest sense, charity—charity toward our fellows, toward those whom 2,000 years ago, and 10 years ago, it was fashionable to call our brothers and sisters. We should not forget those words, those obligations, simply because budgets are tight.

During the darkest days of England's Industrial Revolution, William Blake could, after describing the "dark satanic hills," call for building Jerusalem in England's "green and pleasant land." We have come a long way from nineteenth-century England, but this would be an especially poor time to decide to give up the fight.

Our task is to respond to the challenge of closer scrutiny and higher expectations, but to do what we should always have done. Our programs should always have been effective, fair, and efficient. They should always have been well-coordinated and accurately targeted. They should always have emphasized returning clients to the main stream of the economy. Now they have to do so. We face challenge as well as an opportunity. Let us make the most of it.

PART VI

GUNTER WITZSCH

PROFESSOR, FACHHOCHSCHULE MUNSTER,
FEDERAL REPUBLIC OF GERMANY

THE TERM "basic human needs" contains a concept which has recently attracted increasing attention and received political thrust in international forums ever since a United Nations symposium, held at Cocoyoc, Mexico, in 1974, stated as a primary objective of the new international economic order:

Our first concern is to redefine the whole purpose of development. This should not be to develop things but to develop man. Human beings have basic needs: food, shelter, clothing, health, education. Any process of growth that does not lead to their fulfilment—or even worse disrupts them—is a travesty of the idea of development.[1]

Other forums soon followed suit, and the concept now figures prominently in the discussions at various UN meetings, notably the annual sessions of the Economic and Social Council. The 1976 World Employment Conference, convened by the International Labour Organization (ILO), elaborated the concept in great detail and called on the UN General Assembly to make the policies required to meet basic needs "an essential part of the United Nations Second Development Strategy and the core of the forthcoming Third Development Strategy."[2]

It should be noted, however, that the concept as such is not

[1] John McHale and Magda Cordell McHale, *Human Needs: a Framework for Action,* a report to the United Nations Environment Program (New Brunswick, N.J.: Transaction Books, 1977), p. xxiv.

[2] International Labour Office, *Employment, Growth and Basic Needs: a One-World Problem* (New York: Praeger Publishers, 1977), p. vii.

a new one. Scientific studies were carried out by Booth and Rowntree as early as before World War I and later by Maslow and the McHales in particular, to mention only a few. The 1948 UN Universal Declaration of Human Rights, in Articles 25 and 26, postulated the same elements of basic needs satisfaction as did the Cocoyoc Declaration twenty-six years later.

The basic difference between the earlier and the new approach lies in a shift from the emphasis on redistribution of wealth between nations to a pursuit of international policies to be followed by the developing countries themselves. While the sixth and seventh special sessions of the General Assembly of the UN, as well as the fourth UN Conference on Trade and Development, held at Nairobi in 1976, stressed the importance of a reform of the international economic order, assuming that—as a by-product—increased resources generated within the developing countries with the assistance of the developed countries would automatically alleviate the worst forms of poverty in the former, the new concept emphasizes the need for parallel policies, the necessity of both interstate and intrastate reforms. This approach, put forward most explicity by the ILO, acknowledges the fact that people and not countries are central in the development process.

The new approach also reflects a certain disenchantment with the results of previous development strategies based primarily on economic growth. Although the developing countries as a group achieved impressive growth rates, often at an accelerated pace, this growth was not matched by a concomitant decline in the numbers of people living in absolute poverty. Per capita gross national product in developing countries increased by almost 3 percent each year over the past twenty-five years and accelerated in the 1970s to 3.3 percent; these rates compare favorably with the growth rates of the less than 2 percent that most of the developed countries of the West were able to achieve since industrialization started in those countries.[3] Despite these impressive gains in economic devel-

---

[3] *World Development Report 1978* (Washington, D.C.: the World Bank, 1978), p. 3.

opment, the number of absolute poor people in all developing countries has now reached 770 million. The picture is not very likely to change rapidly. A recent World Bank report gloomily projects the number of people living in absolute poverty in the year 2000 at 600 million and concludes that, even given more favorable assumptions of growth, elimination of absolute poverty in the so-called low-income countries by the end of this century seems impossible.[4]

When we talk about absolute poverty or the nonsatisfaction of basic human needs there is, of course, always the problem of definition. An indicator often used expresses poverty in terms of per capita income. Thus, an Organization for Economic Cooperation and Development (OECD) study considers an average annual income per capita of $150 US to be the amount at which people in developing countries are unable to meet their basic human needs.[5] Absolute figures, however, do not sufficiently take into account the considerable range of buying power in individual countries or the variability in human requirements. Physiological, climatic, social, and cultural conditions are variables which make it difficult to express requirements in single monetary terms. For example, a shelter adequate for living in a tropical climate may be totally unacceptable in a colder climate where construction of an adequate shelter would also cost considerably more.

How, then, do we measure basic human needs? Following the 1976 World Employment Conference, basic needs were defined as "the minimum standard of living which a society should set for the poorest groups of its people."[6] According to the Program of Action of the conference, the concept of basic human needs includes two elements: first, certain minimum requirements of a family for private consumption—adequate food, shelter, and clothing as well as certain household equipment and furniture; second, essential services provided by and for the community at large, such as safe drinking water, sani-

---

[4] *Ibid.*, p. 33.
[5] OECD, Survey of International Development, XV, No. 1 (1978), 1.
[6] *World Development Report,* p. 7, n. 2.

tation, public transport, and health, educational, and cultural facilities.[7]

It is interesting to note that the ILO conference adopted a somewhat broader concept of basic needs than the Cocoyoc Declaration. This is not too surprising since a new concept such as the one we are faced with is subject to interpretations which depend to some extent on individual value judgments. Therefore, even human freedoms were suggested as part of the concept of basic needs.

Attempts have been made to categorize individual basic needs. Thus, Maslow proposed a "needs hierarchy" which goes from basic physiological needs such as hunger, thirst, and sex, followed in ascending order by higher level needs for security and belonging toward self-actualization and aesthetic experience at the top level.[8]

A working group of the Aspen Institute for Humanistic Studies suggested a distinction between a "first floor" and a "second floor" of basic needs. The first floor would contain minimum human needs—food, health, and education—to which each person should be entitled by virtue of being born into the world. The second floor would contain such other basic needs as are defined (and redefined over time) by each nation-state for its own people, within the context of the interdependence of all societies. While the meeting of the first floor needs would be the joint responsibility of the country concerned and the international community, the meeting of the second floor needs would essentially be the responsibility of each nation-state.[9]

One may argue that the question of a hierarchy of basic human needs is of a more academic nature. However, the question may become an issue if basic needs conflict with each other. How do we meet a human need considered basic if its satisfaction means the encroachment upon, or even elimination of, another basic human need? Suppose an increase in ag-

[7] Section I, paragraph 2 of the Program of Action adopted by the 1976 World Employment Conference, cited in International Labour Office, op. cit., Annex B.

[8] See Abraham H. Maslow, ed., *Motivation and Personality* (New York: Harper & Row, 1954), chap. 7.

[9] *World Development Report*, p. xxiv, n. 1.

ricultural production necessary to meet the need for food can only be achieved by using fertilizer with harmful effects on the environment, thereby posing a potential threat to human health. Or, a construction program to provide housing can only be carried out by using arable land, resulting in decreasing the potential to meet the human need for food.

These examples show that any basic needs strategy is intricately linked to the environment issue, and, indeed, one may wonder if a healthy human environment does not in itself constitute a basic human need.[10] It is sometimes forgotten that the 1972 UN Conference on the Human Environment, held in Stockholm, considered mass poverty one of the worst forms of environmental degradation. Indeed, the relationship between poverty and environmental concerns is too obvious in most developing countries. Take, for example, the lack of cheap energy to cook food or to provide heating: the scramble for firewood has led to widespread deforestation in many developing countries and has often resulted in rapidly increasing desert areas, thereby depriving the poorer segments of the population of the very resource base on which they depend for their livelihood. There is a vicious circle: mass poverty is a source of environmental destruction, and this leads to even more poverty.

Eradication of poverty and environmentally sound development must, therefore, go hand in hand. Development without regard to the physical and social constraints of our environment will ultimately result in elimination of the resource base from which man must inevitably gain his sustenance and the capacity to meet basic human needs. This conclusion has by no means become a universally accepted axiom. Thus, the seventh special session of the UN in 1975 adopted an elaborate program of action geared to development efforts within the context of a new international economic order. Yet, the environmental dimension is totally missing in this program. What we need is a concept that ensures development without de-

---

[10] Thus, an ILO report specifically notes that a basic human needs strategy implies the satisfaction of needs of a more qualitative nature, such as a "healthy, human and satisfying environment." *Ibid.*, p. 7, n. 20.

struction of the environment. What we actually witness today in many countries is destruction without development.

At the core of environmental degradation lies the population explosion. No strategy aimed at satisfying human needs will succeed without tackling the problem of population growth. "If population growth does not decline, then the cost of realizing food, health and education requirements for ever larger numbers of people—and raising their standard of living—becomes increasingly difficult if not impossible."[11] It is surprising and discouraging that the populations issue is still not yet seen in its proper perspective, and quite a few governments still refuse to acknowledge the devastating impact of uncontrolled population growth on any efforts to implement a basic needs strategy. There is still widespread reluctance to adopt determined government policies of reducing population growth rates. Although a recent report of the UN Fund for Population Activities indicates some promising signs of a decline in fertility, the lowest forecast for the world population in the year 2000 is still 5.8 billion, compared with today's total of about 4 billion.[12]

The population increase will pose tremendous challenges to the world community and particularly to the taxpayers of its more affluent parts. However, past experience should dampen our hope to expect too much willingness from those who are asked to pay the bill to do so. Development aid has somewhat lost its appeal to the public in many developed countries. The Official Development Aid has consistently fallen short of the target of 0.7 percent of the GNP that the developed countries were expected to contribute. OECD member countries' Official Development Assistance disbursements even declined from 0.36 percent in 1975 to 0.33 percent in 1976 and 0.32 percent in 1977.[13] Deplorable as this may be, it may partly also reflect negative experiences of donor countries in regard to the distribution of aid within the recipient countries. Not rare are cases where development aid

[11] *Ibid.*, p. 5., n. 5.
[12] *Development Forum*, VI, No. 5 (1978), 1f.
[13] *World Development Report*, p. 6., n. 5.

did not reach its ultimate destination. We see inefficiency, disinterest, and mismanagement within some developing countries which are counterproductive to or even obliviate whatever material efforts are made by donor countries. We must overcome the attitude of complacency which seems to be prevalent in certain quarters of both the developed and the developing world when it comes to the plight of millions of the less fortunate. As a high-ranking UN official once pointedly remarked: "What we have witnessed may be more of a concern with satisfying human greeds than basic human needs."[14]

[14] M. K. Tolba, Executive Director of the United Nations Environment Program, in an address at the University of Houston, Houston, Texas, 1977.

Economic and Security Needs

VICTOR I. A. BARRETT

PERMANENT SECRETARY, MINISTRY OF AGRICULTURE, JAMAICA

IN ALMOST every developing country there is increased physical development, accompanied by economic and social change. Economic development in most countries is the key to progress.

In Jamaica there are substantial economic, social, and security needs. The need for more education at all levels, the need for more income, the need for increased provisions of housing, and for health insurance schemes—all are outstanding. The security needs of developing countries, including Jamaica, are similarly outstanding.

In order to feel secure, one has to be assured of ready and capable health services, medical and dental care, mental health care, maternity care, infant care, adequate income, and good nutrition. These exist in most developing countries, and the main aim of progressive and developing countries is to increase these facilities as far as resources will allow.

The economic needs of nations rely on their resources—employment, industry, imports, exports, agriculture, tourism, education. Agriculture, education, and industry are the mainstays of all nations. Every effort ought to be made to develop these.

Advisory services in agriculture, government subsidies in agriculture, and agricultural schemes administered by responsible bodies will all assist in keeping local production at a satisfactory level. Local production should be the key word. Production ought to be encouraged. The more a country exports its products, the more its economy is boosted, providing needed foreign currency.

EMPLOYMENT OF WOMEN

There is a need for policies and programs aimed at increasing training and job opportunities for women in wider ranges of occupations, thus ensuring equality of opportunity and conditions of employment for female workers. The incorporation of more women in the labor force should be a priority.

In raising livestock I have had the experience of proving that dairy cows and calves respond more favorably to feminine care than to masculine care. The tender care of a feminine assistant immensely affects the growth and development of livestock, and increases milk production as a result of the reaction of the appropriate hormones. Women, therefore, should be encouraged and given adequate facilities to participate fully and to acquire training and education in agriculture at all levels.

The social implications of the increased incorporation of women in economic activities should be taken into account. There should be continuous recognition of the interrelationship of the social and economic factors.

There is a need for adequate provision of management skills to assist women to manage cooperatives and self-employment ventures, as well as to provide training for top management posts in commerce and industry. Governments, trade unions, and private sectors should ensure that the economic, social, and security rights of all workers are fully protected.

SECURITY NEEDS

Education is foremost among a progressive country's social and security needs. Programs, curricula, and standards of education and training should be the same for both sexes. Courses for both sexes should include, in addition to general subjects, industrial and agricultural technology, political education, economics, current and prevailing problems of the society, responsible parenthood, family life, nutrition, and health.

There is a need to reorient educational programs whenever the occasion arises, in order to keep abreast of the fast-changing conditions in a changing world.

There is an urgent need to formulate programs to reduce infant and child mortality rates by means of improved maternal care, child health care, nutrition, sanitation, and health education. Special priority attention ought to be given to rural and depressed areas. Dental services, especially in these areas, should be updated and increased. The quality of family life requires the attention of social welfare services whose programs should be coordinated with health and nutrition services. The proper positive educational steps should be taken in order to discourage the use and misuse of dangerous drugs. The increasing problem of adolescent pregnancy should not be overlooked.

SOCIAL SECURITY

Most countries have established a Ministry of Social Security. In Jamaica, there is a national insurance scheme. A certain percentage of the cost is contributed by both employers and employees. Benefits are obtainable if a worker is injured while on the job, as well as in cases of incapacitation, retirement, or death.

A substantial sum of money is allocated to the Golden Age Clubs, and to the Jamaica Legion, whose membership is composed of war veterans.

The Golden Age Clubs, set up for adults fifty years of age and older, are operated along the same lines as youth clubs and hold annual residential and nonresidential summer camps. A meals program for which a special government allocation is made, is also included in this project.

The Council for the Handicapped also falls under the Ministry of Social Security. Rehabilitation officers assist in job placement of the handicapped from centers and workshops where they receive training to equip them with some form of skill for employment in society.

The pioneering and development of social services benefit mainly from voluntary social organizations which receive subsidies from the government of Jamaica, in spite of its very limited resources.

PART II

AHMED FATTAHIPOUR

DIRECTOR, SOCIAL WELFARE AND DEVELOPMENT CENTER ASIA
AND PACIFIC

THE DEFINITION of "social development" is not always sufficiently clear to be universally acceptable. Arbitrary and oblique interpretations of social development generally refer to "noneconomic" aspects of improvement in social welfare. However, the interdependence of economic and social development makes it rather difficult, at times, to delineate sharply social development from economic development.

For present purposes, social development consists of the following:

1. Improvements in the prevention of diseases and in the general health of the public
2. Improvements in standards of nutrition
3. Introduction and/or mass distribution of such facilities as clean piped water, sewers, power, telephone, gas, and so forth
4. Improvements in the quantity and quality of education
5. Provision of equal opportunities for citizens in education and employment as well as other social privileges, regardless of their sex, religion, ethnicity, or social background

6. Improvements in housing conditions, and a fair allotment of space
7. Expansion of, and access to, modern means of transportation and communication
8. Provision of social security benefits and gains
9. Improvements in the provision of basic maternal and child care services
10. Provision of recreational facilities and cultural opportunities
11. The humanization of administrative and organizational set-ups and procedures
12. Promotion of people's participation in their local affairs.

This list is by no means comprehensive. However, it is not possible further to refine and specify the composition of social development here. Nevertheless, one may infer from this list, inadequate though it may be, that there is one common element in all the social services and facilities, and that is the well-being of human beings. It is the man rather than objects or wealth which is a matter of concern to those who are planning or implementing social development policies.

As society moves from traditional small rural communities to more modern types of life, dependence of the individual on his family or kin or community declines. Simultaneously, society at large provides social services and amenities to the individual who is moving toward "independence," with his specific rights and responsibilities.

POPULATION OF ASIA

With 58 percent of the total population of the world, Asia represents the most densely populated area on earth.

The population of the Economic and Social Council Asia and Pacific (ESCAP) region is growing at an average annual rate of nearly 2.3 percent during the 1970s, slightly faster than the rate of nearly 2.2 percent during the 1960s. The total population of the region in 1970 was around 2,000 millions. The figure is expected to rise to 2,500 millions in 1980. This increase equals the total population of North and South

America combined in 1970. The rapid drop in mortality and improved health conditions coupled with a high fertility rate account for the gigantic increase in the Asian population. In speaking of population factors we may remind ourselves that we are concerned with population size, growth, composition, and interaction. It is not only the size of the population that matters to us, it is also their qualifications and characteristics. Cultural perspectives, attitudes, values, norms, and traditions are considered as effective in the development of these societies as manipulation of population policies.

POPULATION CHANGE AND SOCIOECONOMIC FACTORS

Income. Declining fertility increases per capita income from 3 percent to 9 percent after ten years, from 13 percent to 32 percent after twenty years, and from 29 percent to 93 percent after thirty years, depending on the choice of economic developmental models and parameter values. According to ESCAP reports, the short-term benefits of fertility reduction are small, but the long-term benefits are substantial. Fertility reduction means that the national income is shared by fewer persons. The national income may increase, since fertility reduction does not damage the productive capacity of the economy, which is a function of the amount of natural resources, the accumulation of capital, and the quantity and quality of the labor force. Since dependency ratios are lower, capital accumulation is affected positively. The size of the labor force is reduced by fertility reduction after some fifteen years. Improved health, nutrition, and education affect the quality of the labor force positively.

Labor force and employment. Rural underemployment and stagnation of rural per capita income are serious problems in Asia, and may even worsen in some countries in the next decade. Over two thirds of the population in the high-fertility region are inhabitants of farms. Because of migration, however, nonfarm occupational sectors are increasing, in spite of their limited absorptive capacity. Hence there is underemployment in both rural and urban areas.

A number of studies have shown that fertility decline is

closely associated with engagement in nonfarm occupations. Whereas the male population in the labor force outside agriculture is increasing during 1970–80, the female labor force participation rates are expected to decrease from 36.35 percent to 36.05 percent in East Asia and from 23.38 percent to 21.79 percent in South Asia.[1]

Health development. ESCAP reports indicate that per capita, the available supply of medical services, doctors, and hospital beds in Asian countries has remained low in spite of inexpensive public health techniques such as water purification and malaria eradication. As in the case of education and housing, rapid population growth retards health services since it requires sheer expansion of services for more people rather than investment in qualitative improvement of public health.

Migration of medical personnel is also a very serious problem for developing countries of Asia. There are two aspects: internal and international. Quite out of proportion, doctors are concentrated in cities; moreover, they emigrate to more developed parts of the world.

Food and nutrition. Malnutrition and undernutrition plague most Asian countries. However, by 1985 in all countries of the region, except the Philippines, the daily dietary intake will exceed minimum average calorie requirements, and in all countries except the Philippines, Thailand, and Sri Lanka will exceed the minimum average daily protein requirements. According to ESCAP reports, the population of the Philippines is growing the most rapidly among Asian countries. In spite of the increased calorie and protein consumption by 1985, the uneven distribution of income and wealth leads to a high incidence of undernutrition and malnutrition among the poor families with large numbers of children.

Educational development. Rapid population growth implies an increasing rate of school-age population dependent on the working population. High drop-out rates are to be expected with rapid population growth. A shortage of well-qualified

[1]*Labour Force Projections* (Geneva: International Labour Organization, 1971), Part V, pp. 73, 77.

teachers and the increasing cost of plant, equipment, and personnel have positive correlations with population explosion.

Housing development. Requirements for housing in the ESCAP region during 1970–80 will grow even faster than the population due to a decline in the average number of persons per household. The number of households will increase by almost one third between 1970 and 1980. When the need to upgrade the poor condition of most housing is taken into account, the housing needs of many high-fertility ESCAP countries are enormous.

Transport and communication. In developing countries, the growth rate of the transport sector is often two to three times that of the total gross national product. At the initial stage of development, transport development rates very high among the items included in the plans, whereas at later stages, growth of transport services falls behind production of goods and the provision of services.

The most serious effects of rapid population growth are found in urban areas. Rapid rural-urban migration and rising per capita income enable a large number of people to own automobiles to the extent that traffic becomes a serious problem in such cities as Manila, Bangkok, and Teheran.

In the initial stages of communications development, huge amounts of funds are invested, often unprofitably, to build a viable communication infrastructure for the economy. However, as in the case of transport, communication expenses per capita will decline with economic growth.

Social security. The development of social security programs appears to be retarded by rapid population growth. The high rate of dependency of the younger population on middle-age workers and the aged puts burdens and restrictions on social services and social security programs. Also, as family size declines and parent survivorship continues to improve, the burden that economically inactive parents put on their children increases, so that the need grows for the state to assume part of this burden. Social security needs are usually great in the ESCAP region. However, unless and until economic take-off is well under way, scarce resources need to be invested in other aspects of social-economic development than social security entitlements.

Humanization of administrative setup. In some Asian countries, a colonial type of bureaucracy is still dominating. On the one hand, the larger populations in the cities make bureaucracies inevitable. However, with further growth of these societies, decentralization, flexible structures, and liberal procedures are necessary to allow participation of the people in their own affairs.

People's participation. Mobilization of the people to exploit their own resources for themselves is positively related to people's participation in decision-making. Experiments with community development in Korea and the Philippines include effective family planning education in their program. Decentralization and people's participation can provide basic rural community-based services to the society, thus contributing to social development.

WHO BENEFITS FROM SOCIAL SERVICES?

A social development project normally benefits a certain group or region more than the others. Hence it contributes to redistributing wealth and shifting it from one group to another.

It may also be noted that social development policies or measures may benefit both the individuals and the group. For instance, the effects of the eradication of tuberculosis in a certain region, or the introduction of television, are not limited to some individuals who directly benefit from these social services and goods; they also help the development of society as a whole.

Two interrelated elements are noteworthy:

1. Rapid population growth may make the cost of social services prohibitive for social planners and political leaders.

2. Resources available for social development are generally less than are required to meet the needs of a growing population.

VICIOUS CIRCLE OF SOCIAL DEVELOPMENT

Experience in many rapidly growing societies has shown that increasing the rate of population growth slows down the rate of social development, which, in turn, prevents or impedes decline in the high fertility rates, thus causing further rapid population growth. Therefore, for the well-being of the people, society requires constant provision and revision of a matrix of interrelationships among socioeconomic development factors, and population factors and dynamics.

MATRIX OF DEVELOPMENT

Development factors are numerous and varied, and there is no hard-and-fast rule as regards a stereotyped pattern of development for all societies. However, human needs are the same. Whether they live in a developed society or in any of the various stages of a developing society, human beings wish to meet their social, psychological, and physical needs smoothly and regularly. Therefore, a number of common and universal elements or indexes of development can be traced, with the intention of setting policies, planning certain programs, and formulating operational projects. It is in this connection that we deem it useful for national development planners to design both optimal and actual development matrices in order to guide and apply proper allocation of resources. It may be noted that developing countries need to utilize their often meager resources properly, both in order to avoid further gaps between themselves and the more developed societies, and to achieve their desired targets in a most efficient way. Also, in these developmental matrices, social, cultural, and population factors should receive due attention, in addition to economic factors.

In Asia, the concern about elimination of poverty and the attainment of acceptable standards of living sometimes leads to an oversight or underestimation of the value of social-cultural and population factors, even though, in reality, these factors contribute to the well-being of the people as much as sheer economic growth. In Asia, cultural values as regards human interrelationships may even interfere and conflict with the material gains expected to be achieved by economic planning. Therefore, with all due respect for economic planners, unless a comprehensive sociocultural, economic, and demographic plan is designed for a given society during a certain specified period, material gains could lead to unhappiness and social disorganization with detrimental effects on development of the society in the long run.

DEMOGRAPHY AND DEVELOPMENT

According to neo-Malthusian theory:

1. The population of the world is growing at an unprecedented rate, and the ratio of man to natural resources, particularly land, is increasing.

2. The proportion of the young population to older age groups is increasing.

Hence there is further dependence on the productive population, adding to the "poor" of the world.

For the Third World, these arguments are not necessarily correct. The ratio of natural resources to population varies from one country to the other. In the Indian subcontinent, for instance, the ratio is not the same as in Southeast or West Asia.

Neo-Malthusian theory argues that the per-capita output in the agricultural sector is stagnating. However, it should be borne in mind that stagnation in agriculture as well as slow industrial growth and the upward trend of unemployment in the Third World arise for reasons which have very little, if any, to do with population growth or scarcity of land.

In some Western Asian countries, the southern part of the Indian subcontinent, and Southeast Asia (Thailand, and Indonesia excluding Java) there are considerable reserves of arable land which are not being cultivated. As a matter of fact, the very low density of the rural population constitutes a serious handicap in the attempt to increase agricultural productivity. Likewise, production or improvement of social services and facilities becomes very expensive because of the sparse or scattered population.

Technological innovations, administrative reforms, and organizational management skills actually help development of the population more than manipulation of the population growth rate. In other words, to plan for an appropriate size and structure of the population, it is important to give due attention to socioeconomic development factors which may help to impede population growth.

PART III

MELVIN A. GLASSER

DIRECTOR, SOCIAL SECURITY DEPARTMENT, INTERNATIONAL
UNION, UNITED AUTOMOBILE, AEROSPACE, AND AGRICULTURAL
IMPLEMENT WORKERS OF AMERICA, UNITED STATES

FOR MY purposes here I shall consider the world as made up of developing nations and industrialized nations, even while recognizing that this simplistic dichotomy breaks down under examination. In the industrialized countries the trend toward increasing unemployment, unless modified, could result in intensified strains within the social structure, especially in terms of family role functions. The rush to industrialization among the developing nations without concern for the human consequences of such change could result in the basic needs of many remaining unfulfilled even while national wealth increases. The issues before us, then, are not new. Facilitating the fulfillment of individual and social needs has long been our purpose. What is new is the changing economic and social organization within which these needs must be fulfilled.

INDUSTRIALIZED WORLD

Recent predictions indicate that the cybernetic revolution will continue and intensify during the next decade. The development of the microchip in computer technology has resulted in the capability of machines to operate robots. The potential exists for machines increasingly to replace humans in manufacturing. The trend is already established in Japan and North America, as well as in Western Europe.

The displacement of workers by machines will likely grow within other industries. A French government report indicates that automation will cut employment in banking and insurance by 30 percent over the next ten years. In West Germany the head of an electronics firm predicts that by 1990, 40 percent of all present manual office work will be done by machines. In Britain another study indicates that microcomputer technology will result in the loss of one million jobs in manufacturing and an additional 1.25 million jobs in commerce by the early 1980s. In the United States auto industry we see this trend very clearly. Through the use of more sophisticated technology the output of auto workers, for example, has more than doubled in the last twenty years, and there is evidence that this improvement in efficiency will increase with time.

We are therefore faced with a serious challenge. At present in the industrialized world work is an integrating social facet. An individual's position within society is defined to a large extent by the productive role he or she performs. A family's status is intricately tied to the status of the breadwinner. Yet, we are seeing evidence that perhaps fewer people in the future will be permitted the luxury of fulfilling the traditional breadwinner role.

When viewed in terms of contemporary society the prospect of large numbers being unemployed raises the specter of social disorganization. Widespread economic hardship, alienation, and despair would likely result. Such massive poverty would erode family stability and the very bonds of community essential to the perpetuation of society. Yet we must not make the mistake of viewing future social change within the framework of the current social structure. From a more positive perspective and building upon evidence which already exists, it is possible to view the trend toward increased sophistication in automation technology as providing a basis to free man from the bonds of long-term arduous employment to pursue those activities which are uniquely human.

The contravailing trends to the prospect of massive unemployment are already evident. In the United States a reduction in the work week is already recognized as a possible alternative to job loss, as are programs requiring workers to take scheduled time off from work. Preretirement leaves already exist within the agricultural implement industry. In the automobile industry each of 700,000 workers will be scheduled for one required day off per month by the middle of 1979. These are not isolated instances. They are the beginnings of a societal adjustment to the problems of employment in the future.

Concurrent with changing employment patterns within the basic industries will be the rise of new job opportunities within the service industries. We can expect in the 1980s that more people will be employed in previously neglected areas such as home health care, environmental recovery, and day care for children. Others will be employed to service the many new appliances and machines that will develop as a result of new technology.

The expansion of new employment possibilities as well as the technological advances themselves will require that a new emphasis be placed upon the value of continuing education. Retraining programs designed to assist workers to adjust to changing technological procedures will flourish. Continuing education programs will expand. Time will be available to workers to explore concepts and ideas solely for the sake of exploration. Of course, the value placed upon productive labor will remain. However, time spent in self-improvement will be increasingly viewed as socially desirable and rewarded as such.

In the United States, as well as throughout much of Western Europe, there is a growing trend toward earlier retirement. Those countries which have social security programs which permit early retirement have seen a decrease in the average age at which workers retire. In the auto industry in the United States unionized workers with thirty or more years of service can retire with incomes of $700 per month. The early experience of this program indicates that approximately 30 percent of the workers over age fifty take advantage of this voluntary retirement provision within their first two years of eligibility.

Job sharing, earlier retirement, and job development permit the creation of a societal model in which the quality of life is a central concern. However, a shift in value orientation must occur for the model to take real form. The wealth derived from increased efficiency could be used to underwrite an improved standard of living for all. But the priority must rest with people rather than profit.

Within the present-day societies time spent at work is viewed as worthwhile, while "nonproductive" activities are less highly valued. At the extreme, those who are unemployed are frequently stigmatized for not fulfilling role expectations. We must begin to understand that work cannot remain the epitome of valued activity. Retirement and vacations are already accepted as legitimate alternatives to work. These concepts could be expanded so that concurrent with work, people could be afforded opportunities to pursue activities of their choice. Under such arrangements shared family experiences would not have to wait until a scheduled week away from work or until people have completed their "productive years."

Each week or day could be divided between work and personal pursuits. The prospects for increased family stability through two-parent involvement in child rearing are enormous. Numerous other beneficial activities are possible. Creative expression in the practical and fine arts could become a legitimate alternative to work. Service to others through community involvement could become available to a wider spectrum of society. Individual skills learned at work or elsewhere could be unleashed to the betterment of all rather than solely for the creation of profit.

We clearly have a choice. The changing requirements of employment can be devastating to society if we permit the increased efficiency to deny people a share in the resulting increased wealth. The motive for, and result of, improved efficiency must be the better life for all.

I am not speaking of a utopian society. Even with the restructuring of work and the associated development of opportunities for personal fulfillment, there will still remain a substantial need for government-supported programs of income maintenance and training. Those who lack skills or whose skills become obsolete will require training. During such periods family income support must be maintained. The aged and infirm will continue to need assistance. However, in a society where people are valued not only for the work they do but also for their unique personal qualities, such programs will receive widespread support.

Another major challenge will confront the industrialized nations in the 1980s. There is already a growing recognition that personal and occupational health concerns cannot remain isolated fields. Personal habits are a significant element in individual health status. Life style is crucial, both in terms of prevention of disease and the degree to which complications arise should disease occur. Yet, poor nutrition, lack of exercise, the use of drugs, alcohol, and cigarette smoking are too often the norm within many industrialized societies. In the last fifteen years we have become more aware of the health hazards of the workplace. Exposure to chemicals and other toxic agents not only endangers workers but also jeopardizes the health of their families. We must continue to educate people about, and encourage their participation in, proper health practices. We must see that quality personal health care is available to all. Effective standards must also be developed and enforced within industry which will assure the health and safety of workers.

DEVELOPING NATIONS

The rise to prominence of the Third World nations is being spurred through national and regional social movements. The developing nations are striving for improved living standards and self-determined economic growth. But in their rush to industrialize they must not repeat the mistakes of the old colonial powers and the rest of the industrialized world. To do so would be to replace dependence with a new form of individual and cultural exploitation. The major challenge confronting the developing nations, therefore, will be the planned and controlled development of industry so as to maintain as closely as possible existing sociocultural patterns.

A clear danger is that the pressing problems of hunger, disease, overpopulation, and inadequate shelter will be considered so crucial that they will be dealt with as short-range entities requiring isolated, immediate solutions. The answers are likely to be more constructive when they are seen as priorities in a comprehensive plan.

The economic growth of developing nations cannot become an end in itself but a means for improved living standards for their people. Adequate food, housing, and health care must be the goal. But at the same time the social-psychological impact of rapid social change must be kept to a minimum.

In some countries, new manufacturing plants are being located in isolated areas. Cheap housing is typically constructed for the new work force. Usually only young men move to these industry-created towns. They become separated from their extended families. The result is tremendously disruptive for the families and the traditional community. Children lose contact with meaningful role models. The workers lose the emotional security of proximity to significant others. The strain on social relationships can become severe, both in social and in personal terms.

One way to mediate this type of problem is to establish nation-wide planning for the location and growth of industry. Such planning would take into account the indigenous culture and build upon existing social strengths. The location and type of industry could be designed to fit existing population distributions. Family stability could be maintained through establishment of support services within the industrialized area. Communal day care, education, and health services would be given the same emphasis that is given to growth in manufacturing.

While we all recognize that any change affects the social network, I am stressing the need for balance between the elements of the existing culture and the change required for industrial growth. Educational programs could serve both as training grounds for the skills that workers will need to compete for new jobs and to perpetuate our arts and humanities. Work need not become the central dimension of self-worth as it has in many industrialized countries. Rather personal fulfillment and social ties would be emphasized.

The developing nations have the opportunity to assure that social growth remains an equal priority with economic growth. In many countries extended family relationships are the means for providing support for those unable to support themselves. We must recognize that industrial growth may affect such social ties to the extent that government-sponsored income-support programs may become necessary.

In many industrialized nations, management decisions are subject to government approval under laws that take into account the possible effects of corporate action on public welfare and on optimum distribution of social and economic resources. Similar legislation is needed in the developing nations as an essential instrument of national social and economic policy.

Private corporations should not be allowed to use community-owned air and water as sewers. There are numerous examples throughout Western Europe and the United States of the devastating effect of this type of irresponsible action. The developing nations will have to control the use of their natural resources through consideration of the ecology on an equal basis with economic growth.

The pollution of the environment is not solely a problem external to the workplace. New industrial processes and chemical substances are introduced in manufacturing on a daily basis. Many of these present clear hazards to the health of workers in the developing nations. Procedures must be established so that there are guidelines for testing the processes and substances and for banning their use where they are shown to be unsafe.

Even if a balance between people's needs and the movement toward economic development is accomplished, the 1980s could be another decade of hunger and extreme poverty within the underdeveloped world. While industrial growth could provide the long-term solutions to these problems, in the short run economic aid and technical assistance from the industrialized world will be required.

No nation will face the challenges of the next decade in isolation. We live in an interdependent world. As citizens of that world we must seek and encourage cooperation across national boundaries. While I have outlined the concerns I believe will confront societies in the next decade, I want to make it clear that there is one dominant theme. The needs of the people must be our foremost consideration.

The task is not an easy one. I think that perhaps the late leader of the United Automobile Workers and champion of human rights, Walter Reuther, summarized our task best when in the late 1960s he said:

We prize as the primary goal of a society, the unique and priceless worth of each individual and the family of which he is a part. We recognize that as a society becomes more complex, as huge industrial giants develop, as technological change gives vast new importance to machines and production and things, we must constantly wage the good fight to produce change and modification in our social institutions to see that people are not lost sight of. The objective must be to provide more satisfying lives for all men and women.

PART IV

DAVID S. HURWITZ
DEPUTY ASSOCIATE COMMISSIONER, OFFICE OF FAMILY ASSISTANCE, SOCIAL SECURITY ADMINISTRATION, DEPARTMENT OF HEALTH, EDUCATION, AND WELFARE, UNITED STATES

ECONOMIC SECURITY concerns each of us personally and most of us professionally.

People do not speak lightly or freely about their economic needs, but few subjects interest us so completely and with such intensity. National governments and ideologies are made and undone by these needs, and by how they are met or not met. It is a subject important enough to warrant discussion at summit meetings. Not surprisingly, it is a complex subject—one colored strongly by emotion. For beyond and surrounding the security of a job and work-related income, there is the concern for continuing the income when, for whatever reason, work is not possible.

Ida Merriam, who was with the Social Security Administration in the United States for many years and is an expert in the area of income maintenance, describes the problem:

A modern technological society is dependent upon the existence of large regular transfers or income flows to individuals and families, beyond the system of payment for current work. With complete self-sufficiency no longer possible and family income support generally restricted to narrower circles, a system becomes essential for providing a substitute income when earnings are interrupted or cease. This need overlaps with another, much older set of needs—the need for income support and assistance to those who work but earn too little or who, for whatever reason, have less to live on than society at that time regards as minimal.

There are, of course, many ways of meeting these needs. The ones we shall consider here are: work, income, Social Security, and taxation, as well as the economic growth costs that may be associated with them. We shall focus on specific areas, policy development and planning; implementation and service delivery; research and evaluation; and regional and international cooperation. My comments on policy development and planning will apply to the other areas as well. For understandable reasons, what I have to say may be more appropriate to the United States than to other countries.

In the United States, at the present time, social welfare plays a supporting rather than a leading role in these activities. It is not the primary policy development and planning mechanism for work, income, Social Security, or taxation, and some areas, such as taxation as a method for meeting human service needs, may be unfamiliar to many in the social welfare field. Yet in each one, social welfare does play a part, a part that few

other fields are equipped to play, and that is to propose and
urge that program policies are humane, that they are equitable, that they are designed to help the individuals being
served, and that they seek to alleviate present distress and provide some hope for the future.

Social welfare agencies do not ordinarily provide leadership
in the manpower field, but they can help to assure that job
and work programs are designed to provide opportunities to
improve skills and enhance earning capacity and not to force
people into low-skilled, undesirable, dead-end jobs. With the
steady increase in single-parent families, headed most often by
a woman, they must exert pressure to secure equal job opportunities and pay for women. They must also work to counter
community attitudes that would tie financial assistance to a
willingness to work, under any circumstances, no matter how
onerous, undesirable, or unsuitable a job may be for the person seeking assistance.

If they are alert to opportunities to upgrade and improve
social welfare services in their efforts to expand work opportunities, so much the better. A number of years ago we were
able to achieve a notable increase in day care services when
Congress, in its search for a way to expand job opportunities
for mothers with children, was convinced that an expanded
day care system would help substantially.

Since studies of welfare recipients have established that
many recipients prefer work to welfare—and in fact 10 percent of the mothers of our AFDC program (Aid to Families
with Dependent Children) work full time—one might assume
that social welfare agencies would be deeply engaged in job
creation and manpower development, but they have not been.
We have been trying for nine years in the United States to
amend our welfare law to provide a substitute for a system
that President Carter has characterized as "overly wasteful,
capricious and subject to fraud." To replace that system he has
proposed a program that emphasizes work and that would
provide "every family with children and a member able to
work . . . access to a job." Social welfare agencies have contributed to this welfare reform effort, but again, they have not

been the principal architects for policy planning and development. Perhaps that has some advantages since our income-support programs in the past, including the programs administered by social welfare agencies, have not been well-received—although for very different reasons—by the recipients we seek to help, by the taxpayers, by the media, and perhaps even by some of us who work in the field.

Although a primary policy consideration in developing policy for income-maintenance programs ought to include an estimate of the economic cost—how much a society can afford in income redistribution without adversely affecting economic growth—we are not at that stage now. Since economists, like social workers, still do not possess the exactitude of a science, no one really knows how much a given society can afford. Social welfare's response in the past has almost universally been, "too little," and it seems to me that has been the correct response in most instances. But we should have more forceful evidence than that. We have not, for example, answered the question of what is "adequate" for maintaining a minimum level of health and decency for a family or how wide the gap is between that amount and what we actually pay to people. In many parts of our country, even where the amount paid to people in need is admittedly below that needed to maintain a minimum level of health and decency, we have not been able to raise it significantly. Only a federal standard, supported largely by federal funds, seems practical. That is another element in our current welfare reform proposals.

In the area of Social Security, we face a related but more predictable dilemma. Here, too, our efforts must be directed to a more universal, more equitable, and more adequate system. Social welfare's concern in recent years has been directed to making human services available to those who receive Social Security and related benefits. This is still on the problem agenda, but there are other policy issues we should be addressing, including the question of adequacy. Our overriding concern in recent years has been how to finance the system and meet a changing demographic picture that projects fewer workers supporting a larger and larger number of beneficiaries. This problem and its solution are of great concern to social welfare agencies.

Then there is taxation—an area somewhat neglected but rich in potential. Our conventional concern has been to encourage social welfare contributions by making them tax exempt. In addition we have worked to construct a system in which the tax laws are not disadvantageous to those who are already poor. Since we are concerned with income redistribution, we favor a progressive tax system rather than a regressive one, one that will take more from those who are able to pay taxes than from those who cannot. But the tax structure offers other opportunities. Tax policy can encourage job creation, the employment of disadvantaged and handicapped persons, and other opportunities to help those in need.

In recent years the tax system, and particularly the income tax, has been used to extend income redistribution. We have employed an earned income tax credit to help those people with limited income who pay taxes but need more spendable income. The tax credit increases to $400 when income reaches $4,000 and then progressively decreases to $0 at $8,000 of taxable income. (In 1977 we also considered a flat payment even to those who paid no taxes, but that was never enacted.) In addition to the earned income tax credit, jobs and a national minimum payment standard are a part of our welfare reform proposals.

We have, in addition, considered the income tax as a permanent base for income redistribution. However, the complexities of the means- or needs-tested programs and their administration may inhibit consideration of a so-called "negative income tax" as a method of redistributing income to the poor and near poor. In addition, the cost of establishing an income floor for all needy people may be prohibitive. But the feasibility of such a system has been discussed and, I am sure, will be discussed again.

If social welfare has not been the principal contributor to the development of policy, has it contributed to the implementation and service delivery of programs designed for income maintenance?

There are two trends that have critical impact on this issue. The first is the growing importance of the professional manager in the operation and direction of our programs and agencies. The second is the increasing reliance we all must place on modern technology, such as computers to operate our agencies. AFDC has a caseload of about 3.5 million families and provides assistance to more than 10 million people, spends about $11 billion a year, and employs, at all levels of government, more than 100,000 people. Our Social Security system covers about 90 million people, pays benefits to 34,000,000 people every month in the amount of $75 billion per year, and employs over 80,000 people. These systems must be operated as any other large enterprise is—by a great variety of skilled professionals who perform very sophisticated tasks, tasks which social welfare agencies and professionals have either not been equipped to provide or not been interested in providing.

Just as social welfare has had only limited impact on economic security policy, it has also made only limited contributions to the implementation of these programs. It has, in addition, limited its contribution in the areas of research and evaluation, both in money and in effort.

If social welfare professionals from other countries are any indication of priorities in their home countries, then economic security is not high on the list of social welfare priorities in other countries either. Of the scores of visitors whom we see at the Department of Health, Education, and Welfare, few are specialists in, or vitally concerned about, economic security and income maintenance.

If social welfare plays a limited role in these activities, has it done so by choice, because of a limited interest or concern, or because it is neither invited nor permitted to play a more active role? Or has the field of social welfare, with its concern for the individual and commitment to the medical model of individual assessment and therapy, made a conscious decision that income security can be better managed by others?

It is true that social, economic, and related problems associated with lack of income or limited income have shown remarkable durability and persistence, and despite our plans and efforts, and those of others, poverty has not been eliminated even in well-endowed countries and during a time of prosperity. Because these problems do persist, people look for reasons to explain their continuing presence and content themselves with meaningless clichés such as: "They [the social welfare agencies] make the programs so bad so that they will keep their jobs"; or, "The system can't work because the people who run it are so incompetent or corrupt"; and even the recipient, seeking help for his problems, is blamed for the shortcomings of the system.

Such criticism, common to many of our programs, can wilt even the most idealistic. Has that happened in the field of social welfare and have we consciously redirected our efforts to areas that are more congenial and less subject to community hostility?

Since the service programs we now have are financed largely from public funds, and research and demonstration efforts are heavily supported by public funds, and since public social services have developed from the income-maintenance programs and the effort to meet dependency needs, can the service programs survive without being tied to income-support programs? Our recent experience with revenue sharing in the United States suggests that human services rank low on the local communities' priority list, and at least a part of the recent taxpayer revolt in the states seems to be directed at human services and the poor. What will the future of the service programs be if they are independent seekers after public funds— particularly if one believes, as many people do, that adequate income-support programs might reduce or even eliminate some social services since frequently services are used as a means to supplement inadequate income? Would more adequate income-maintenance programs pose survival problems for social welfare agencies?

With specific reference to income security, does social welfare have a mission that transcends good advice, or is it content to accept as its proper and appropriate role that of trying to influence the policy-makers to make their proposals more equitable and humane?

Social, economic, and political action are obviously not three coequal opportunities since both social and economic proposals must compete in the political arena. Any major change in our efforts to improve the state of human well-being must negotiate the political route before it can be accepted.

All of the programs we are concerned with today are public programs, largely, if not exclusively, funded by public moneys. That means that in order to effect significant change in these programs, there must be a political decision to support such action. An increase in an assistance grant, the authority to purchase social services from private sources, the expansion of a day care program—whatever program improvements we propose or develop—must be supported by a political decision.

Before this era of expanded information, we might have been able to improve programs on the basis of an emotional or ethical appeal that supported improvements because it was the "right" or "good" thing to do. Now that is not sufficient. Appropriating bodies want to know if something is cost-effective; whether other sources can provide the service; whether it is advantageous to contract, go outside the agency, or, in some cases, whether the function should be carried out by some other type of agency.

Without sufficient data and information and a commitment, we can no longer secure support on the basis of noble promises.

In social welfare we have used terms like "social action," "social strategy," "community organization," as though they had the power to effect significant social change. Have they really done so? Often we have been reluctant or perhaps unable to exert significant impact on the political processes that did result in decisions affecting social change. In economic security matters, social welfare is less a force now than it has been; it is more like an interested bystander with some helpful suggestions. The 1980s will be a time when social welfare can play a more significant role in this very critical area. But it will require more than good intentions.

As a start, we must begin to recruit, and to use more freely, people whose training and knowledge can supply the technical competence that has not been used fully in social welfare activities. For those in the field, training in the management of large and costly programs may be more essential than casework competence. Even more necessary, however, is the leadership that is capable of operating in a political milieu. Social welfare programs must compete for public funds and community acceptance with many other programs. It is in this melee that it will be successful or fail and it is the income-support programs, so essential to so many people, that may determine the future of social welfare.

Every era in social welfare is one of crisis—we are a crisis profession. We are chronically committed to challenges, and this is one we cannot evade without jeopardizing something crucial for our own professional survival. If we are not willing to be the battering-ram for a better and more equitable world society by espousing the cause of those who cannot speak for themselves and have few if any others to speak for them, then we cannot hope to further the cause of "social welfare." If we are reluctant or unable to use, with wisdom, the resources that are now available, then we have already seen that there are others who will chance it. The specter of a large and impersonal bureaucracy grinding out benefits of many kinds may not be in the future, it may be now.

In the tradition of social work, I close not with an answer but with questions. Is social welfare's mission today the same as it was fifty years ago? If it is, should it be? Or have the world and social circumstances changed so much that we ought to reexamine, for the next couple of years and in quiet rather than in crisis, what that mission should be? I am suggesting that we do so—now.

PART V

PHILIP A. IDENBURG

CHAIRMAN, WELFARE POLICY HARMONIZATION COUNCIL,
HRWB, THE NETHERLANDS

MY DISCUSSION will concentrate on problems having to do with employment in the industrialized countries of Western Europe and North America. This is an important restriction, since it is practically impossible to consider the problems of these countries without taking into consideration the conditions of developing countries. As a matter of fact, the situation of the poorest in the rich countries—the "fourth world"—is increasingly more connected with that of the Third World.[1]

A further limitation is given by the theme of this ICSW conference. The decade of the 1980s will commence within a year and a half—a very short period from now; practically today—which does exclude deeper consideration of the problems which will confront these countries at a somewhat later time.

The number of unemployed persons in what the International Labour Organization (ILO) calls the "industrialized market-economy countries" is at present considerably higher than at any time during the previous forty years.[2] In the twenty-four member states of the Organization for Economic Development (OECD) at the moment this is more than 5.5 percent.[3]

---

[1] "The poor in the United States are in a unique position to speak about the predicament which threatens all the poor in a modernizing world." Ivan D. Illich, *Deschooling Society* (paperback; New York: Harper & Row, 1972), p. 6.

[2] *Employment, Growth and Basic Needs: a One-World Problem* (Geneva, Switzerland: International Labour Office, 1976), p. 81.

[3] OECD, Paris, Half-yearly Report, December, 1977. Quoted by J. Bartels, *Economisch Statistische Berichten*, February 25, 1978.

The rate of unemployment, moreover, is constantly rising. The number of unemployed in the nine member states of the European Economic Community (EEC) doubled during the previous four years.[4] Furthermore, the number of non-workers is considerably higher than that of those who are actually registered as unemployed.

In all developed countries the proportion of those absent due to sickness and those permanently out of work due to ill-health is growing. For example, in the Netherlands, the number of those permanently unfit or sick is about three times as high as the number of the unemployed.

Taking these three categories together—the unemployed, the unfit, and the sick—the percentage of nonworkers has doubled in ten years from 14 percent to 28 percent of the employable population[5]—a matter of serious concern.

Unemployment is not equally shared among different segments of the population. Quite the opposite. In most countries unemployment among women,[6] youth, and minority groups is considerably higher than the average. The increase in unemployment among these groups is also faster.

As an example, in the Federal Republic of Germany in 1977 a slight decrease in unemployment among men was compensated by the increase in the number of unemployed women.[7] In the nine countries of the common market taken together the number of unemployed among the young tripled in four years against a doubling of the total number of unemployed.[8] A cumulation of these elements makes it practically impossible for young males and, especially, females of minority groups to find jobs.

A plurality of publications on unemployment considers it to be a problem of economics; as a waste of human energy, a loss

---

[4] E.E.G., Commissie; Verslag over de Ontwikkeling van de sociale toestand in de gemeenschap in 1977 (Brussels and Luxemburg, 1978), p. 47.

[5] Wetenschappelijke Raad voor het Regeringsbeleid (W.R.R.), "Maken we er werk van?" Rapporten aan de Regering, No. 13, 1977, 1A, p. 160.

[6] OECD, *op. cit.*, p. 87.

[7] E.E.G., *op. cit.*, p. 45.

[8] *Ibid.*, p. 47.

of income. But should we not consider it foremost as a problem of human well-being?

Twelve years ago the Frenchman Fourastié predicted a world in which the average number of working hours in a lifetime would be reduced to 40,000.[9] Now that we are approaching that utopian situation, only few people seem to value it. In spite of all criticism of the dehumanizing aspects of many work situations, research in the Netherlands showed that 70 percent of those out of work judged their situation negatively.[10] In a report of the British Tavistock Institute of Human Relations the psychological effects of unemployment are described as similar to those of bereavement. "The initial reaction to the loss of one's job can be traumatic."[11]

American research estimates that a sustained one percent rise in unemployment correlates with a 4.1 percent increase in suicides, a 3.4 percent increase in the number of patients admitted to state mental hospitals, a 4 percent increase in the number of those jailed, and a 5.7 percent increase in homicides.[12] Since there is a strong relationship between unemployment and poverty, the conclusions of research instigated by the EEC are of great interest here. More than any other likely factor, such as sex, age, or educational level attained, a low income appears to correlate strongly with feelings of discontent and frustration.[13]

All these indications support the conclusion that unemployment is a serious detriment to feelings of well-being, now and in the near future.

Essential for finding the right solutions for the problem of unemployment is discovering the real causes of it. It is a matter of debate whether we have succeeded in finding these

[9] J. Fourastié, *Les 40,000 heures* (Paris, 1965).

[10] A. L. J. van Buchem, *Effekten van het voorduren der werkloosheid* (Tilburg, 1975).

[11] John Hill, "The Psychological Impact of Unemployment," *New Society*, January 19, 1978, p. 118.

[12] M. Harvey Brenner, "Personal Stability and Economic Security," *Social Policy*, VIII, No. 1 (1977), 3.

[13] *Eurobarometer*, No. 8, January, 1978, p. 5 en 13 en Commissie van de Europese Gemeenschappen, De bewuste waarneming van de armoede in het Europa van de negen (Brussels, 1977).

causes. Apart from seasonal unemployment, economic theory distinguishes three forms of unemployment: (1) frictional unemployment, due to shortcomings in the functioning of the labor market; (2) cyclical unemployment, explained by the periodic slumps in economic activity; and (3) structural unemployment, which has been attributed to a variety of factors.

Economists seem somewhat at a loss in facing the last two types of unemployment and their explanation. But since the 1974 oil crisis, arguments for a structural explanation of unemployment are gaining wide support. As an explanation for the strange concurrence of stagnation in economic activities and high rates of inflation (stagflation) several causes are mentioned:

1. The decline in world trade, probably as a result of a changing international division of labor
2. The fourfold increase in the price of oil
3. The shrinking stock of raw materials
4. Too high investments in labor-saving technologies
5. A growing awareness of the negative effects of economic activities upon the environment and human well-being.[14]

The EEC as well as the OECD is considering the possibility of a reduction in the expected economic growth rates for the next years. If these gloomy predictions come true and we seriously have to reckon with a definitive reduction of economic growth, the whole economic market system and its attendant form of democracy will be in jeopardy.

In this system labor has always been vulnerable. Therefore, in most countries a coalition of liberals and socialists has worked together—especially since World War II—to build an elaborate system of social security, to absorb the negative effects of economic activity. The cost of these insurance schemes as well as of all other provisions of social welfare has been paid from the surplus of the economic production. In a growing economy this was sufficient for a gradual increase in income transfers.

---

[14] Illich calls this the third form of poverty, "the right to useful unemployment." "Poverty then, refers to those who have fallen behind an advertised ideal of consumption in some important respect." Illich, *op. cit.*, p. 4.

As long as the requirements of the economic system were fulfilled work could be considered as one of the means of attaining the goal of economic production and growth. Unfortunately, there is growing evidence that social pathology in the welfare states increases. "No one believes we have fully developed the range of necessary services."[15] Felt needs and expectations tend to outrun the level of productivity.[16] There is even a growing number of people who think that the negative effects of economic growth will be constantly larger than the possibilities to offset them by social provisions.[17]

One should seriously ask whether those measures which were taken to offset the negative results of a production-oriented economic system are not becoming increasingly part of the problem. When economic surplus is becoming endangered it can be questioned whether the system is able to fulfill its basic requirements. Thus, it should be asked whether the system itself is at fault. Should we not seriously consider whether or not the provision of work as such rather than an increase in productivity should be the primary goal of economic policy? This at least is the challenge of the previously quoted ILO report. This idea seems to be supported by what could be called the new work morality. More and more it appears that not only the availability of work but also its quality—one wants to experience a sense of autonomy—becomes an essential prerequisite of economic activity.[18] There is plenty of evidence of the potentially satisfying nature of work.[19]

There are three groups of tentative solutions to the problem of unemployment. First are the traditional solutions. These comprise measures like stimulating the demand for work, lowering labor costs, or better adjusting supply and demand on the labor market. A welter of indirect measures can be ranked

[15] Mayer N. Zald, "Demographics, Politics, and the Future of the Welfare State," *Social Service Review*, LI, No. 1 (1977), 114.

[16] Eugen Pusić in a review of Morris Janowitz, *Social Control of the Welfare State*," *Social Service Review*, LI, No. 4 (1977), p. 700.

[17] Tibor Scitovsky, *The Joyless Economy* (London: Oxford University Press, 1976); Fred Hirsch, *Social Limits to Growth* (Boston: Harvard University Press, 1976).

[18] ILO, *op. cit.*, p. 87; Jean Rousselet, *l'Allergie au travail* (Paris, 1974).

[19] Scitovsky, *op. cit.*, p. 91 ff.

under this approach, such as better education, better employment, investments in quality industry, and so forth.

A second group of measures is directed at a redistribution of work (twin jobs), shortening of work time, and a limitation of working years by lengthening compulsory education and sabbaticals. One could also consider lowering the pensionable age, although in the United States compulsory retirement at a specified age is deemed discriminatory.

A third group aims at relaxing the relationship between work and income by introducing a guaranteed minimum income for everybody.[20] One could perhaps call these utopian solutions.

A number of these measures seem to be contradictory in nature.[21] This will hamper an effective strategy in countering unemployment. Furthermore, since business is relatively powerless to take most of these measures, unemployment will necessitate a stronger involvement of government with what is left of a market economy. It is certain the final word on our present economic ills has not been said and is not likely to be said in the near future.

Not being an economist I assume that the problems in the field of social work have been caused by structural changes in the whole economic system. This offers a double challenge to workers in social welfare:

1. There will be a systematic dwindling of financial resources for the work we all do.

2. We will be called upon to contribute to what in essence appears to be nothing less than a cultural revolution.

I do not think that the second problem will manifest itself fully during the 1980s. The challenge, therefore, will be to understand as early as possible the tokens of the times.

Some of these issues are:

1. We seem to have grown up in a basically optimistic mood. Consistent economic growth during the last 30 years, if not the last 100 years, has taught us that deferred gratification is only a temporary matter. *Hodie mihi cras tibi,* today mine, to-

[20] Social and Cultural Planning Office, *Social and Cultural Report 1976* (Rijswijk, the Netherlands, 1976), p. 62.
[21] W.R.R., *op. cit.,* p. 27.

morrow your needs. Our social game has not been, as some theorists would say, a zero sum game. In such a situation sharing wealth with the poor was not too heavy a burden. With continuing stagnation, though, the question will arise as to how society will face this serious predicament, in which the fundamental requirements of the game threaten to disappear.

2. One of the aspects of our optimistic social vision is the fundamental belief in the malleability of our societies. Three years ago, at the ICSW regional seminar in Yugoslavia, Robert A. B. Leaper stressed that one of the basic assumptions in our discussion seemed to be a belief in the rationality of human action and an optimistic assertion that human beings, if generally left free to decide on social issues, will reach positive and workable decisions, even in the face of human divisiveness, conflict, and violence.[22] Do we not see everywhere how, even apart from the economic crisis of the moment, the basis for this pragmatic optimism is being taken away?

3. How will we deal with social change in the future society?

Due to our basic optimism and to economic growth during the previous two decades our societies have changed more than during many decades before. Unfortunately, the last few years have shown a gradual erosion of progressive attitudes in favor of more conservative attitudes.[23] Social welfare work has been inspired by a generally positive striving for innovation. Do we not run the risk that what has been built up in this area will turn into an unprogressive if not conservative establishment?

In his latest book Ivan Illich castigates professionals for their Byzantine powers: "The credibility of the professional expert, be he scientist, therapist or executive is the Achilles heel of the industrial system."[24] But Illich certainly is not the only one to question the ability of our societies to make the basic transformations which are required.[25]

4. The fourth challenge we are facing is due to stagflation

[22] Social Development in Europe and the Mediterranean Area, 8th regional symposium, ICSW, Paris, 1975.

[23] *Eurobarometer, op. cit.,* p. 20.

[24] Illich, *op. cit.,* chap. 2.

[25] Peter Hall, ed., *Europe 2000* (European Cultural Foundation, Duckworth, 1977), p. 245 ff.

and unemployment. Who in the coming years will decide how our societies will develop? One of the greatest challenges seems to be to find new bases for the rapidly eroding legitimacy of our governments.[26] In many countries we can witness a serious quest for a new type of citizenship.

Everywhere we are seeking new opportunities to participate in the government of our communities and organizations. Many of us will be called upon for continued support for this process of fundamental democratization. No matter how significant this development may be, there is a real danger that increased fascination with the beauty of smallness will cease at the expense of attention for the global scale on which problems of unemployment also have to be faced.

Professor Michael P. Fogarty, who cooperated in 1944 in drawing up the famous Beveridge report (one of the founding stones of our present society), last year remarked to me: "Then we did not have many problems with what we wanted. We were in agreement on that. The problem was to put everything in order. Now there are different questions. What we are dealing with is the question what we will do in the coming decades. What shall be on the social agenda?"

We cannot take our welfare states, in which many of us play an important role, for granted any longer. Perhaps we should start with asking ourselves whether the growing issue of unemployment does not require us to make the whole structure of our welfare state *the* political issue of the 1980s.

[26] Wetenschappelijke Raad voor het Regeringsbeleid, "De komende 25 jaar," Rapporten aan de Regering, No. 15, 1977, p. 56 ff.

PART VI

MOACYR VELLOSO CARAOSO DE OLIVEIRA

CENTRO BRASILEIRO DE COOPERACAO E INTERCAMBIA DE
SERVICOS SOCIAIS, BRAZIL; ASSISTANT TREASURER-GENERAL.
INTERNATIONAL COUNCIL ON SOCIAL WELFARE

SOCIAL SECURITY is one of the most important means of assuring the fulfillment of our economic needs and guaranteeing our security.

Social security was born of the imperative necessity to come to the aid of the employed and then of the entire population of a country when major risks such as sickness, unemployment, disablement, maternity, or death deprive the family group of its means of existence. Social security is the sum of the measures adopted by the state, entrusted to specialized organizations, specially created or subsidized, in order to provide for the vital needs of a country's population and thus help it to meet any difficulties arising from its way of life. It functions through an integrated system of social insurances, of social service benefits, administration, and finance, toward which the populations concerned and the state itself contribute, directly or indirectly.

We can cite as typical systems of social security those of New Zealand, a pioneer since 1939; France (1945); the United Kingdom (the Beveridge Plan, 1947; put into operation in 1948); Australia; Spain, Czechoslovakia; and many other countries. To this list we should add the more recent example of Brazil which, following a systematic evolution throughout recent years, has nonetheless still adopted the former denotation of *prevoyance sociale,* which consists of a true system of social security, covering practically the whole population by an integrated form of social insurances and social services managed by the Ministry of Welfare and Social Assistance.

Although a goodly number of these social security systems date back to the nineteenth century, most of them developed rapidly immediately after World War II. At present they cover the major risks which lead to a temporary or permanent interruption of salary. The risks to be covered, the services, the procedures to follow, the types of organization and financing—all these are subjects of public debate and become, sometimes, the focus of government decisions and decrees.

In 1964 a document on "the relationship between social security and social services," produced by the United Nations Economic and Social Council, stated: "Whatever the form of social security that may be installed, and the stage of development to which it may have arrived, it is necessary to associate social service with social security." Furthermore, Maria de Los Santos Legero, in her exhaustive doctoral thesis at the University of Madrid (in my opinion the most complete study on the subject), points out precisely that:

The maintenance of earned income is considered to be one of the principal objectives of social security; this objective is now possible by combining measures particular to social security with those of social services. Just how far would a security program be effective if the benefits of social services are not adequate? . . . Aside from the classic allowances, the social services appear as a new benefit of social security; social security extends into a new dimension and assures the collective benefits, which have an important social significance, beyond the classic individual allowances. The new ideal of social security is to consider social security as a collective benefit.[1]

It is my opinion that social security is truly an essential instrument in the formulation of the economic and social policy of each country. Social security, in fact, constitutes a real redistribution of incomes among the population in a goodly number of countries. It covers vital needs, both for those who work and share in its financing as well as for those who are retired, disabled, or unemployed. Without it, what would be the

---

[1] *Revisa Ibero-americana de Seguridad social,* Vol. XX, No. 6 (1971).

economic plight of the entire population? In allowing many to regain a good state of health, and thus to become active again, the standard of living is permitted to remain stable, thanks to the benefits distributed to all.

PART VII

ROBERT VERGER

DIRECTOR, CAISSE NATIONALE DES ALLOCATIONS FAMILIALES, FRANCE

IN APPROACHING this topic we are struck by its compass. Through it, in effect, numerous aspects can be introduced concerning the human condition, this condition whose great diversity and astonishing fragility are well-known.

Throughout time, man has been conscious of his limits; he has had to struggle in order to protect himself from the scourges of nature, and to assure his subsistence. In primitive societies this consisted of a limited battle against a hostile and unknown environment, with thousands of hazards of hunger and survival.

In our modern societies, the struggle is better organized, but it appears no less fierce or difficult. These incertitudes of existence are both material and metaphysical: to survive first of all, certainly, but also to try to know what man is, and where he is headed. Humanity is tormented by the presence of many risks, and haunted by the sureness of the most serious of all of these, and yet the inevitable, death.

Man reacts differently according to his beliefs and his attitude, be it voluntarist or determinist. He arms himself with a creative hope or he seeks refuge in a certain sterilizing wait-and-see policy. He either fulfills himself or he withers away. Between primitive societies (or those that have remained poor) and the rich nations, however, the dominant preoccupations are of a totally different nature. What are secondary risks for the former have become major for the latter. What was once tolerated has today become intolerable.

Behavior has been radically changed by industrial society:

1. The increase in liberty and the act of enterprise have led to new risks for the individual and for the community.

2. A corrective system for covering these risks has taken root beside, and in close connection with, the economic system.

BEHAVIOR AND THE CHANGES IN SOCIETY

THE UNSETTLING SIDE EFFECTS OF ECONOMIC GROWTH

A general perspective. The development of the industrial society has brought about profound imbalances. Undoubtedly, the economist Francis Perroux showed most clearly how the concentration of activities in their present geographic centers has led to a profound destabilization in other empty or neutral zones.

Elsewhere, economic development creates specific organizations and somewhat destabilizes the individuals concerned. The sociologist Edgar Morin perfectly formulates the dialectic of order and disorder as a factor of evolution. The disturbances of this evolution are often traumatic, as was the labor of women and children during the nineteenth century, the rural exodus, industrial accidents, and, in our time, the injuries to the natural environment caused by industrialization, nuclear dangers, and so on. This is the hard reality, but without it, without this minimum of disorder, could economic growth occur?

The businessman's perspective. Whoever goes into business freely is obliged to take numerous chances. Certainly the risks are varied and different, according to the type of business, according to the personal involvement or capital accumulated, according to the nature of the product and of the business environment. But whatever it may be, the system's base, the pursuit of profit, includes as a corollary the risk of loss or bankruptcy.

Collectivist industrial societies had to find a substitute for the indicator of individual profit; this is no other than the general interest, that is, the planned collective interest. But when these objectives are not attained, the plan may also be eclipsed, and this is another real risk.

The employee's perspective. For those who draw the principal part of their income from their ability to work, the risks are many: exodus, migration, reconversion, unemployment, illness, old age, accident, and so on. Liberalism often has no pity for the individual, who runs up against the hard necessities of production. But collectivism, with its dehumanizing oppression, limits the choice of occupation, and restricts the possibility of self-fulfillment.

The family's perspective. Industrial society has profoundly transformed the concept of the family. It has put an end to the family, in the widest sense of the word—formerly a tribe, in the heart of which a community spirit was practiced.

The family group has contracted; this is the phenomenon perfectly described by the sociologist Émile Durkheim toward the end of the nineteenth century. The extended family has given way to the nuclear family. This withdrawing to the couple, linked to urbanization, leads to the notion of the restricted family, which has become a small consumer unit, remarkably more menaced and more fragile.

NEED FOR PROTECTION

Therefore, whether concerned with society considered as a whole, with the individual, or with groups of individuals, incertitudes remain, and consequently protection is seen to be indispensable. The means of protection have seen a progressive development that we cannot recount here. Let us note only that certain corrections preceded the risk and have not, therefore, necessarily followed. Thus in Germany, Bismarck's creation of social insurance definitely preceded the acceleration of industrial growth. Social security, which was born in France just after the war, constituted a decisive factor in the economic development that followed. As a general rule, however, means of protection first see the light during difficult economic periods. It was so in the United States where the concept of social security developed with the New Deal, at the moment when the industrial world was going through the deepest depression it has ever known.

It even happens that this social policy is conceived as a remedy for an insufficient demand for consumer goods, and that it thus serves also as a reinforcement for economic recovery. Thus, societies organize themselves to protect themselves, and to protect individuals, in order to make insecurities resulting from economic growth more bearable. In the language of cybernetics, this is what could, on the whole, be referred to as a process of self-regulation.

EXTENSION AND LIMITATION OF SECURITY

It seems necessary to make a distinction between collective security and individual security. The former often includes the latter, and there is evidently a profound interdependence between these two terms.

THE SECURITY OF STATES

An individual feels all the more personally protected when the community he lives in benefits from effective protection. The security of a nation benefits its citizens. The military defense capability gives credit to the idea of pacific protection, tranquilizes, while economic strength assures a guaranteed standard of living.

International rules attempt to regulate interstate relations. Unfortunately, these rules are fragile and uncertain, since transgressions cannot always be excluded: any state may profit from a position of unctuous rectitude. An organization of states can, however, embody groups of nations and put defense treaties or commercial agreements into effect. This involves as much organizing markets and developing facilities for joint production as warning against dangerous competition or excessive constraints.

THE ROLE OF THE STATE

The over-all protection of citizens. The organization of states, each in relation to the others, constitutes a sort of situation characterized by balances and influences which are more and more delicate. Nothing valuable can be durable unless the notions of interdependence and indispensable solidarity prevail. Man, however, feels risks that touch him in his own life, or in his physical entity, more directly than the collective risks that he quite naturally tends to consider as other people's problems.

Each society has its feeble, its disinherited, and the duty to protect them is imposed on all civilizations. However, the evolution of our modern societies leads toward a sort of spreading anxiety. The weak are no longer the only ones to ask for protection, and security has become a sort of creditor's right extended to all members of society. The number and extent of risks have taken on such an amplitude that no citizen, not even the best equipped, apparently, can pretend to face them alone, and dependence on the community becomes unavoidable.

The protection of firms. Security of income and the assurance of an income-producing activity concerns as much the capitalist and the self-employed worker as the employee.

He who invests in his own business risks both his capital and his source of income. That is the "name of the game" in the capitalist system. Employers, moreover, base the legitimacy of their power on the existence of this important risk. What compensation do they have a right to expect in case of difficulty? It seems that the covering of risks cannot be unlimited. One cannot, in effect, claim the benefits of liberalism and at the same time demand financial support and blind protection. The firm represents, however, a productive unit whose goods profit, first of all, its employees to whom it gives a livelihood; secondly, it contributes to the whole nation. This latter attribute gives it a right, then, to certain guarantees, accorded in the spirit of the general welfare.

The protection of individuals. Every citizen claims protection as a right. Every mishap, whatever its nature may be, calls for compensation. But the manner of compensation may differ according to whether or not it implies the personal participation of everyone. This is the famous dilemma between insurance and assistance, between active protection and passive protection.

These terms can and ought to coexist, and their relative importance evidently depends upon the ability of those persons protected to contribute. We must also beware of the perverse tendency leading to the extension of assistance, giving the individual the false comfort of irresponsibility.

To this problem of a qualitative nature is added a quantitative problem. The whole of the population and no longer only the least favored now demands protection. The rise in the standard of living and the change in consumer habits have lifted to the rank of the indispensable that which was formerly felt to be superfluous, or a supplementary requirement.

While the initial measures of social protection try to cover the most dramatic risks, in an over-all manner, and consequently imperfectly, the attempt is now made to map out the whole terrain and to put into operation the available aid (which is more and more individualized), with the help of a larger number of parameters. The idea of prevention, which constitutes a considerable progress in itself, gives credit to the idea that the risk itself may eventually be abolished.

The equilibrium. The abundance of economic goods causes the risk, however, of bringing forth an increase in security requirements.

One might wonder about the sense of an economic system whose essential objective is to assure the financial cost of a system of social protection. The situation of various states illustrates a sort of paradox. The most prosperous and richest states have fewer social needs to cover, but are, however, those that can devote the largest share of their income to covering those needs; whereas the poorest states, which have come to terms with the greatest needs, have a low financial capability. There is a problem of equilibrium and of limits.

What proportion of the national revenue of each country should be allotted to social transfer? What should be the respective shares of direct incomes and indirect incomes? What is, in the total of health costs, the share which must be financed by the community and that which must be borne by the individual? In France, if these costs keep up their present rhythm of growth, in a few years they will absorb the total budget of the state.

We have arrived at the essential points of our reflection. How can we sufficiently avert risk, either to make it vanish or, at least, make it insignificant enough to be bearable?

This undertaking demands a great deal of prudence and skill from the governments responsible. All systems create their own idiosyncrasies and include their own contradictions. A system of progressive social protection must avoid many pitfalls:

1. Accused of maintaining or increasing existing social inequalities, it nevertheless sees itself as entrusted with the mission of reducing these.

2. Motivated by the desire to do much, and thereby pushed into undertaking a great deal, it is ridden with obstructions and complications that partly diminish its effectiveness.

3. The suitability of the means to the needs, and the good adaptation of the measures granted to the problems aimed at, makes all the difficulty of the solutions evident in relation to the interest of the populations concerned and with respect to individual liberties.

Since we have brought up the dilemma of liberty versus security, we shall conclude by saying that soliciting security at any price is lethal to liberty (and to the dignity of the person) when it is translated into an incessant and continual call for protection from above. Men cease to be men whenever society, in order better to guarantee their safety, forces them to renounce their liberty.

Education, Culture, Values, and Communication

PART I

WERNER W. BOEHM

PROFESSOR OF SOCIAL WORK AND DIRECTOR, CENTER FOR
INTERNATIONAL AND COMPARATIVE SOCIAL WELFARE, RUTGERS
UNIVERSITY, UNITED STATES

IN ORDER to tackle the subject of this discussion I availed myself of the services of a professional "matchmaker." I wanted to see whether a linkage could be achieved between the four areas which constitute the subject matter and then match it with the theme of the ICSW conference. The matchmaker informed me that such a feat is impossible. Nevertheless, I shall attempt it, and have selected education and values, two concerns which have occupied and preoccupied me for some time. I shall embrace these two topics by dealing with some of the overarching problems that social work education faces in many parts of the world and how these problems are at one and the same time not only problems of policy and technique, but also problems of value.

We recognize that there are sizable differences in the levels of economic and social development in many parts of the world. We also recognize that these differences directly influence not only the form but also the content of education for personnel engaged in social welfare. In the United States in recent years we have increasingly moved to a recognition that the provision of income transfers combined with the provision of services in kind requires categories of knowledge and skill which go beyond, and are different from, what is traditionally assumed, taught, and learned. As we ask the question, "What are the appropriate mixes between programs in cash and in kind or, to put it more simply, between service and money?"

we realize that we need persons with technical skill in policy analysis and planning. As we become aware that we need to staff large bureaucratic structures we realize that we need more than before, personnel with management skills. At the same time, we seem to perceive realistically that our society expects us to be less of a curing profession and more of a caring profession. This helps us to revalue the importance of concrete services for vulnerable segments of the community including, for example, children, families, the aged, delinquents, and all people who suffer from drug abuse.[1] We are beginning to be comfortable in shifting our emphasis increasingly from a heavily psychiatric orientation to a more balanced social or psychosocial orientation which helps us to produce personnel with skill in helping individuals, groups, and communities to obtain and use services designed to contribute to the achievement of functioning in their life roles and tasks and beyond that to the achievement of meaningful lives. These developments and shifts in thinking are coming late in the United States. The notion of social development which has now achieved considerable currency all over the world lends itself rather well to examination of the question: what are the major risks of life and what services and programs do people need to obviate or at least reduce these risks? It seems that social development more than social welfare is a concept useful for the achievement of human well-being.

If premises such as these are at all valid, it seems to me that in different parts of the world education for social welfare, or as we say somewhat euphemistically in the United States, education for the human services, must seek to prepare personnel for three functions: social habilitation, social rehabilitation, and social construction.

SOCIAL HABILITATION

Under social habilitation I include those activities which make for the building and development of the capacities of in-

---

[1] For a more detailed description of the concept of caring see Robert Morris, "Social Work Function in a Caring Society: Abstract Value, Professional Preference and the Real World," *Journal of Education for Social Work*, XIV, No. 2 (1978), 82–89.

dividuals and groups who in the course of their lives, either by force or by the inexorable process of change which affects all of us, will need to abandon customary roles and learn new ones in order to function and to survive with dignity and a modicum of effectiveness. This includes all of us who will have to go through the changes which come with maturing and aging. This includes all of those who as a result of political, economic, or geographic upheaval have lost their habitual pathways and are forced into new and often unknown and frequently frightening ones. Some will be able to make these changes unaided, but many will require the ministrations of a caring profession through services in kind and cash and societal provisions in the form of program structures which can be utilized without aid or with the aid of a professional, semiprofessional, or volunteer. I believe, for example, that we will need semiprofessionals and professionals in various combinations to help people bridge the gap between services and their ability to use them.

It does not follow that because services exist they will automatically be used. Thus the old notion that service structure and individualization of service availability should be viewed separately in practice and education needs urgently to be laid to rest. Any society, no matter how primitive or how sophisticated, needs first a service structure, second a delivery system, and third ways of bringing the two together.

SOCIAL REHABILITATION

Social rehabilitation is a range of activities with which we are most familiar. This set includes some but not all of the traditional services performed by caseworkers and group workers and also some community workers. I am not one of those who proudly proclaim that casework is dead or that it should be. I am among those who believe that more members of society regardless of socioeconomic level or of sociocultural membership at some point or other in their lives suffer problems of dysfunctioning and are incapable temporarily or permanently of carrying out their usual life tasks. For that reason they need assistance in defining their problem and to help them make use of service programs. I also believe that such a view of social rehabilitation conceives of intervention in behalf of individuals and families as reflecting a focus on social relationships, their order and disorder, rather than on the underlying psychology or preoccupation with the question of the role of the unconscious in the causation of reality problems.

SOCIAL CONSTRUCTION

Here I am suggesting a function which is claimed but seldom executed by the profession of social work. What I have in mind is essentially a function of social policy, the careful analysis of unmet needs and the design in keeping with this analysis of programs which are geared to meeting needs in the social realm. It goes without saying that this function also implies social reconstruction; that is, the improvement and redesign of social programs that have proved to be inadequate, obsolete, or contrary to expectations, programs which do not achieve the goals they were designed to achieve. We have learned from the close links between social and economic phenomena that social workers must learn about economics and need to become familiar with, and adept in, the political process since ultimately it is in the political arena that social construction will be decided.

I am aware that this way of looking at what we are doing or ought to be doing may not be readily accepted. But it seems to me that increasingly an approach such as this may be needed if we are to be able to address the three problems which in varying degrees and in varying ways seem to beset the world today:

1. The problem of poverty and economic insufficiency, although different in scope and nature is a world-wide phenomenon.

2. The problem of social insufficiency, also a world-wide phenomenon, is manifested often by a sense of alienation and indifference, nonparticipation, and an excessive desire for privacy, a sense of resignation from the community and from the world.

3. The problem of unrequited life satisfactions is called in

the United States the problem of the unattained potential by those who have the economic and social wherewithal to attain it. We experience as a result the concomitant loss to self and society.

I believe these three problems are what Alexander Solzhenitsyn had in mind when he criticized American society for its moral decay. We do not know too much about the relationship between moral and social decay, but we suspect that there is a relationship. We have no patterned solutions to these problems, but increasingly we realize that provision of resources, adequacy of their delivery, and help in their utilization may in the long run be more effective means of reducing social decay for most people. Thus what I propose is indeed societal change and social intervention of an individualized nature, but the latter is a far cry from individualized attention which reflects a psychotherapeutic cast.

If the three functions I have identified have any meaning at all they will in due course have an impact upon social work education and its content here or anywhere. But what has all this to do with values?

I like to think that the very position I have taken reflects a value stance; namely, that equality of opportunity matters, that the attainment of human potential matters, that to facilitate human development matters. It is customary these days for social workers to beat their breasts and indulge in masochistic self-denigration; *mea culpa,* the more collective the more satisfying. I hope you will forgive me if I do not join in this self-indulgent posture. I believe that no profession is more committed to the brotherhood of man and, at the same time, to the uniqueness of the human person and the respect due to each individual, than our profession. I think we have reason to be proud of this commitment. If we deserve criticism, and if we want to engage in self-criticism, for the sake of deriving from it a dubious if transitory and essentially illusory satisfaction, it is because of our insufficient capacity to transmit values such as these into practice and to monitor their practice. I have always felt that the French adage *"Tout comprendre c'est tout pardonner"* is a pernicious prescription for inactivity. It plays into our propensity to equate understanding with excuse. We have a duty to try to understand, but we also have a duty not to deprive ourselves of our capacity for righteous indignation and our commitment to change which flows from it.

In many parts of the world not only the numbers, but also the types of social welfare personnel are increasing. There are professionals, technicians, aides, and volunteers. I submit that in our understandable zeal to help achieve technical competence for all, we have at times failed to help all of us to obtain a sense of the nobility of our enterprise and to achieve a sense of pride stemming from the fact that we sometimes risk opprobrium by practicing values which elsewhere too often are observed only in the breach. I like to think that we can do better. I like to think that we want to do better. Vision coupled with skill and compassion harnessed to knowledge are what we seek to implement in our work.

As a Jew who was nurtured by two great European civilizations, the German and the French, and who was aided to come to flower by the great American ethos which fosters man's potential, it occurs to me to reflect once again on the fact that in Hebrew a word for charity does not exist. The appropriate Hebrew word is *tsedakah,* which means justice—social justice, which implies both goal and means, a striving for change because justice is never fully achieved yet always in need of seeking.

PART II

OTTO H. DRIEDGER

PROFESSOR, UNIVERSITY OF REGINA, CANADA

WHEN ONE considers education, culture, values, and communication in the context of human well-being, one is immediately struck with the power in these four forces in relationship to human well-being. These forces have the potential for fantastic development and change, but similarly, they have a great potential for maintaining equilibrium. In a way, one could compare these forces to the forces in an atom. If the forces counterbalance each other there is a stable element. If, however, the atom is split or fused, spectacular changes occur and powerful forces are released. If these forces are released in a controlled environment the energy can be used to meet numerous objectives. If the energy is released in an uncontrolled manner the explosive power is used to meet a different set of objectives.

The socioeconomic and political contexts in which education, culture, values, and communication find themselves have an important influence on the direction of the potential. This context also has a great deal to do with what will happen in the 1980s. In a postindustrial society where there is continuous rapid change, the effect will be quite different from the impact in an agrarian community. Education and communication can be used as tools by politicians, by industrialists, by religious leaders, by communities themselves, or by any other groups to influence the values and culture of the people. They can be used for the benefit of the people or for the enhancement of the individual's objectives.

EDUCATION

Let us examine the educational force more closely. Frank Adams, in his book on Highlander Folk School,[1] suggests that education does not begin in schools; the teacher must learn to work inside the experiences of those being taught. In basic terms, initial learning requires the child to learn basic communication skills by learning the language. Learning the traditions of life-style values and vocational skills begins in the family.

Later the child is also taught to read, which opens the world of study to him. He can then learn about the world around him and the world beyond him, both physically and in abstract

[1] Frank Adams, *Unearthing Seeds of Fire: the Idea of Highlander,* (Winston-Salem, N.C.: John F. Blair Publishers, 1975).

terms. Additional media, such as radio and television, now have further impact on the possibility of learning for the individual child.

Writing is an extension of the verbal language skills acquired earlier in life. Here the individual learns to communicate with his neighbor and with the world, so his contribution may be known. Communication through other media such as radio and television is an extension of his ability.

Arithmetic is the fourth basic ingredient of the child's learning.

The purpose of basic education in acquiring skills for self-study, for communication, or for calculation, and of learning values or the criteria by which one judges events, is to give the child the basic preparation to develop competence in living. Not too much "competence in living" is acquired in the school—there the focus is on learning skills and knowledge.

Education of youth. Further education beyond the elementary basics has become an important objective in most societies. Particularly in a complex society it is important for youth to gain a great deal of knowledge that has been developed by mankind over the ages. In fact, there is so much knowledge available now that each individual may attain a high level of specialization. Early in his education a broad spectrum is presented so that the youth will have a better basis from which to select the specialization he would like to pursue. His skills in self-study, particularly at the postsecondary level, are developed much more extensively, especially if he goes to college or university. The importance of libraries and, in some cases, computers becomes very important. In selected skill or vocational areas the training can become very highly specialized in order to produce experts in a vast array of fields. Skills in communication, particularly verbal, written, or computer communication, are further developed. New perspectives and understanding of the world are presented in order to enhance the youth's understanding of his society. It is considered important for him to learn how to analyze societal processes quickly and to acquire competence in making judgments, but also competence in vocational terms. It is assumed that he also develops identity, culture, values, and roots. Little emphasis is placed on this aspect in the education of our youth; for in educating youth we have traditionally used universities, technical institutions, community colleges, vocational training institutions, apprenticeship or job training, and similar job processes.

Adult education. In more recent years there has been a growing surge of education for adults. Increasingly it has been recognized that with very rapid changes in technology and an acceleration of changes in values and life styles it is important to keep up with the information in one's field of specialization. The increased knowledge in medicine, pharmacology, and energy resources, for example, illustrates the importance of this point. Because of rapid change, it is also important to develop continuously one's analysis of the societal context in which one works and assess one's perspective of issues in society.

In some societies adult education has become a "second chance" to learn what has been taught to youth and children in the normal process. Some adults have not had the opportunity to obtain elementary, secondary, or postsecondary education and therefore literacy programs, vocational training, and professional education have been made available for adults in a "second chance" context.

Again, with rapidly changing technology, many jobs become obsolete in industrial communities and retraining or reeducation is necessary for vast numbers of citizens.

In the literature one finds a wide variety of approaches to adult education, and an extensive bibliography is available. One can refer to "second chance" education in the United Kingdom, to the concept of "conscientization," by Paulo Freire, in South America; here I am speaking of his philosophy on education and adult education; concepts of continuing education, lifelong learning, recurrent education. A wide range of methods has been used to respond to adult educational needs. Folk schools have been instituted, particularly in Scandinavian countries; extension departments in universities; technical institutes, with many part-time adult students; polytechnics and people's universities; as well as the open-university idea in the United Kingdom. Some of these institutions use correspondence, radio, and television communication extensively in making their courses accessible to persons who cannot leave their home communities. Part-time studies have been used extensively by some universities to make programs available to persons in rural communities rather than expecting the students to move to the university cities.

EDUCATION FOR HUMAN WELL-BEING IN THE 1980s

In my view, the challenge of the 1980s in the educational field in order to bring about further human well-being is that it will be the decade of adult education. In many universities, for example, education for adults and part-time education have had second-class status. Educational institutions have been designed basically for children, and secondary and post-secondary education for youth. With the impact of persons such as Paulo Freire, Ivan D. Illich, Malcolm Knowles, and countless others, education, I believe, is finally breaking out of the rigidity and enslavement of narrow principles and policies which are no longer adequate. One important move toward enhancing human well-being is for the illiterate adult not only to learn to read and write, but to learn how these tools can be helpful in his social and economic situation. Freire used literacy education to assist people to recognize what they could do about their poverty, for instance. Horton did the same in the Highlander School. Education can also reinforce self-confidence rather than highlight feelings of inferiority. Postsecondary education may assist the person toward greater human well-being in the 1980s by providing him with options to educate himself for career shifts, increasing his competency in his chosen career and life style, or enhancing his well-being by access to aesthetics and art.

Human well-being may also be advanced through cultural education, which is beginning strongly for the aged, for persons who want skills in order to enjoy hobbies.

COMMUNICATION

There has been a fantastic advance in communication technology. Combined with the highly industrialized nature of many countries this advanced technology has resulted in an explosion of communication. Radio, television, access through satellites, computers, microwave, microfiche, and microfilm, tape and video, as well as countless other technologies have made this information flow and communication explosion possible. There is an information overload which is difficult to control. If a researcher wants material on a particular subject he can plug into information stored in numerous systems and be deluged with a bibliography of thousands of books, articles, and papers on the subject. One computer company has a data bank in two locations in the world on all the problems that have been encountered with their computer. If anyone, anywhere in the world has a problem with their company's computers, one can communicate the problem and immediately receive information on how to deal with the problem. Medical emergencies can be dealt with by long-distance communication, so an individual can get emergency care in an isolated area with professional advice from a medic located in a city medical center hundreds of miles away.

The communication explosion has resulted in world systems of communication. These systems are used for information sharing and communication of knowledge, for entertainment and leisure activities, for communication of values or political views. The famous saying that "the pen is mightier than the sword" has never been as true as it is today. The word "pen," however, must be interpreted in a much broader context, and the access to knowledge is gained not only through abstract writing but through verbal and visual communication—and with much greater impact.

Such powerful means of communication in so many media results in immense opportunities for development and positive change, for self-help, knowledge, or action. It can also be used for gaining control over others, self-aggrandizement, and brainwashing.

CULTURE

A society expresses its values through its culture, life style, patterns of behavior, and institutions. The economic, social, political, and cultural structures are given form through the culture that emerges. These expressions include art, literature, dance, language, and religion. They provide an identity and confidence for the individual and the community or society.

Human well-being through culture is under siege. With the world-wide high level of communication that is available and the fact that communication reaches everyone—not just the literate or highly educated person but every home, through radio or television—has an unheard-of impact on the culture and values of the community. Education is not limited to an education in skills or knowledge, but communicates values which may be significantly different from values held in the community and culture. Industrialization and urbanization, as well as the emphasis placed on economic development, have a strong influence on the values and the cultural expression of the community. We are moving toward a more international, global "village." The "one-world" concept moves us toward cultural similarity and uniformity.

The cultures are under siege, but there are also new opportunities for expressions of culture. Our competence in the use of technology for expression of cultures has been developed substantially in some countries and suggests that skill in the use of technology for cultural development will be enhanced during the 1980s in many countries.

VALUES

In a rapidly changing society values are under constant review. The questions of the reason to be, the reason to act, the value of self, the value of others, perceptions of the world, the judgment base for the future, are constantly shifting. It is one's values that actually form the basis of defining human well-being, and views that I might hold or you might hold on what is human well-being may very well differ from a third person's definition. One person may define well-being in economic terms, another in relationship terms, and a third person may find a different set of values most important.

Here are a few examples of values presently under examination:

1. The population explosion in many countries moves them toward an examination of the values held in regard to birth control.

2. Medical advances have made it possible for persons to be kept alive for long periods of time even though they may be unconscious. This raises questions related to the definition of death and to the maintenance of life.

3. In many societies a much higher percentage of people reach age eighty or ninety and therefore, with retirement at age sixty-five, the question of the meaning of life between the ages of sixty-five and ninety-five is raised.

4. Social work commonly views human issues in terms of human needs, and society should meet the needs of each individual. This "needs" orientation is being challenged by an emphasis on rights. Many values in society besides human service orientations are challenged by rights movements. The articulation of children's rights, women's rights, the individual's rights, collective rights, and so on, are forcing the reconsideration of societal values. Havemann and Riches, in a paper on this subject, suggest that a major reorientation of social work is needed. We often speak of rights, but we plan services on the basis of a "needs" orientation.

SYNTHESIS

In view of what has been said, I suggest that education and communication exert powerful pressure on the values and culture in a community or society. For example, what effect do situation comedies on television have on children's views of family life? Usually the "families" are divorced, separated, or "living together" unmarried. If a community values married family life, what impact does television have on that community? Violence on television could be considered as well.

The values and culture in the community, in turn, have a strong influence on communication and educational processes. This could be viewed as the dynamic tension in a society which maintains a *status quo* if the powers and interrelationship remain fairly stable. A strong urge of values or cultural influences can be communicated effectively to change policies. An example is the impact of environmentalists on economic development. In weaker communities, on the other hand, external communication and educational processes may overwhelm local values and culture and be replaced by the stronger culture. American influence on Canadian culture and values through the news media, but particularly through the entertainment media, have had a considerable impact. On a more local scale, the impact on Inuit communities in Northern Canada, on their culture and values, of radio and television from the Southern Canadian culture has been dramatic. This can have a positive or a negative effect.

What does this have to do with well-being? Frequently, greater economic well-being or development, higher education, or increased communication can be accompanied by a breakdown of local values and culture, a disintegration of family life, or a deterioration of the structure of the local community.

It appears that during the 1980s we shall be moving toward a broadening of concepts of well-being beyond economic well-being; we are also moving toward increased breakdown of some communities through their interaction with dominant societies. There are some trends toward incorporation of a dominant society's values into the life style of weaker cultures or communities (for example, the Canadian Indian).

ISSUES ARISING FROM THE DISCUSSION

One may want to discuss the standards by which well-being is judged and the differences in this judgment based on one's values and culture. One may also want to take up the issue of information overload, with its emotional impact and the ways in which increased communication enriches as well as impoverishes the individual or the community. Television has broadened the scope of information, knowledge, and experience of our children, youth, and adults. It has also impoverished them by giving them a passive role rather than creative involvement. It also makes unique, exceptional experiences commonplace (passé).

With the explosion of communication, education, and information there is a widening gap between the illiterate and the vast number of professionals, experts, specialists, and super-specialists. All this specialization has in many instances decreased the perspective that specialists have on society, on the fragmentation that occurs, and on the lack of communication between specialists, even though they are actually in related fields. The book *Human Service Professions* raises this issue, referring to the fact that a wide array of professions is involved in the human services. Social workers, psychologists, health service workers, mental health specialists, and many other professionals work in human services with specialized professional identities. They are suspicious of each other but have similar concerns and objectives as well as theories and practices. The challenge of the 1980s could be a movement in professions to break monopolies, develop interrelated service; and so on. Professions are being challenged by governments and the public.

One may want to discuss the impact of influences brought into the local community or society through communication and education and consider the potential for growth and also the potential for deterioration in that context.

CASE STUDY

A brief case example from Western Canada may be of some value here. A large number of native North American Indians lived in Western Canada prior to the influx of thousands of immigrants from Europe who settled on the Canadian prairies in the last 100 years. The Plains Indians had a sound economic base to their society. The cornerstone of their economy was the buffalo. They had a well-organized social and political structure with a well-integrated system of values and culture communicated to the children by the grandparents and elders. There was a strong community identity and a positive sense of well-being.

With the influx of Europeans, first as fur traders and hunters and subsequently as settlers, the economic base of the Indian community was destroyed. From an abundance of buffalo numbering in the hundreds of thousands, the buffalo were reduced to a few hundred. The influx of settlers led to an arrangement with the Indians whereby they received reserves of land. They no longer roamed the plains but were located on reserves. This changed their social and political structure.

The Europeans thought it important that the Indian children have access to the educational pattern developed in Europe, and therefore they were taken to residential schools. This European type of education had a further impact on the values, life style, and culture of the Indian community. With the basic economy destroyed, the shift to permanent settlements on reserves, and the fact that young children were being educated in residential schools rather than in the community, led to a strong disintegration of the community, and lack of identity and purpose for the Indian. The well-being of the Indian in this period was very negative. Many social problems emerged.

In the last fifteen years there has been a resurgence of cultural and religious values in the Indian community. Education and communication are being used by the Indian community for redevelopment of an identity. Political leadership is strengthening, and the economic base of the Indian community is beginning to take form. There is wide variation in the development of this identity from one Indian community to another. In many communities there is still a high degree of disintegration. The well-being of many of the Cree Indians is increasing, possibly not primarily because of their economic situation but to a very large extent because renewed strength in their own culture and values, and their emerging identity assists in a rebirth of pride, confidence, and competence.

When one considers human well-being for the Indian in Western Canada, one would have some cause for optimism for the continuing reestablishment of an identity and a community that is a synthesis of the old and new. This would mean a restructured culture, value system, and educational process within a reestablished political, economic, and social context.

CONCLUSION

It is difficult to speak of the four forces under discussion in an abstract way. One must look at these issues as they affect a particular society or community. What is happening in *your* society? Are the values and culture in *your* community being overwhelmed by education and communication? Is there a process of development and change so that there is an increasing level of human well-being? Can the recurrent education process be harnessed to provide a dynamic force for human well-being?

Will the power of education, communication, culture, and values be spent in maintaining an equilibrium in world communities? Will they reform in processes that lead to greater human well-being in the 1980s, or will they fly apart in explosions and disintegrate communities?

PART III

K. E. DE GRAFT-JOHNSON

HEAD, DEPARTMENT OF SOCIOLOGY, UNIVERSITY OF GHANA, GHANA

MY THEME covers four major areas of socialization and social control. Each subtheme is a major subject in its own right, but there is a thread that runs through all four subthemes and links them. What kind of education we want will depend on the society we envisage for the future, and the future society we have in mind will depend in part on the kind of education we give to the youth. For education in its broad sense is a dynamic process of interaction between people and their physical and social environment. What people are as individuals and as communities, their values, habits, abilities, motivations, and achievements, depends on the culture into which they are born and the social values that support their culture.

Education and communication are processes designed to induct individuals into the culture of their communities and help them internalize the existing social values as well as imbibe new ones.

All over the world people have been expressing dissatisfaction with their educational systems. Advice on what is wrong and what will put it right is not lacking. Questions raised relate to purpose, relevance, content, and form. It is not easy to predict the future form of society and to give people today training that will be needed tomorrow. Too often what educators offer is the experience and wisdom of today in the hope that this will still prove useful tomorrow. If only we had a clearer idea of the future, education could be made more relevant. But we have too many prophets, too many diverse projections of tomorrow. To avoid the confusions and uncertainty we need to determine what we want; that is, what kind of Man do we want, and what kind of society?

Education is a process that aims at helping us develop our potential personal resources of mind and body to achieve greater self-fulfillment. But this aim is not always realized through the actual offerings which an educational system makes. Formal education has usually taken the form of general education with an intellectual orientation. Such education largely suited those earmarked for leadership, the privileged body of elites whose needs do not reflect the concerns of the mass of the people.

Education and socialization of the young were not necessarily separate activities in most societies until a few centuries ago. Even today there are communities in which no formal educational systems exist. In such communities certain problems that formal educational systems pose do not arise. In creating separate institutions to cater to the training and education of the young, many societies unconsciously introduced a divisive force into their social relations. This is more clearly seen in

Third World countries where having formal education is a critical factor in determining one's life chance. This division between literate and illiterate is, of course, an unintended social consequence. The inisistence, now almost universal, that basic formal education should be recognized as a human right and the declaration of intention of many governments to make basic education both compulsory and free are concrete proof of the desire to bridge the gap which education has introduced, and to give each person a chance to better himself.

The aims of education have often been spelled out and elaborated with varying emphases. It is not my intention to go through a similar exercise. It is sufficient to recognize the three main aims of education:

1. To develop the personal faculities of the young in reasoning and judgment, and in appreciation of what is "good"
2. To provide them with knowledge and skill necessary for making a living
3. To inculcate attitudes of mind and behavior patterns that will make them useful and congenial members of their communities.

The actual slant given in any educational system depends in large measure on what the leaders of the country deem to be the necessary qualifications for life as they see it. But educational institutions, like so many other institutions, develop a life of their own, and may develop latent functions not altogether in keeping with the declared national aspirations.

Much of the criticism of formal education today has stemmed from the lack of inspiration it gives to the youth. Adults who choose to continue their education are more likely to do so with a clearer view of what they want, and their objectives are often limited to the acquisition of certain skills or knowledge for particular purposes. For them, there is no sense of compulsion or coercion, but perhaps of necessity.

For the education of youth is a way of introducing them to their society, its values, its purposes, and its opportunities. If the vision they get is of a society of people involved in a meaningless ritual of activities with no ultimate purposes, then there is a danger that their attention will flag and their loyalty to the system will wane. Education will not fulfill its purpose if it fails to give hope and confidence to the young.

Let us consider one main issue. What is there in it for Man in these endless systems and processes of education, accultura-tion, and conditioning which are supposed to shape him into "something"? Is it just to make him a convenient tool to serve the purposes of society? If so, what is it that makes society so sacrosanct that Man must be made to serve it, when without Man it is nothing? I cannot see how society can be an end in it-self. The value of society lies in its service to Man. Its existence and its claims can only be justified if they serve the higher purposes of Man. Therefore I see Man's interaction with his society has having meaning ultimately only because it provides him with the milieu for his moral growth.

Education, as a system that enables us merely to acquire more knowledge and skills, is to me only incidental to the pur-poses of Man. If it were not, we would claim that the educated man of today is more fulfilled than the educated man of 2,000 years ago. I doubt if anyone would want to press such a claim.

To say that *more* knowledge and skills are incidental is not to say that knowledge and skills are incidental. Each generation defines and seeks the knowledge and skills within reach and with which to interpret and control the environment, and in doing so places its own peculiar stamp of mind and heart, expressed in its material and spiritual culture, on the contem-porary scene. For Man, then, it is not the answers, important as they are, which count. The answers given by each genera-tion to the critical questions of their day are always subject to review by following generations. It is rather the search for the questions, the effort to find answers, the quest to reach new horizons of knowledge, experience, and meaning—this is what gives Man his sense of fulfillment. This is why education must never end for anyone.

How does education help in this quest for fulfillment? I would say that this is to be seen in the way that the existing culture and the values reflected in it are subjected to interpretation, scrutiny, and change in the process of their transmission.

In the realities of everyday life, and in the struggle to keep body and soul together, the larger issues of education and culture become submerged in the need for the skills and knowledge required for material existence. This latter is of more immediate importance, but fulfillment of these needs is subject to diminishing returns, as the unbridled materialism of the industrial countries has proved.

If man must not live by bread alone, he must still live by bread. And for most people, the first concern with education is that it must at least equip them with the means to make a living. The respective merits of emphasizing cognitive as against skills development in school has been the subject of a great deal of debate. The emphasis placed on the one or the other should depend on situation and need.

It does not seem to make much sense, especially in developing countries, where technical skills are scare, to lay greater emphasis on a classical or grammar school education instead of creating more vocational schools. But this attitude stems from historical accident rather than actual intent. G. D. H. Cole, writing on the aims of education some thirty years ago, noted the problem:

From university down to primary school, we have no clear conception of the purposes for which education is being carried on. The entire school system, from primary to secondary and "public" schools, is permeated by a fear of vocationalism which would be laughable if it were not tragic. For the "culture" which opposes itself to vocational training is in fact in part the survival of a form of preparation for life deemed appropriate for a small leisured class possessed of great power, self-assurance, and certainty of its own superior claims, and in part the outcome of a type of limited vocationalism, directed towards a few of the older professions, which was worked out before the spread of the professional status over a much wider range of callings, and before the advance of science had created a great new range of professions calling for radically different types of training and mental approach.[1]

[1] George D. H. Cole, *Essays in Social Theory* (New York: Macmillan, 1950), p. 48.

Unfortunately, the developing countries do not seem to be in a hurry to give up this dubious inheritance.

The bread-and-butter issues of life require that education should be linked to, and serve the development aims of, countries. Thus the slow returns on educational investment in many Third World countries is not only disappointing but alarming. Most countries in Western Europe and North America have a per capita gross national product (GNP) in excess of $6,000 per annum. In most Third World countries the per capita GNP is under $300. There is a ratio of 20 to 1. Between, say, Sweden and Upper Volta the ratio is 60 to 1! The structure and facilities for education in these developed countries are based on their ability to pay. Third World countries have copied these structures, and even though their costs are sometimes lower, their ability to keep up the system and expand it give no cause for optimism. In fact, unless the structure and facilities are drastically altered, formal education for the majority of their peoples will be an impossible dream. Yet they balk at the effort to try out schemes for simplifying the structure of education and adopt the adapted apprenticeship schemes suggested by progressive educationists like Ivan Illich,[2] which aim at educating pupils at an older age on the job with suitable doses of functional literacy which can then later on be augmented as their need and interests develop.

This is a very serious problem. Unless we find ways of bringing education and literacy to all our populations, millions will be condemned to live as second-class citizens for generations to come. We must seek an answer. How do we ensure education for *all* children and adults in spite of the relative poverty of so many countries? Do we dare accept the challenge to make the whole world literate in one generation? Failure to seek quick solutions to this widening gap between the developed and developing countries would only aggravate the paralyzing agony of feeling left behind that plagues Third World countries.

The problem of the relevance of educational content may

[2] Ivan D. Illich, *Deschooling Society* (New York: Harper & Row, 1970), chap. 3.

not be so acute for the industrialized countries, but even here, the right mixture of cognitive and skills development in any given package of education has yet to be determined. Beyond these bread-and-butter issues of education are the finer issues of the cultivation of the mind and the stimulation of the human psyche. Cole speaks of "an education which will minister to happiness through the creative use of leisure."[3] The school system can and sometimes actually does blunt pupils' appreciation of culture and their cultural growth, especially where it puts on inspid programs in lip service to cultural activities.

There is now, happily, growing recognition by governments that cultural activities need to be programed and budgeted both in and out of schools, that cultural development is an aid to the development of creativity in youth. As Augustin Girard notes in an excellent little publication by UNESCO,[4] new cultural programs linking school and community are being tried out in a number of countries. But these experiments are too few. There is need to expand such programs.

If man must work, he must also have time for self-expression through cultural and other activities. But leisure time and its use have taken new forms, especially in industrialized countries. Girard laments the alienation of leisure in modern society as such activities become organized and commercialized:

Work has become a means of buying more, or buying something else, and leisure offers the occasion for greater consumption. Buying a car, holidays by the sea or a winter holiday in the mountains have become the mandatory symbols of access to a consumers' society, so cried up by advertising. In this way leisure, far from assuming a cultural value, becomes the occasion for further alienation and helps to aggravate social inequalities, since it is precisely the less favored who lack the resources underpinning such a form of leisure.[5]

He goes on to make a plea that we "give leisure back its value as an element of culture, that is, its role in the re-creation of

[3] Cole, *op. cit.*, p. 56.
[4] Augustin Girard, *Cultural Development: Experiences and Policies* (Paris: UNESCO, 1972), pp. 47–78.
[5] *Ibid.*, p. 15.

the personality, individual expression, and social communication."[6]

Culture as a concept has been subjected to many interpretations and many abuses. In its wider meaning, it embraces the full span of life styles and living conditions of a people, socially acquired and socially transmitted. But the essence of any culture is its basic values, the principles upon which its priorities or choices are based. It is this that determines the particular character of its laws, government, art, science, customs, religion, morals. But the material products of the people with which they live and enjoy and defend themselves also help to shape the culture and therefore the character of the people.

People are born into a culture, and as they grow up they imbibe its essence by learning and imitation with the aid of some teaching. Culture, it has been said, is the spectacles through which people see life and interpret it. It follows that a culture that becomes sterile, moribund, or static will inhibit and cripple the growth of its citizens, instead of being the vehicle for their upliftment.

Culture poses a dilemma for many people in societies undergoing rapid change. They cannot afford to miss the boat of progress. They need it for surviving in a modern and hard world. At the same time, their culture, however restrictive, is what gives them a sense of identity, which makes them what they are. This problem is particularly acute for social and ethnic minorities all over the world. The harsh choice is to give up their identity and live, or to keep their identity and die. Some, indeed, as we know from recent histories, have chosen the latter. Need this be so? Surely, the need for national integration and conformity should not be completely incompatible with a degree of accommodation that provides variety and depth to human life.

But even where such special problems do not exist, and one is dealing with a culture that is considered progressive and modern, rapid change becomes a source of insecurity. For culture, among other things, is the anchor to which people tether

---

[6]*Ibid.,* p. 16.

their social values. To uproot it too rapidly is to leave people with a feeling of hanging on hooks which no longer exist.

On a more general level, the less developed countries face a special dilemma. They see modernization as a threat to their way of life. For modernization, coming along with colonization, has become indistinguishable from Westernization. The bogey behind it is the modern industrial machine; it is becoming increasingly pervasive, powerful, demanding, almost totalitarian in its effects on modern society. Its dehumanizing effects have been deplored by many sensitive writers. Do we succumb to the machine culture and dance to its tune, or can we humanize it?

The many and pervasive changes going on around us threaten many social values. But social values need not be defended if they serve no useful purpose. Change there must be; the problem is to be selective, to know what to preserve, what to accept, what to reject. That task cannot be arrogated by any one group in a society. It is a point on which youth are adamant today. If they are to accept the values of their forebears, it must be on their demonstrated worth, not on authority or mere tradition. Of course, there are many values in society whose appreciation only comes with experience. Against the impatience of youth, and the assertions of the aged, a dialogue is needed to produce a creative compromise.

Culture today is also threatened by the mass media. Techniques of communication have increased considerably. They are both a blessing and a curse. Writing on moral education today, W. R. Niblet notes:

You cannot bring the world to the world on the cinema screen without injecting people with the idea that different kinds of conduct are *possible*. Newspaper reporters with an unblinking eye, and TV programmes with a roving one, shoot the suspicion into the mind of many a family that this long-established convention or that is not as unbreakable as they thought.[7]

But these same media have the capacity to spread information and bring culture to millions who could not otherwise be

[7] W. Roy Niblet, *Moral Education in a Changing Society* (Salem, N.H.: Faber & Faber, 1963), p. 17.

recipients. There is a danger, though, that the intensive barrage of information, advice, suggestion, along with misinformation, half-truths, and mischievous suggestions create too much confusion. Fortunately, it has been observed that many people today maintain a healthy skepticism about the mass media. But this does not solve our problem. There is still need to know what to accept, what to do. It is an unending quest to determine what is good.

Does education provide the guidelines? Culture, which is the vehicle for our personality growth, is threatened with new, intruded values. This veritable indigestion of cultural postures, customary practices, habits, and social values which has been aggravated by improved communications poses a challenge which must be met. The older generation cannot simply denounce these other values and pretend they are not there. The fact is that we are gradually approaching the conditions for a universal culture and universal values. The necessity for global communication and interaction requires us to go beyond the mere habits and practices of people to discover the common grounds from which the divergences developed, and to redefine for our universal purposes the rules and values that should guide us. Differences there will be. That is desirable, if mankind is not to die from sameness and boredom. But the challenging task for social welfare is to help in articulating and propagating universal values and using these to restrain the excesses of modern societies. It is, after all, part of the quest, the unending quest for self-realization and understanding of his universe of things and ideas that provides Man with his sense of perennial fulfillment.

PART IV [1]

OLAVI RIIHINEN

PROFESSOR, UNIVERSITY OF HELSINKI, FINLAND

THE FOCUS of social policy has traditionally been on the lowest manifestations of welfare; in other words, we have been above all interested in deficiencies in satisfying physiological and safety needs. The interest in the satisfaction of safety needs has perhaps been the most outstanding feature of social policy. During the last decades expenditures for social security have increased continuously and rapidly. Mass poverty in the early decades of industrialization drew attention to the need for alleviation of misery and want. Therefore, equalization of the material quality of life was, with good reason, adopted as the central task of social policy.

The law of inertia tends to prevail in social life, too. There seems to be a certain cultural lag in the social policy of the welfare states. Social policy operates as if there were only basic needs of one kind—safety needs. No doubt safety needs are essential for human welfare and happiness; their satisfaction is also important for the successful satisfaction of other basic needs. Nevertheless, the optimization of human welfare requires that we also take other basic needs explicitly into consideration.

Quite recently there have been certain indications that the scope of social policy would be widening. When discussing the quality of life, researchers have also paid attention to the problem of more adequate satisfaction of "belongingness" and

[1] Summary of a longer background paper, "On the Highest Forms of Human Welfare" (University of Helsinki, Institute of Social Policy, Research Reports, No. 4, 1978).

love needs. People in modern, urbanized societies have quite generally felt lonely and isolated. Thus opportunities for satisfaction of belongingness needs have, with good reason, been included in the quality of life. But in practical social policy there are only a few examples of plans for more adequate satisfaction of such needs.

The highest human basic needs, the self-actualization needs, have been almost totally omitted in the discussion about the quality of life. There may be many reasons for this omission. There are researchers and decision-makers who do not know what self-actualization really means. The concept in itself is quite unfamiliar, and researchers have written only a few essays on the subject. Therefore, decision-makers have not been able to appraise its importance for human welfare. In order to make the concept clearer and more familiar, researchers must ponder the significance of self-actualization for the totality of human welfare. Because of its unfamiliarity the concept has had an elite sound, and it is possible that therefore it has been avoided in social policy.

Those most worried about inequality in the society apparently gravitate, more than others, toward following traditional lines in social policy. It is very probable, however, that the most striking inequalities in all developed societies are in the satisfaction of the highest basic needs. Welfare states have, to a degree, succeeded in equalizing the opportunities for satisfaction of physiological and safety needs, but they have hardly tried to equalize the opportunities for satisfaction of self-actualization needs.

Since self-actualization needs (self-realization needs, growth needs) are the highest human basic needs, it seems realistic to regard their satisfaction as the highest manifestation of human welfare. Self-actualization means that a man realizes more of his potential. It is a question of making use of his often latent capacities for development. The sufficient satisfaction of lower and more prepotent needs is a prerequisite for satisfaction of self-actualization needs. There are, however, other prerequisites, too—cultural values especially.

Probably the only empirical study of self-actualizing individuals is that of Maslow, and even that does not make use of available methods of empirical research. He examined sixty-one persons whom he considered to be self-actualizers on the basis of a preliminary scrutiny. His selection of the sample is quite easy to criticize. The group seems very elite in a sense and is overloaded with upper-class intellectuals. But after all, his method probably was adequate for discovering some essential features of self-actualizing individuals. Besides, Maslow's discoveries get support from other researchers.

Self-actualizers are to be a great extent characterized by the same features which, according to some researchers, belong to so-called "psychologically healthy" individuals. Thus these people are capable of a less biased and more efficient perception of reality than people in general. This ability to make realistic observations is perhaps more a sign of the state of their need satisfaction than a sign of high intelligence.

According to Maslow's analysis there is a certain group of characteristics that seems very typical of self-actualizers. Maslow describes these traits under the headings of "the quality of detachment," "the need for privacy," "autonomy," "independence of culture and environment," "will," "resistance to acculturation," and "the transcendence of any particular culture." On a social and cultural level these qualities could be described by one concept: lack of concern regarding pressures toward conformity. Well-developed autonomy is perhaps the most typical quality of self-actualizers.

Erich Fromm's discussion on the humanistic conscience and the productive character illuminates important aspects about the relationship of self-actualization and autonomy. Fromm distinguishes the authoritarian conscience from the humanistic conscience. The authoritarian conscience consists of those internalized values and norms which a person has learned from his environment. The internalization of values and norms as such, of course, is completely normal and part of man's socialization. The fact that such internalization, to great extent, leads to irrational and blind approval of what the environment dictates to people is a questionable phenomenon. This internalization will lead to lack of independence and even to a feeling of guilt, characteristic of persons who adopt the authoritarian conscience. The humanistic conscience is more independent of the environment's values and norms; it is more autonomous; it does not approve of irrational authorities, no matter whether they are social, religious, or political. In Fromm's opinion, only a humanistic mentality, free from authorities as such, can achieve the potentialities for true human fulfillment.

It is noteworthy that the distinctive features of the self-actualizing person—autonomy and privacy—constitute central ideals of individualism and liberalism. In the nineteenth century Mill and de Tocqueville expressed their fear of the increase of conformity.

If a person is autonomous, if he very much appreciates privacy, he is likely to have difficulties in his relations with other people. So how does a self-actualizing person get along with other people? According to Fromm the matter is clear: autonomy is a prerequisite for love and good interpersonal relations. When internalizing false values and norms man falsifies himself, and only by releasing himself from these false values and norms will a person be able to love other people. Maslow's observations support Fromm's view. The persons studied by Maslow were democratic and empathetic in the essential sense of the words.

There are many other characteristics which are typical of self-actualizing people. They have a particularly intensive relation to their work, although they do not differentiate greatly between work and leisure. In a way, work is play for them, although they consider their work a mission. Another characteristic may partly explain this paradox: self-actualizers are exceptionally creative people, and therefore they see their work as a gratifying game, while ordinary people feel that work is a burden.

If social policy in the welfare states is going to be successful in increasing human welfare from now on, serious attention apparently has to be paid to better satisfaction of the highest basic needs. It is probable that there are cultural values and some institutions that strongly impede people's self-actualization. These are probably stronger hindrances to self-actualization than lack of satisfaction of the lowest basic needs. For example, the modern mass media belong to the questionable institutions in this respect, because they have unforeseeable effects in spreading patterns for conformist, unautonomous behavior. Many of the hindrances to the highest basic needs are associated with mass society. The highly autonomous and individual nature of the process of self-actualization is perhaps contradictory to several conforming features of mass society.

Human Relationships: Individual, Family, and Community

PART I

ANNE KOHN-FEUERMANN

HEAD, SOCIAL WORK DEPARTMENT, VIENNA

THE CHANGES in the development of the family have become a fashionable topic. There are many schools of thought; some cry that the family is dead or disintegrated or disintegrating, topsy-turvy, experiencing a renaissance, muddling on as ever, or rising anew as a phoenix from the ashes. The fact is that families are grappling with more or less energy with their problems of survival—as they did in ages past—but nowadays additionally not only with the economic situation, but also with their social and emotional ties and needs that surface into consciousness more and more as time goes on.

From this point of view new outlooks and new forms of behavior become important to the individual as well as to society. This culminates very decidedly in attitudes toward reproduction and sexuality. In the last three or four years many countries passed laws that legalized abortion under certain preconditions. In Austria, for example, abortion is no longer an indictable offense if counseling is performed by a qualified medical doctor within the first three months of pregnancy. This means that the utmost importance attaches to introducing and developing family planning and marriage and family counseling services. There is, however, consensus that abortion itself is not exactly a desirable means of achieving the preferred family size. Therefore, the work to introduce family planning counseling may truly be considered pioneer work. This is just as true in developed countries as in developing countries. Needs, although perhaps having different expressions because of different social, cultural, religious, economic, and traditional backgrounds, are present and must be taken care of.

It was accepted from the beginning that fertility-regulation programs cannot have only a medical character, but must also have a social connotation and on this assumption services were built up. It is accepted that the treatment approach must be of a holistic nature, which implies, needless to say, an understanding of social behavior patterns as well as concentration on the individual's state of health.

While in many countries fertility-regulation programs are a matter for the health authorities, in other countries, including Austria, family planning and family counseling services are equally a concern of the social services, a combination that so far has proved entirely benevolent. From this point of view and in order to enable the authorities to improve the services to the public and most of all to progress from thereapeutic services to prophylactic services whose main aim is prevention, certain investigations first of all into motivation began to be of interest.

A small project was carried out to investigate the motives of fifty-five women who came to the family planning center at one of the maternity wards in Vienna. The object was to find the different reasons that prompt women to decide to interrupt their pregnancies. All were under considerable pressure, for they were all within five to ten days before expiration of the three-month period allowed by the law for an abortion to be carried out. Apart from this, the investigator,[1] a psychologist, was interested to find out what emotions such women experienced from the moment they first suspected pregnancy until the final decison whether or not to have an abortion performed. How did they feel in that time, what did they do, with whom did they talk, whom did they need? The aim of the investigation was to gain information with respect to these particular stress situations in order to see how existing services could be improved and adapted to needs of clients.

[1] Dr. Beate Wimmer-Buchinger, "Motivation zum Schwangerschaftsabbruch" (unpublished).

The average age of the women was twenty-six, the youngest being fifteen, and the oldest forty-two. Forty-seven percent of these women were married; the average duration of the marriage was eight years. Twenty-seven percent had a stable partner, and 9 percent were living in a common household. Fifty-five percent had children, two on the average. Surprisingly, this very random sample was quite homogeneous since nearly all belonged to a lower middle class.

Occupationally, 41 percent were commercial employees; 22 percent, housewives; 17 percent, in training; 30 percent, unskilled workers, 2 percent, apprentices. The interviews were carried out by a psychologist and a sociologist and covered the following areas:

1. Situational constraints: income, occupation, housing situation, age, state of health, numbers of children, and education
2. Psychological factors: anxieties as regards the mother role; anxieties as regards a change in the woman's life situation; anxieties as regards change in the partnership; aspects of their own childhood situation; needs for stable family relationships
3. Partner problems: trust and satisfaction in the relationship
4. Moral norms and ethics: individual ideas of moral values, but also meaning of influences of family, church, and so on.

The results of these interviews were interesting. Married as well as unmarried women stated that their decision to have an abortion was prompted mainly by "situational constraints." If the given facts are analyzed further it turns out that for 36 percent the occupational situation was the deciding factor; for 20 percent, the housing situation; and for 20 percent, income and education.

It was very interesting that education was significantly more important for the unmarried women than for the married ones. Apart from this, 60 percent of the women stated that their accommodations did not allow for an additional child.

Second in importance as the reason given for the decision to interrupt pregnancy were psychological factors. In this, married women were in the majority. It may well be that a married woman's decision is more reflective of a view to the whole family situation and how the family would be affected if confronted with another child or if a child were withheld. It was interesting to know that statements such as, "Did not have a happy childhood myself" and "My child shall have it better" showed a significant difference between unmarried and married women. The explanation could well be that unmarried mothers are more strongly prompted by the need to offer a child, especially a first child, security and a complete family. For married women with chilren, different psychological factors seemed to be significant, such as one's being "too old" or that there would be too many limitations if there were another child. Other studies also mention such factors.

Third place in frequency were problems of partnership, such as anxiety that if there were a child, the partner might lose interest or the relationship could suffer owing to the presence of a child. Again in these arguments, unmarried women showed significantly more agitation than married ones.

That the women, by and large, invest their relationship to their partner, obviously justifiably, with a great deal of trust is shown by the fact tht 89 percent of these women had discussed pregnancy and abortion with their partners. For half of the sample the communication seemed to lead to a decision based on mutual agreement. In 50 percent of all cases, both voted for interruption; 25 percent stated that it was the man who wanted the interruption, and for 25 percent it was just the other way round.

It was interesting to find out that the majority of the women could correctly judge the partner's attitude. Whether married or not, most of the women were at first rather happy at the prospect of a child, while the partners' reaction was not necessarily positive, perhaps indifferent. Many of the women also seemed to be of the opinion that their feelings were considerably more emotional than those of their partners.

The area of norms and moral values decidedly played a minor role, which may be due to the fact that the sample was entirely of urban origin. It may well be, of course, that a sample taken from a rural setting might show different results.

The second part of the study investigated the origin of the unwanted pregnancy. It turned out that 52 percent were due to a so-called "pill interval," during which time no sufficient contraceptive care had been taken; insufficient information is at the bottom of this. Thirty-four percent tried to use some inadequate form of contraception, while some practiced abstinence part of the time. The remaining few used chemical contraceptives or rubberware.

On the average, 7.6 days after they had expected their last monthly cycle to begin, the women suspected a pregnancy. For some, it was thirty to forty days before the idea crossed their minds. Ninety-two percent accepted the disappearance of menstruation as an indication of pregnancy, some felt sick as well, and some noted a particular sudden irritability. To make certain, 75 percent visited a gynecologist and 12 percent used a test; the rest knew anyway. In considering what was to be done about pregnancy, 62 percent immediately thought about abortion; the others took a while to come to the decision.

None of the women, neither at the moment of suspecting their pregnancy nor at the moment of certainty, considered consulting a counseling service, but rather talked at first with their partners or else with parents or friends. Only after they had come to a decision did they visit a counseling agency.

It appeared—and I think this is a very important aspect— that the women had hardly any information regarding the objectives or the location or the possibilities of counseling agencies. Only 47 percent had heard at one time or another something about the existence of counseling services, and this mainly through the mass media. Only 12 percent knew of information pamphlets, and of these a number worked in social or medical services.

Among the consequences, outstanding was the fact that the main motivation for demanding an abortion was neither fear of, nor hostility to, the child, but social pressures, such as professional, training, and educational situation, financial responsibilities. This shows the change in situation and role understanding of women. No longer is a woman solely concerned with children, kitchen, and home, but she is decidedly concerned with job satisfaction and also beset with many fears and anxieties with respect to her status and position in the working world. The majority of women who do not have children already want a child at a later date, when they think that the chances of achieving better standards for the children will be greater.

This shows also a high moral responsibility on the part of the women, although they request an abortion at a special point in their lives. Not only a number of investigations in other countries (Sweden, Britain, the United States) indicate this trend, but also an Austrian publication that became available quite recently.

Rainer Münz and Jürgen Pelikan investigated 250 women who had been pregnant once. The basis for this investigation was a number of other investigations on large numbers of women, such as a survey of 10,000 Viennese women in 1973 as well as a written survey ten years ago of 1,372 married female wage earners. All these investigations were attempts to find out motivations for having children and also how many children were desired for any one family. The population that was interviewed at the time showed that the average number of children wanted was 2.2 while the average number understood as realistic was 1.79 and the average achieved amounted to 1.34. The discrepancy between the desired number of children and the achieved number could not be explained satisfactorily. It was presumed, however, that members of higher social classes have more children than those of lower social classes because they want more children, while those of a lower social class have more children than they wish because they are only in a minor way able to prevent conception.

That study showed as an important factor the fact that the number of children varied definitely according to the size of living space. The results of all these investigations mean that the extent to which a woman is prepared to adapt her own desirable fertility is determined by her social situation.

We find that this leads also to new developments that should give us a lot to think about. We find, for example, that a growing number of women are not only determined to have a child, but at the same time do not wish to continue living with the child's father. This attitude seems to be on the increase. In 1967, 11.5 percent of all children born in Austria were illegitimate; in 1977 the figure had risen to 14.17 percent. The expected increase in abortion did not take place, and it seems that to have a child while remaining quite openly unmarried is more and more accepted, although, however, it again seems to remain a privilege for the better educated middle-class woman, who is economically well able to look after herself and a child and thus remains "independent"—at any rate independent of a man.

What this is going to mean for the children in question, and for society, remains to be seen. H. E. Richter, the German psychoanalyst, asks some very pointed questions as regards these single-parent-child relationships, such as problems of identity, of projection, of substitution of one's own self, and so on.

This should lead to the discussion of the development of the father and the role assigned to him in modern society, where the father seems to discover that it is no longer entirely desirable to be on a pedestal, mainly as the producer of progeny and provider of economic security. It seems that to have and to hold power is no longer the father's prerogative, nor does he seem to want it. Far more does it seem that he wants to be part of the circle that radiates warmth and well-being, and not to be an outsider, even though a very powerful one.

One more aspect has a close connection to all those already mentioned and that is sex education. Whether we talk about family or family development, or family planning, or planned parenthood, sexuality is part and parcel of the problem and cannot be isolated from the context of interpersonal relationship. The problem of sex education—when and where it is to begin, who is to give what information to whom—certainly causes concern over wide areas. Some countries, such as the Scandinavian countries, may report success, but other countries are having their difficulties. Owing to their ignorance, adolescents cannot and perhaps prefer not to ask questions about sex, and most youngsters feel that their parents and teachers are about the last people they can turn to for advice.

Bearing this in mind, we started a small experiment under the auspices of the health and welfare authorities of Vienna. A gynecologist and a social worker, both very young and of a sympathetic nature, were detailed to give a program of sex and fertility information to a class of fifteen-year-old girls who had finished compulsory schooling and were undergoing career training. Before the course started, the girls were asked whether they perhaps preferred to have as instructor one of the teachers of whom they were very fond and with whom they had a pretty good relationship. They refused point blank and chose the team unknown to them. The doctor gave his medical information and was listened to with respect. When at the end he asked whether he should stay for discussion, he was thanked warmly, but it was indicated that there was no further need for him. Left alone with the social worker, the group of approximately twenty girls gradually loosened up and began to discuss their problems. And here is the point I wish to make:

The official attitude has long been to keep adolescents in ignorance, confining sex education, if any, to the mechanics of reproduction, and this was what these youngsters knew anyway. But they neither knew how to deal with their newly awakened erotic preferences nor how to assess them, nor could they deal adequately with the feelings of guilt and shame with which they had been burdened since childhood.

When they discovered they could talk about these feelings as well as about their problems of interpersonal relationships concerning either their peers or their parents' generation, there was no stopping them. We felt that we had at long last found a way to overcome resistance toward the solution of a very important human problem and we are going to continue these efforts.

PART II

SANFORD KRAVITZ

DEAN, SCHOOL OF SOCIAL WELFARE, STATE UNIVERSITY OF NEW YORK, UNITED STATES

FAMILY DEVELOPMENT and community development are areas of concern for social welfare, and in my judgment a bridge should be constructed between these concerns and our policy and practice.

For the past eighteen months I have been engaged with my colleague Siobhan Oppenheimer-Nicolau of the Ford Foundation in an examination of the essential elements necessary for neighborhood revitalization in depressed and poverty-striken communities in several cities in the United States and on several reservations for American Indians. We have examined the recent successes and failures of a variety of competing United States government demonstration programs.[1]

We have tentatively concluded that governmental fragmentation of programs aimed at social development, physical development, and economic development has been a major contributor to a long history of the ineffectiveness or failure of such interventions. In our report we describe what we believe to be a definite, critical interrelationship among these three essential sectors of activity as we see them expressed through the programs we have examined.

In my efforts to clarify the concepts of family development and community development, I began to search the literature for references or information which would provide additional

---

[1] Sanford Kravitz and Siobhan Oppenheimer-Nicolau, "The Community Development Corporation: a Strategy for Integration," a report prepared for the Ford Foundation, September, 1977; mimeo.

insight or support for the hypothesis that family development and community development are critically interwoven. In a paper on the concept of social development, as used in the international community, Paiva says that development is used to connote "the development of people, institutions, and their environment."[2]

Four major concepts—structural change, socioeconomic integration, institution building, and institutional renewal—are seen as crucial to the development process. These are broad, somewhat esoteric concepts. The practitioner or policy developer eventually must move to a more practical concern with specific interventions. In an intermediate step, Paiva goes on to state conditions which describe the development process:

1. There must be a concept of comprehensiveness, a holistic approach, which includes knowledge of the systems of related factors necessary for meeting a goal. He adds that the economy will dictate some selectivity in the balance of social and economic components essential for such a unified approach.

2. Specific targets for what is regarded as crucial for desired outcomes at a given time must be identified and integrated with the comprehensive approach.

3. The elements of a multiple programmatic strategy must be sequenced and should reinforce each other toward a productive and creative interdependence.[3]

It is the thesis of *this* discussion that a major concern of social policy and social welfare practice should be the conscious identification of these development strategies into a holistic, sequenced development process. This thesis has several subthemes. These are, somewhat globally, the role of social welfare today, family development work, and community development.

Exactly ten years ago, our distinguished colleague John Turner, chairman of the United States Committee of the ICSW, described social work in the United States as a profession at the crossroad. He said that the real test of a profession

---

[2] J. F. X. Paiva, "A Conception of Social Development," *Social Service Review*, LI (1977), 327.
[3] *Ibid.*, p. 330.

is its ability to be relevant to the problems of society it is granted sanction to remedy. Turner, in what was a substantial criticism of social work practice in the United States, described the role of social work as, all too often, the protective caretaking of the non-able-bodied. He argued that the ideas of caretaking and rehabilitation are too limited in definition as it becomes clear that it is not just people who are deprived, ill, and unskilled, but our communities, our social, economic, and political structures, are also sick, dysfunctional, deprived, in need of crisis intervention and in need of rehabilitation. "If social work is to become more responsive to the human crisis it must operate from a concept sufficiently broad to embrace the range of front-line institutional functions that are required to produce and to maintain a socially productive man in a humanized society."[4] Turner went on to state that social work in the United States is located within a system that places personal inadequacy at the core of the explanation of the failure of the individual to satisfy his needs for housing, health, education, justice, or communal participation.

I suggest that it would be useful to ask ourselves whether in the education and practice of the social welfare worker we underemphasize the importance of substantive knowledge about normal social systems and the problems attendant to their utilization. Among these, of course, are housing, employment, education, health care.

I must be cautious about a lapse into a critical review of the shortcomings of the social welfare profession, at least as seen from the narrow parochialism of practice in the United States. I am more interested in determining what can be the appropriate social welfare roles in the arenas defined by the ICSW. It is in the subject of this discussion that I find us driving closer to our roots. Perhaps we can gather together the important strands, to locate those central themes that will allow for the reality and necessity of specialization and skill development but which are fixed within a frame of reference. We need to rethink the central concerns of our practice. From my

[4] John B. Turner, "In Response to Change: Social Work at the Crossroad," *Social Work*, XIII, No. 3 (1968), 9.

narrower United States viewpoint I often see it as a crisis of survival of the profession. Others may see it as an opportunity for reassessment. Still, even though our perceptions may differ, perhaps we can reach agreement that a look at future directions can be useful. Whether we are concerned about improvement, reform, or survival we need to explore new approaches to underpin the future direction of social welfare policy and practice.

I submit that the two related themes of family development and community development should be examined and possibly integrated because they may offer us direction.

It is of interest to note that despite a monumental body of Western sociological literature on the family, a reasonable review of that literature and consultation with sociologist colleagues who specialize on the family tell me that there is little written on family development or on the family in its community context. The United States social work literature of the 1970s has few references to the family in the context of family development. We have, however, an extensive family *treatment* literature. Sanford Sherman notes in a review of family therapy that "in its conceptual framework, [it] raises its clinical eye level one notch in the social organizational continuum, moving from the atomized level of individuals to the nuclear level of the family. Family therapy stakes out this level of concern."[5]

A note on the decades of discussion on the future of the family in our society may be important here. I quote from Lillian Rubin's book on working class families:

> The either-or quality of the debate about the family seems inappropriate. Will it live or die? Is it an institution of oppression or the only place of refuge and belonging in an otherwise frightening, alienated and alienating world? . . . it seems clear that questions which force such alternatives upon us distort and simplify reality and deny the subjective experience of most people who live in families. In fact, the family as an institution is both oppressive and protective and, depending on the issue, is experienced sometimes one way, sometimes the other—often in some mix of the two by most people who live in families.

[5] Sanford N. Sherman, "Family Therapy," in Francis J. Turner, ed., *Social Work Treatment* (New York: Free Press, 1974), pp. 459–60.

So it is also on the question of its life or death. The family . . . will not die nor will it live in precisely that mode we all know so well. For like all institutions . . . its form is a product of its historical time and place and of its relationship to other institutions with which it connects and intersects.[6]

It is important to note that we should not be talking about *the family,* as much of the Western literature does, but about *families* as they are found in the class, racial, and ethnic structure of our several societies, both the similarities and differences, single-parent families, older families, individuals between family settings.

A book by Kenneth Keniston and the Carnegie Council on Children reiterates in detail the pressures on a large minority of American families, the poor, the nonwhite, the parents of handicapped children.[7] We are given substantial documentation of the environmental and economic odds against large numbers of American families. They estimate that a quarter to a third of all American children are born into families with financial strains so great that their children will suffer basic deprivations. Such data are deeply disturbing for an affluent nation.

The report notes that it takes extraordinary parents to raise children growing up in the slums of American cities, Appalachia, migrant camps, or Indian reservations. That some do succeed is a tribute to the strength and the nurturing networks of families and the strengths of community life. Despite this widening awareness, many of our programs and certainly much of our training for practice point at the personal inadequacies of families without attention to the social and economic forces that are root causes.

In pursuit of ideas about family development I have searched the social work literature and the sociology literature for ideas, concepts, and strategies of family development. A UN General Assembly resolution in 1965 stated: "Families, children and youth are not only beneficiaries of economic and

---

[6] Lillian B. Rubin, *Worlds of Pain: Life in the Working Class Family* (New York: Basic Books, 1936) pp. 6–7.

[7] Kenneth Keniston *et al., All Our Children: the American Family under Pressure* (New York: Harcourt Brace Jovanovich, 1977).

social development programs but a vital potential resource for such programs . . . that investment in. . . . families, children and youth is therefore essential for long-term economic and social development." Thus family development is a prime objective of community development and vice versa. That is, we must enhance the well-being of people by raising their standard of living through social justice and a more equitable distribution of the resources of the society. Family development programs must be designed to give the family, individually and collectively, the opportunity to participate as healthy, educated, contributing citizens of a community. Therefore, an essential function of social welfare is the development of human resources by assisting families to improve their lives as they contribute to the general development of the community.

This perspective is based on a "developmental" assumption of basic strength and health and not on a "medical model" which assumes pathology. In this preventive mode, the family development model makes provision for unanticipated social problems and minimizes the need for curative or remedial services. Family development services and programs should treat families as a whole and offer aid in preventing the disruption of family life by the variety of negative influences which have not equitably shared in the resources of the larger society.

The central purpose of family development is to strengthen the unity and the integrity of the family members in the context of the economic and social life of the community in which they live. It is essential that family development programs build on, utilize, and strengthen traditional, spiritual, and cultural institutions in the community.

There is a well-recognized set of biologic, social, and spiritual needs that must be met for family development:
1. Adequate nutrition
2. Protection against disease and a favorable health environment
3. Personal security
4. Opportunity for social and economic participation
5. Opportunity for meaningful work
6. Opportunity for participation in activities which con-

tribute to community cohesion and enhance inter-familial communication

7. Opportunity for access to education
8. Provisions for social mobility and flexibility
9. Opportunity for intellectual development and education
10. Opportunity to retain and develop cultural traditions
11. Opportunity to fulfill spiritual needs
12. Avenues for aesthetic satisfaction
13. Opportunity to participate in and enjoy visual and performing arts, art, and architecture.

This list describes goals rather than discrete programs. They do, however, form the basis for the development of discrete programs which can, collectively, contribute to meeting these needs.

It is recognized that many institutions contribute to the satisfaction of these needs. What is critical is the necessity for social welfare to recognize the place of these needs and the crucial social work role in providing for them if we are to participate in this developmental perspective.

When I reviewed these issues with the chairman of the ICSW Conference Organizing Committee, Moshe Kurtz, he chided me that I was giving insufficient attention to the critical importance of spiritual well-being. He has suggested that we must give increased attention to preparation for parenthood and to a commitment to a climate for wholesome relationships between parents as essential conditions for family development—what Dr. Kurtz would call the "sentimental emotional component."

Keniston and his colleagues in their study of the family in the United States describe in detail the obscuring of the "ecology of childhood." I would add the ecology of the family—that ecology is the over-all social and economic system that exerts the crucial influence on what happens to parents and children. The study asserts that until policy-makers and planners shift their focus to the broad ecological issues, the pressures on children and parents, our public policies and programs will be unable to do more than help individuals repair the damage that the community environment is constantly inflicting.[8]

Families, and the circumstances of their lives, will remain the most critical factors in determining children's fate. Social welfare policy and social welfare practice must deal with the family in the context of its ecology.

COMMUNITY DEVELOPMENT

The term "community development" has come into international usage to connote the processes by which the efforts of the people themselves are united with those of governmental authorities to improve the economic, social, and cultural conditions of communities; to integrate these communities into the life of the nation; and to enable them to contribute fully to national progress. This complex of processes is made up of two essential elements: the participation of the people themselves in efforts to improve their level of living with as much reliance as possible on their own initiative; and the provisions of technical and other services in ways which encourage initiative, self-help, and mutual help and make these more effective.[9]

The frame of reference, like the family, is not new to social welfare or to the ICSW. It is, indeed, one of the principal arenas where Third World nations have made substantive contributions to our practice, our vocabulary, our sensitivity. That community development strategies and policies bear an irrevocable relationship to family development policy is central to my theme.

An examination of the ecology of the family forces a focus on the issue of physical and economic well-being. A sense of physical well-being is an essential cornerstone of family development. A characteristic of fragmented social policy efforts is that social, physical, and economic initiatives are seen as unrelated, at least in the United States. Are we unique?

[8] *Ibid.*, p. xiii.
[9] Marshall Clinard, *Slums and Community Development* (New York: Free Press, 1966), p. 117.

The physical characteristics of a community or a neighborhood have social, psychological, and economic impact. The physical qualities of both shelter and related amenities help shape the lives, the attitudes, the potential of individuals and families.

As the United Nations conference on human settlements noted,[10] a human settlement is, by identification, where individuals and groups live. It is where people spend the greater part of their lives, where social and economic activities are most densely concentrated, where the opportunity for individual and collective satisfaction and advancement is greatest, where the most intense conflicts appear.

A physical community represents more than wood and bricks and mortar. It is a complex of streets, stores, places of worship, safety, clean water, adequate sewage disposal, police protection, shopping, transportation, beautification, parks and playgrounds, cultural and artistic resources, protection against pollution, and adequate schools and environmental opportunities for spiritual gratification.

As Peter Marris has noted, a central question for us as social workers, beyond interventive efforts in the lives of families, is how are people helped to establish the relationships which make up their lives, adapting to change without breaking the thread of meaning which gives them hope and purpose.[11]

If families are to have this thread of meaning in their lives, if they are to sustain relationships which satisfy their needs, they must do so in mutual cooperation where they are, in their neighborhoods and towns. They must come to terms with one another, balancing their interest. They must both gain and feel some semblance of control over the social, political, and economic relationships which determine their lives.[12]

One group of these community development needs typically falls within the purview of public authorities. Often

---

[10] *People and Places: Social Work Education and Human Settlements* (New York: International Association of Schools of Social Work, 1977).

[11] Peter Marris, "The Ideology of Human Settlements," *ibid.*, pp. 3–4.

[12] *Ibid.*, pp. 14–16.

such public activities are fragmented, haphazard, and bear little relationship to the ideas of family development. By decision or by default, families, community residents, are non-participants in defining how community development needs are to be met. This form of community development, the sense we are speaking of, has paid little attention to, and has often been so designed that it has a negative influence on, family development.

Our recent United States history is replete with the sorriest examples of urban renewal, massive public housing, and the construction of freeways and take no account of the spatial relationships needed by families. Planners, local officials, and government agencies continue to operate, and government funds continue to flow, in ways that bear little relation to the concept of community building as envisioned here. I have seen and read of enough examples from Western Europe to know that this condition is not unique to the United States.

To see the family within the ecology of its community goes far beyond advocacy of housing for the elderly or the provision of housing subsidies for the poor. It means a profound and committed awareness of the impact of the community on the lives of families. We are talking about:

Decent shelter for all families
Sanitary water facilities
Streets and sewage systems
Transportation services
Recreation and cultural facilities
Accessible shopping
Security and protection
Neighborhood schools and parks.

The revitalization of rundown neighborhoods, the preservation of the quality of life in the small towns and cities, *these* are essential to family development. The integrity and vitality of family life that are so essential to our survival are experienced in the neighborhoods of large cities and in small towns and villages.

I would be remiss if I neglected the other pivotal area that is a major subject of current concern in the United States but one that has generally been outside the purview of social work; that is, employment and economic development. Viable communities are economically secure communities. There must be opportunities for jobs, for job training, and for productive employment in the private sector when possible and in the public sector when not. There must be facilities to perform the daily economic activities of community life. The neighborhoods of our cities and our towns require economically productive housing, food services, banks, and retail stores. In addition, clinics, hospitals, theaters, and institutional care facilities of appropriate scale all can make economic contributions and create jobs.

To what degree, as you view your responsibility, does it include opportunity for active involvement in economic development policy, be it community, region, or nation?

The issues of sex roles and family planning are inextricably linked to family development and community development. The recent designation of the International Women's Year is in itself an admission that in the workings of most societies, past and present, tradition has accorded women an inferior role and status, and that the time for change has come. The campaign for women's rights has been part of the historic movement for human rights, first in industrial societies and then in the developing sections of the world. It is within this framework of basic human rights that I shall discuss the issues of sex roles and family planning.

FAMILY DEVELOPMENT

We usually refer to the "family" in our many different cultures as a unit born of the recognized union of two persons in marriage, the legality of which may be established by civil, religious, or other means. This marriage unit is nearly universal for both men and women, although the institution of marriage is defined differently in different cultures. In some countries any type of union outside marriage would be unacceptable, particularly for the woman. However, in other countries, consensual unions have been prevalent historically and have been generally acceptable.

Three types of families are most prevalent in our Western society:

1. *Extended families.* Several generations of various degrees of kinship may live in the same or adjacent households. In general, the lower the social and developmental strata, the greater the probability that the couple will choose the extended family. This tendency probably reflects prevailing, unquestioned, traditional values as well as the more pragmatic (and needed in poorer families) advantages of larger adult groups in the family: namely, assistance in household and child-raising chores and mutual financial assistance and exchange.

2. *Nuclear family.* This is the two-generation family composed of parents and their children. Current trends in many societies indicate that the nuclear family is the predominant type in urban areas and that the tendency toward nuclear families is similar but not so strong in rural areas.

The predominance of the nuclear family has been attributed widely to the growing urbanization and industrialization throughout the world. While I am sure that both factors have contributed to the increasing choice of nuclear units I believe that these alone do not account for the spread of the nuclear structure, particularly in rural and nonindustrialized areas. I believe an important factor is the value placed on autonomy and privacy, the natural, mature desire to have freedom from control by parents, and the economic circumstance that preclude the establishing of extended families.

Additionally, the extent to which surrogate parental figures in the extended families, such as grandmothers, play a socializing role with the offspring of the couple may perpetuate traditionally regressive values and outmoded attitudes that would impede social change and full human development.

3. *The single-parent family.* A phenomenon distinctive of re-

cent decades is the increase in single-parent families headed by either a divorced or a widowed spouse, by the spouse left behind as a result of the desertion or migration of the other parent, or by an unmarried person. Usually, single-parent families are headed by women.

Until recently woman's role has been perceived by society as entirely that of childbearer. Traditionally, the majority of world societies have not only perceived woman in this role, but have effectively locked her into that one and only role through the legal mechanisms of that society that would in effect make the woman legally and totally subservient to her husband, economically dependent, and in some societies vulnerable to abandonment should her fertility not produce the sons desired by her spouse. Biologically, the woman is the only one capable of conceiving and giving birth. The error lies in the fact that women have been locked into *only* the one role of motherhood and have therefore, of course, been deprived of educational and vocational preparation, equal pay and job opportunities, and so forth.

Undoubtedly, much progress has been made in improving the situation and status of women. Laws have been and are being changed to accord women equal rights with men in political, economic, social, and family life. Age-old traditions, attitudes, and practices are slow to change, however, and the gap between law and reality remains very wide. Nevertheless, progress has been made, and there are observable changes worth analyzing.

Locked into her only role of childbearing, the role of the female was oriented very largely toward her capacity to reproduce and to provide sustenance for her family. Before the age of twenty, the female carried a full load of adult responsibilities; by age twenty-five, she generally would have given birth six or seven times; by age forty, she might already be exhausted by illness, poor nutrition, childbearing, and heavy work in the fields and at home. She died early. To the males went the responsibility for decision-making, for protecting the home, for providing material benefits.

However, the scientific revolution brought epidemic diseases under control, reduced infant mortality, and made possible individual control of fertility. This coupled with our obviously exploding population thereby decreased the need for women to bear as many children as they possibly could.

In essence, this basically implies two important changes:

1. It decouples the marriage relationship from a *solely* procreative role, and allows it to have the dual role intrinsic to it: a love partnership role and possibly a procreative role. It allows it to be a partnership between a man and a woman who choose out of love, friendship, and compatibility to share their lives in companionship, respect, and love.

2. Control over fertility permits the couple to decide when they will have children and how many they will have. Differing from the past when all intercourse spelled pregnancy, this decision can be made maturely and at the proper time when the couple are ready physically, emotionally, and economically.

All human beings have the basic human right to control their own fertility; likewise, every child has the basic human right to be born wanted and loved, and into a family that will be able to give him his basic human rights of adequate food, adequate shelter, adequate educational opportunities, and the affective guidance and love necessary for his/her healthy emotional development. This, in effect, frees woman from the rigorous physical necessity to bear a second generation regardless of choice, and frees her to decide with her mate when and how many offspring they wish, not out of imposed societal demands, but out of the desire to have children and the realistic assessment that they will be able to raise those children adequately.

Raising children adequately is an important and complex issue for it means not only feeding and physically nurturing a child, but also providing the necessary affect and guidance that will enable him to grow into a physically and mentally healthy, mature human being. As we know from the many investigations conducted in this area this is a complex, difficult task. It is not enough simply to provide food, shelter, and education to one's children; the guidance and love the child must receive are just as crucial to his development as the food he must eat in order to grow physically. This therefore implies that during the first years of the infant's life, both parents must of necessity make a major adjustment in their daily schedules in order to have the necessary time to guide and nurture the infant through the first five or six years of his emotional growth.

Our responsibility after all, once we decide that we will procreate, is to ensure that those we procreate have everything they need. This is our responsibility to the children we conceive. It is also our responsibility to society to bear a generation of healthy and emotionally mature individuals who will have the capacity to improve this world of ours and to ensure the survival and development of humankind. It is the generation that follows us that will have the delicate and arduous task of ensuring the survival of this planet and the further development of its people.

In turn, maternity must be recognized as a social function, and the protection of this function must be recognized as a basic human right as well as a social duty. This means that measures must be taken to create and extend the right to maternity protection where this does not exist, and to improve the scope and standards of protection where it does exist.

Moreover, this means that women as well as men need full and free access to information and facilities regarding family planning and the right to decide freely and responsibly on family size and the spacing of births. The influence of family planning itself, both as ideal in the sense of enlargement of personal choice beyond biological accident and as something urgently desired for reduced population growth, is now apparent. Its practical realization for all still lags behind its need.

A development central to female concepts of birth control is the concomitant freeing-up of women, who until recently were bound to the home for the major part of their lives by multiple births and the subsequent years of child rearing. Consequently, with women having fewer children, and spacing the births of those children, there is now the possibility for a woman to engage in productive activity outside the home once the crucial early child-rearing years are over and she has more time on her hands.

Progress has been made, and I believe that some of the changes in the role of women in the family do indeed substantiate a claim of progress. I think it is important not simply to look at what women must be liberated from, but particularly what responsibilities this liberation entails.

Being free in this world carries with it the responsibility of working for the betterment of the community and for the improvement of family life. It is possible to disagree as to whether life begins at the moment of conception or at the moment of birth, but there is no disagreement about what is required to sustain life from birth onward. As women achieve freedom from their historic oppressions, their energies are essential for the strengthening of family and community life. The development of the avenues and opportunities for such participation is a high priority for social welfare.

It may be useful to determine the degree to which our national policies reflect an explicit family policy or a haphazard patchwork of institutions and programs designed under conditions of crisis.[13] In the same vein we may examine whether there is an explicit community development policy that is linked to the needs of families. Such an exploration may indeed be useful in the process of learning from one another.

As I reflect on our United States experience, I must believe that the systems we work in and our fragmented responses produce victims faster than we can salvage them. As John Turner noted a decade ago, much of our current efforts are devoted to salvage.

I firmly believe that whatever the national, social, and political context of our policy and practice may be, there is need for a continuing examination of the relationship of family to community. The family social work that I see as the core of prac-

---

[13] Alfred J. Kahn and Sheila B. Kamerman, *Not for the Poor Alone* (Philadelphia: Temple University Press, 1975), p. 175; Charles Schottland, "Economic Programs to Maintain Income," in Paul E. Weinberger, ed., *Perspectives on Social Welfare* (2d ed.; New York: Macmillan, 1974), pp. 189–231; Keniston, *op. cit.*, pp. 213–21.

tice is not family therapy as in the current United States mode and it is not family life education as it is currently promoted by family agencies in the United States. It does examine all the elements in a family's environment that can contribute to health, stability, growth.

I do not exclude appropriate family therapy, nor do I exclude family life education, nor individual counseling. We need social workers who are capable of working with children and families who have been severely damaged by their environment. Such activities can, in my judgment, only be appropriate within the much larger areas we have already discussed. Our practice and our policy must fully recognize the continual interaction among family, community, and the economic substructure. We must take as a basic tenet of social welfare practice that such specialization cannot be conceptualized as discrete without considering as part of *a development—not a treatment*—strategy the ways in which other sectors make an impact upon it. As we examine family systems we must continually go beyond the conventional boundaries of the family system to the community in which the family functions. In this way, specific features of family life, such as illness, alienation, poverty, access to the labor force, are read not as isolated categorical variables of the environment but as features of the community with which families must interact successfully for their survival.

As we train our workers we must make sure that the family is understood in its sociostructural context. We must be critical of both education and practice perspectives that contribute to viewing our role as that of protective caretakers of the culturally deprived. Our view of social welfare practice at the wider level, be it community organization, social planning, or social policy, must begin with the family and view the family in the context of the community and economic framework within which it must struggle for survival. Our efforts to affect social policy would express both in policy and practice an integrated concern for the family in the context of its ecology.

Many of my comments reflect the parochialism of my experience. I apologize for comments that may be overly specific to the United States. To the extent that they may deal with cross-national concerns, I hope they have been useful.

I deeply believe that as social welfare practitioners and leaders in the development of social policy we have the central role in the task of integrating family development, community development, and economic development policy. To play this role, to be leaders, we must know where we wish to lead our followers.

PART III

PETER KUENSTLER

SOCIAL DEVELOPMENT OFFICER, DIVISION OF SOCIAL AFFAIRS,
UNITED NATIONS, SWITZERLAND

A REAL challenge already exists, and will no doubt grow ever larger during the 1980s. That challenge is the increasing extent to which social welfare and social work are seen and carried out as a professional practice of human relationships. For many, this will come as a contradiction; and it is a sad commentary on the failure of professionals to provide a satisfactory definition of what is meant by "profession" and "professional" that these terms are still so widely taken to be in contradiction with "human" and "humanity." This contradiction arises in many cases, not so much because of the money or payment component of professionalism as of its large-scale bureaucratization. This, in turn, while more obvious and more frequent in state and governmental services, whether national or local, is not a malady from which private, voluntary, and nongovernmental social welfare agencies are exempt.

This, then, is the first challenge: Is it going to be possible within the context of large-scale and highly professionalized social welfare services to practice, in any real and ethical sense of the words, human relationships? How, for example, are professional practitioners to reconcile their rights and claims as employees, often employees of large-scale and dehumanized organizations and bureaucracies, with their vocational duties of confidentiality, availability to clients, and the building up, seeing through, and eventual valid termination of an individual, essentially human and personal relationship with each of their clients?

An extension of this challenge into a second one is that of the capacity of social welfare and its practitioners to promote and strengthen networks of human relationships within the vast and growing complexes in which increasing numbers of their fellow citizens live and, above all, work. Whether we see it in the context of the growth of cities, in the take-over and merging of industrial and commercial units, in the construction of standardized and gigantic housing complexes, the phenomenon is sensed and suffered to some degree by ever larger numbers of people in almost all the countries of the world. The meaningless and repetitive work at a desk or a machine and the isolation of the individual within a teeming city of thousands or millions of inhabitants are all too often diagnosed as the main factors in a widespread social malaise. The critics may with justification claim that the root causes of this malaise can only be removed through fundamental and structural changes in the political and economic systems which produce these symptoms; meanwhile they constitute a challenge to our skills and sensitivity in the field of human relationships. This challenge is not only to seek to remedy or alleviate the human suffering which is involved and to overcome the crisis situations which are created for individuals and for families. The challenge extends to providing the essential ingredients of human relationships which will be required if the profound political and economic changes which are seen to be necessary are to be brought about without bringing in their train suffering and deprivation which may be virtually as great as the suffering and deprivation they are intended to replace.

This second challenge can be translated into a series of further and perhaps more realistic questions: Is it possible to develop within the public services a capacity and a willingness on the part of, and specifically among, those who have the power and the responsibility to change the situation and environments of their fellow citizens, a capacity and a willingness to listen to what individuals and groups at the local level have to say? Is it possible to devise forms of training that will mold or remold the traditional attitudes of the personnel of central and local governments and other large bureaucracies, be they commercial, industrial, or engaged in voluntary welfare activities, so that they will accept and understand the significance and the potential usefulness of small voluntary associations and informal organizations within the community, rather than seeing such associations as rivals, competitors, or enemies?

If the future of providing basic services for the mass of mankind, in health, in welfare, in education, lies in the utilization of front-line volunteers and local people as village, block, or community workers, what will happen to these people in the long run, when, drawn as they are from among the intended beneficiaries of the services, they have become competent in their particular local activity? Will they have a career structure, going on to paraprofessional and professional roles and thus cease to fulfill their original function? Or, will they be expected to stay on as vital but comparatively unrewarded front-line workers? This may well become a question of some magnitude if the recruitment of this level of worker really proceeds at the needed rate; and it is indeed a question of human relationships.

Again, if participation is accepted as a key element in the development of social welfare, and the concept of human relationships moves away from a "we-they" relationship to what Martin Buber called the "I-thou relationship," what does this imply for the organization of social services in the 1980s? Will it be easier to get this participation and the personal touch for single and separate services (old people's welfare, services for youth, child welfare, care of the disabled), or can that be more easily achieved within an integrated, multidisciplinary organization?

Again, if we accept participation as the key and essential element, what are the implications for social welfare research? What, in terms of satisfactory and satisfying human relationships, is implied by the idea of participatory social welfare research; that is, in which people and their relationships and attitudes to each other are not just treated as objective data of research to be examined and assessed by outside researchers?

These and similar questions are of a very general nature: if we move on to specific issues, the challenges become much more difficult to face. As one example, in developed and developing countries alike, unemployment looms large as a major social problem. After a period of wishful thinking, the highly industrialized market-economy countries seem to have accepted that it is no short-term or temporary problem. One analysis after another shows that the hardest hit are young people entering the labor market; that among young people girls are worse off than boys; that ethnic and other minorities suffer more than their peers; and that those who come from culturally and educationally disadvantaged backgrounds and who have little or no success in school suffer worst of all. If ever there was a case of cumulative inequalities and disadvantages, youth unemployment is a clear-cut example. Politicians and economists proceed to devise solutions, or seeming solutions. Some say that nothing can be done and that the whole market-economy system has to be changed and that only a state-planned economy will resolve the unemployment problem. But the challenge will continue to be: who is responsible for the human relationships aspect, for doing something, for instance, about the desperate deterioration of self-respect which afflicts the unemployed young person in the midst of a rich and consumption-oriented society? Certainly some people are concerned, if only to prevent the civil disturbances or violence which can be so easily generated by this type of frustration and despair—but which social welfare department or organization is ready and able to do something positive and creative about it in terms of human relationships, of restoring or preserving young people's sense of their own worth and of their role in society?

To take another example, again from the problem areas of

Europe and North America in particular but one which may soon spread to other regions, how is it possible to deal more humanly with the so-called "problem" of the rapidly growing proportion of aged people in our populations? Why does society regard it as a problem? How can we avoid what appears to be an almost automatic reaction of taking away meaningful and satisfying social roles from the elderly, of preventing them from continuing to have a significant economic and productive function, which in most of our societies is the key function which provides prestige and self-respect? The right to retirement has been a social challenge in the past; now perhaps the new challenge is the right to a form of retirement which does not amount to ostracism or exclusion from human relationships.

A further and universal challenge of the same nature is that of the acceptance and rehabilitation of the disabled in our societies. The United Nations has proclaimed 1981 as the Year for Disabled Persons, and it will challenge us to ensure the fullest possible participation of the disabled in all aspects of economic, social, and political life according to their individual capacities, so that they are not in any way excluded from the full range of human relationships.

Finally, as a colleague reminded me, we cannot face challenges of the kind I have mentioned unless we have the relevant information to know what are the problems and their dimensions. So we have to face, too, the challenge of being able to collect the relevant facts and present them in a usable form. And here Israel has presented an excellent example, in their chart, "Social Profile of Cities and Towns in Israel," of one effective way of responding to the challenge of establishing and improving our social reporting. Is it in fact possible to improve our information base concerning social welfare needs and services on a local basis so that we can break down the vast national and international statistical tables into small-scale realistic and accurate instruments which will ensure that as we improve the economic and material infrastructure of welfare, we do not sacrifice the values and qualities of the I-thou relationship?

PART IV

CATHERINE McGUINNESS
PRESIDENT, NATIONAL SOCIAL SERVICE COUNCIL, IRELAND

I SEE it as significant that in dealing with the challenges of the 1980s the importance of the individual's human relationships within the family and within the community is recognized. If we look at the historical growth of state health and social welfare schemes we will find that these schemes have generally been devised as solutions to the problems of the individual, and have not looked at the individual's relationship to the family and to the community. Pensions were provided for the elderly individual, medical treatment for the sick individual, state support for the unemployed individual. Later some provision may have been added for the economic dependents of the individual, but generally speaking, social welfare provision was seen as the individual solution of individual problems. It was not appreciated that human well-being also depends on family and community relationships.

In the developed countries, the growth of such social welfare schemes took place in the latter half of the nineteenth century and in the earlier part of the twentieth century. It is interesting that this, the period following the Industrial Revolution, was also a period when the family group, in particular the extended family group, was weakening and gradually ceasing to be the protective and supportive unit which it had been in earlier forms of society. Of course in many countries the family retains its old strength to a considerable degree, but it seems to have been an unfortunate corollary of industrial development that it produced a corresponding weakening in the sense of family and the sense of community.

In 1975 I attended the World Council of Churches Assembly in Nairobi, and there took part in a group which studied human relationships within the family—the effect on the family of such trends as the ending of polygamy, the movement for women's equality, industrial employment, and mobility of labor. What emerged most clearly was that within such an international group the word "family" carried a wide range of meanings. Africans spoke of family/tribal groupings; Indians, of the extended family of brothers, wives, and children living as a group. At the other extreme, North Americans spoke of children who had never met their grandparents, children of repeatedly broken marriages, of ceaselessly mobile nuclear families. Ireland, I felt, occupied a more or less middle ground in this family range, so that perhaps in Ireland we can still see the strengths—and weaknesses—of the old system even while we learn to cope with the problems of the new. There is no need to emphasize the role of the family in Israel; the whole history of the Jewish people could be read as an illustration of the tenacity and strength of family. The very expression "the Children of Israel" tells its own tale.

Yet only in recent years have we begun to see the need for a social welfare system which sees the family and the larger community as a whole. Our services still tend to deal with individual problems, though in practice the social worker can well see that the individual problem is part of a family or community problem. A caseworker is sent to investigate school truancy; the problem is not just a truant child but an alcoholic father, or a mother involved in prostitution, or perhaps a whole community where traditional academic schooling is seen as irrelevant. A recent survey carried out among twelve-to-sixteen-year-old Irish boys with criminal records showed that there was an average of eight children in their families (four times the European Economic Community average); 84 percent of their fathers and 98 percent of the boys themselves were unemployed; 66 percent were illiterate, and none could read and write well; and 92 percent had a brother and/or father in prison. These children lived in a well-known problem community, and the survey results were not particularly surprising.

What is important is that no attempt to deal with any of the boys' individual problems could succeed without also dealing with their family and community problems.

The London *Sunday Times* published an article on the British National Health Service on July 30, 1978. The article dealt largely with the burden placed on the National Health Service by old people—their accommodations, their hospitalization, coping with their everyday needs, their loneliness. These old people were referred to as "the crumblies." That a whole society should not only push out its older people from a normal place in the community but should see them as a burden and calmly refer to them in such callous terms is surely one of the disgraces of the developed world.

As in recent years the importance of the family and community groups has begun to be understood, social welfare policy has changed in the direction of seeking community participation in the care of the individual. This is a healthy trend so long as it is not allowed to become an excuse for abdication of responsibility by the welfare authorities. Help and problem-solving are still essential, both by central and local government agencies and by voluntary agencies within the community itself. This help must be given in context, seeing the individual as part of the family and part of a number of interrelated community groups. The less developed countries, where social welfare services are still being built up, should be able to learn from this experience and treat the individual not as a lone creature but as the center of a complex net of human relationships. It is three centuries since John Donne wrote, "No man is an island"; he is still right.

Our family units and the structures of our communities may change, and change radically. The challenge of the 1980s is to develop comprehensive social welfare policies to meet these changes and truly to promote human well-being.

Another challenge seems to be growing stronger in the past few years, particularly in the more developed countries. The difficult policy question of allocation of economic resources and selection of priorities faces all governments. Those involved in the creation of social welfare policies and the provision of social welfare services naturally seek the continuous improvement of existing services and the extension of new services to other areas of need. For all of us it seems axiomatic that social welfare spending and the creation of comprehensive social welfare services are central priorities of government policy. It is easy to forget that others may not see it that way, and may, in fact, regard social welfare expenditures as marginal to the major aims of economic development.

In the developed countries of the West, at any rate, there is an increasingly vocal expression of the opinion that social welfare spending is absorbing too large a proportion of economic resources and that the state has gone quite far enough in supporting the weaker members of the community. This outlook can come to the surface in various forms. In its simplest form it may be expressed as a feeling that the responsible and hard-working citizens are being grossly overtaxed in order to feather-bed the idle, the improvident, and the work-shy. Few will be entirely critical of providing services for the elderly—after all, we will all be old some day. Rather more are critical of increases in health expenditures; this is seen to have gone beyond acceptable limits. Increased support for the unemployed and their dependents is a constant target for criticism. There is a widespread feeling that unemployment benefits are so high that many are financially better off than if they were working, and that wholesale welfare handouts are supporting a whole class of idlers who have long ago given up any idea of supporting themselves. We may be aware that these opinions bear no relation to reality but we would be foolish to ignore their existence and, I feel, their growing strength.

The resistance to social welfare spending may also surface in more subtle ways. It may take the form of an accusation that a large proportion of resources is consumed in wasteful administration, that far too small a proportion actually reaches the people in need. This accusation is made not only against central government services—the old familiar target for allegations of bureaucratic waste—but also against the major voluntary bodies working to alleviate human need: Oxfam and Christian Aid are but two examples.

Another attitude toward social welfare spending which is

fairly widely manifested is the idea that if economic growth and development are going ahead, then with a little corrective and residual spending here and there, social welfare needs will be looked after automatically. This is a more difficult outlook to deal with since it is generally based on the idea that if full or nearly full employment can be provided in the economy all other problems will be solved. This idea contains the truth that unemployment has been a major evil in recent years, and that a solution to the unemployment problem must be a main priority for any government. It also contains the truth that solving the unemployment problem would free resources which could be spent on improving social welfare services.

It is easy to forget that economic growth in itself does not mean the allocation of greater resources to social welfare; it can just as easily mean that the rich get richer and the poor fall still farther behind. This is true on an international scale as well as on a national or community scale. A social welfare policy which aims at a fair distribution of increased wealth throughout the community is a conscious decision, not merely an automatic reflex of economic development.

I have deliberately put this challenge to the further development of social welfare policies in rather harsh terms because I see the growth of these public attitudes as a major challenge of the 1980s. It is of little use to talk in terms of a caring community if large numbers of community members are in fact becoming more and more "don't care" in their attitudes. We must, I think, realize that in a period of general economic difficulty and recession people's own fears and struggles will often surface as attacks on what they perceive to be unnecessary spending of their money on policies which they do not support. If we fail to understand this challenge and cope with it we may well find that our planning for comprehensive social welfare systems is a mere creation of castles in the air; public support for the implementation of these plans may simply disappear.

I do not pretend to offer any universal solution to this problem. I merely say that we ignore it at our peril.

In surveying these challenges for the 1980s I have discussed the need and the desire to plan social welfare policy as a coherent whole, as an over-all strategy to promote the well-being of the individual in the family and in the community. For this purpose we seek to use not only the central resources of the state but also the resources of voluntary commitment within the community itself. This concept of coherent over-all planning both for the use of resources and for the provision of services is a relatively new one. It is only in recent years that we have realized fully that the piecemeal provision of social welfare remedies for specific, acutely perceived needs is not a real solution.

Precisely because we are still only exploring this area of social welfare planning we may often find that the results of our policies are not entirely predictable. To put it simply, things do not always turn out the way we intended. In the area of policy creation there is a need to be humble and to recognize the fact that we are still only groping our way. We need to learn from our mistakes as well as from our successes. Only in this way can we overcome the challenges which will face us in the coming decade.

PART V

ROSA PERLA RESNICK

PROFESSOR, SETON HALL UNIVERSITY, UNITED STATES

WE MUST recognize that the field of human relations is likely to make a great contribution to the promotion and implementation of our goals around the world in the next decade.

What do human relationships mean? It is interesting to note that neither the *International Encyclopedia of the Social Sciences* nor the *Encyclopedia of Social Work* nor current dictionaries have a definition of this concept. *Webster's Dictionary*, however, defines the two words separately:

Human. Characteristic of, or having the qualities of, mankind; a person.

Relation. Connection as in thought, meaning; the connection between or among persons, nations. Relationship.

Nevertheless, for those who work in the field of social welfare or, more specifically, in the field of social work, the concept of "human relationships" is very familiar, and one that we use to guide us in helping our clients, no matter whether we deal with individuals, families, or communities.

Helen Perlman has said:

In the sense in which we speak of "relationhip" in social casework (and it is probably the concept that appears with greatest frequency in all of casework's oral and written discussions), it is a condition in which two persons with some common interest between them, long-term or temporary, interact with feeling. . . . Relationship leaps from one person to the other at the moment when emotion moves between them. . . . Whether this interaction creates a sense of union or of antagonism, the two persons are for the time "connected" or "related" to each other.[1]

For social workers, educators, and psychologists the importance assigned to learning how to establish and maintain professional relationships with individuals and families, and use them with the purpose of providing help, is certainly common knowledge today, and yet not too easy to put into practice. It is equally difficult to develop the feelings of acceptance, respect, and empathy which are so fundamental to establish a genuine rapport, to communicate easily, and to start a meaningful dialogue between two human beings, as is so masterfully presented by the Israeli philosopher Martin Buber.

It is even more difficult to deal with human relationships among groups, where conflicts and interpersonal and communication problems usually arise. The same holds true when we enter the field of intergroup relations, where one has to work with people who come from different ethnic, religious, cultural, educational, economic, and political backgrounds. Serious problems of human relationships in different parts of

---

[1] Helen Harris Perlman, *Social Casework—a Problem-solving Process* (Chicago: University of Chicago Press, 1957), pp. 65–66.

the world are well-known where relationships among various groups of the population have become increasingly difficult in recent times.

Itzhak Navon, president of Israel, had told us with pride that the people who live in Israel come from 102 different countries and speak 81 different languages, making an extraordinary effort to integrate themselves into one nation, united by a common past and looking forward to a common future. This is a beautiful example of a people that have gained much success in their thirty years of independent life. According to Navon, however, the most difficult task that lies ahead is to live in peace with their neighbors, but he was optimistic that peace will come as a result of the personal relationships and talks at the international level among the political leaders of today's world. What is the role played by human relations in this process? I think it is obvious that they are playing a fundamental role to promote, facilitate, and improve the communication of dialogue among those leaders.

The learning of human relations is a lifelong process being achieved since birth through education, socialization, community participation, and so forth. In social welfare we recognize today that many projects have failed because human beings were not given the opportunity to participate in plans affecting themselves for the dialogue had not been established; man himself should be the agent of his own individual and social development. It is precisely in this process where human relationships must indeed play an important role respecting man's individual self-determination, freedom of choice, and need for self-expression.

I think that the social well-being we aspire to achieve in the 1980s should be based on adequate human relations at all levels; the recognition of individual, regional, and national socioeconomic and political differences, and the joint effort of all nations to live fuller and more meaningful lives.

Aurelio Peccei, the president of the Club of Rome, recently suggested that "the 150 national states, a symbol of today's world divisions, are in contrast with the actual reality of interdependence and with the spirit of solidarity, communication and human relationships at the world level without which there will be no authentic possibilities for the future."[2] We should, therefore, recognize that human relationships are an absolute, indispensable factor if we are to translate into practice the consciousness of world interdependence through respecting the will of increasing numbers of countries to preserve their political autonomy and development models.

PART VI

GEORGETTE ST-ARNAUD

TITULAR PROFESSOR, THE SCHOOL OF SOCIAL SERVICE,
FACULTY OF SOCIAL SCIENCES, UNIVERSITY OF LAVAL, CANADA

THE THEME of the XIXth International Conference on Social Welfare concerns human well-being in the 1980s. What will be the economic and political actions that are likely to promote it? More particularly, how will community, family, and individual human relationships be linked to development policies, distribution of services, subjects pertinent to research, and regional and international action?

In this discussion the culture and experience of a French-speaking, North American will necessarily come to the foreground, even if only through the sources of the supporting examples. Although I apologize for not always giving a universal character to the topics dealt with, Canada, by its geographical situation and its origins, does have affinities with the United States and with Europe.

As a result of demographic changes, how does the evolution of family and social relationships appear, and what problems will be created by this evolution in the society of tomorrow?

[2] Speech given by Aurelio Peccei, International Convention on Problems and Prospects of Modern Society, Rome, Italy, 1978.

What are the measures of social security, social policies, and services that will take on particular importance in the next decade?

THE EVOLUTION

If the populations of various continents are compared, and if they are pyramided into three subgroups—the young, less than fifteen years old; the active population, from fifteen to sixty-four; and the aged, sixty-five years old and over—one finds, at one extremity of the pyramid, Europe with 24 percent of its population aged less than fifteen, while Africa has 44 percent. At the other extremity of the pyramid, the aged make up 12 percent of the European population, and 3 percent of the African population.

In Canada, the number of young people has been rapidly decreasing for several years. Our population, though younger than that of the United States, is characterized by a continual increase in the active group. In 1990, and for the first time, 60 percent of the population will be between eighteen and sixty-four years of age.

How does the evolution of social and family relationships appear following these demographic developments? The traditional family formed a complete world in all societies.[1] It established vertical relationships between the generations; satisfied almost all emotional needs for affection, protection, and procreation; furnished the necessary consumer goods for housing, nutrition, and clothing. Its members themselves provided the necessary services of looking after children, education, and often elementary health care. Finally, the family provided for its own security through savings.

During the centuries, the family evolved. First, it required the parish or village to take charge of certain services; it obliged the society to organize itself to provide education and health care, and then to assure the security of its members by means of various allowances. In the twentieth century, society tends to supplant the traditional family in almost every field.

[1] See Marc A. Lessard, "The Family and Quebec Society Today," *Social Service*, XXVI, No. 1 (1977), 14–27.

Social and human relations go beyond the family structure and establish themselves more and more on a horizontal level; that is to say, between those persons who have common bonds through similar age, responsibility, or role.

The family itself has been considerably modified. For example, in the highly industrialized countries, family planning has had the effect of modifying the equilibrium of the demographic pyramid, making it thinner at the bottom, with the reduction in births. Instead of having a single type of family, composed of parents, children, and grandparents, there is a whole variety of family models.

Couples of today can opt for a life together as two, three, or many; choose a common-law, civil, or religious marriage, divorce, remarry; etc. The family may be a commune, a nuclear family, or an extended family, even though our socioeconomic arrangements do not help in the inclusion of grandparents at the present time.[2]

Taking Canada as an example, the divorce rate has increased a great deal since passage of the law on divorce in 1969. It was 139.8 per 100,000 inhabitants in 1970, and in 1976 it was 235.8 per 100,000, an increase of 68.6 percent in six years.[3]

Other statistics predict that one marriage in three will end in divorce or break-up.[4] The number of single-parent families is on the increase in Canada: it was 10 percent in 1974. The majority of these heads of family are women.[5]

In line with these facts there is a growth in the number of working women, especially among married women. In 1953, in Quebec, the female population in the work force was 24.6 percent; in 1975, it was 38 percent.[6] Nearly a third of the world's working population was composed of women in 1970. It is predicted that the absolute number of women in the work

[2] M. Berlinguet, "Evolution of the Family and the Practice of the Social Services," *ibid.*, pp. 30, 31.

[3] *Statistics on Personal Data,* Vol. II, Marriage and Divorce (Ottawa: Statistics Canada, 1976), p. 30, table 12.

[4] See Commission on Legal Services, second annual report, March 31, 1974 (Quebec: Commission on Legal Services, 1974), pp. 68, 69, as quoted in *Social Service,* XXVI, No. 1 (1977), 39.

[5] *The Economic Condition of Women in Quebec* (Quebec: Editeur officiel du Quebec, 1978), I, 11, 128.

[6] *The Active Population,* Vol. XXXI (Ottawa: Statistics Canada, 1975), p. 65, table 38.

force will increase at least until 1980.[7] We are seeing, then, a transformation of the traditional roles within the couple. An international study has revealed the proportion of time devoted to employment, to personal activities, and to homemaking and pedagogical tasks. In this study there is a comparison between men and women who have children and who are employed outside the home and who live in France, Poland, the United States, and the USSR.

Szalai's study has brought out the following data: A man devotes between 4 percent and 6 percent of his daily time to household tasks; a woman, about two or three times as much. As for remunerated work, a woman devotes, on the average, 30.8 percent of her time; a man, 35.8 percent. A woman has 54.7 percent of her time available for her personal needs; a man, 59 percent.

Another change which has come about in society is the state's taking charge of training and education of the population. School attendance has become compulsory in most countries. Many countries have entrusted the universities with developing technical, scientific, and professional competence of their citizens. Expressed in these terms, the level of education has visibly increased during the last few years. To take Quebec as an example, in 1971, according to the statistics, 11.4 percent of Quebec's women between twenty-five and thirty-four years of age had a university diploma. On the other hand, among the population aged sixty-five or over, only 3.6 percent of the men and 0.8 percent of the women had an equivalent diploma.[8] From the statistics of 1971 it can be said that there are approximately four times as many men as women sixty-five who have a university diploma whereas among the adult population from twenty-five to thirty-four years of age, this ratio is only two and a half times in favor of men.

In many countries there has been a recent increase in the level of education, more noticeable among women than among

[7] *Le Travail des femmes en France* (The Employment of Women in France), pamphlet edited in collaboration with the Committee on Women at Work (Paris: La documentation française, 1973), p. 79.

[8] *Statistics Canada, the 1971 Census,* Vol. III, Part 7, April, 1975, pp. 11–12, Table 1, as quoted in the *Economic Condition of Women in Quebec,* I, 99, table 111.1–16.

men. This partly explains the revaluation of women's professional competence in the work force.

Demographic developments, and changes that have come about in the family, have led the state to accept its responsibilities regarding our senior citizens, as it has done for other population groups. It is in this way that old-age pensions, as well as various private and public insurance schemes, have appeared. At the moment, social gerontology is evolving; it helps in adapting our services for older people. The increase in longevity will soon have to be taken into account. It is estimated that between 1971 and 2001 the number of persons aged from seventy-five to eighty-four will increase by 113 percent and that of persons eighty-five and over, by 156 percent.[9]

Let us note the preponderant role of the state in the organization of services and the resultant problems of costs. How will the state resolve these problems in a manner that is financially and psychologically acceptable?

MEASURES OF SOCIAL SECURITY, SOCIAL POLICIES, AND
SERVICES

The growth of the active population and the fluctuations in the economy inevitably risk creating problems of unemployment. In order to mitigate the lack of income thus caused, unemployment insurance has been instituted in the majority of industrialized countries.[10]

In the past, an attempt has been made to lower unemployment by lowering the age of optional and compulsory retirement; but with the aging of certain populations, this measure has become onerous. Other efforts have been made to lower unemployment by increasing the length of schooling for the young. Another means is to spread the number of available jobs among all the individuals suitable for work, thereby adjusting salaries. These solutions are already being applied in certain countries. Some are decreasing the active population

[9] Nicolas Zay, "Social Gerontology: Its Present and Its Past," *Social Service,* Vol. XXVI, Nos. 2–3 (1977).
[10] "Social Security in Ten Industrialized Countries," *Union des Banques Suisses* (Union of Swiss Banks), May, 1977, p. 70.

by closing the gap between the age of entry into the work force and the age of leaving it. Others allow a greater number of adults to share in the work, thereby reducing unemployment. These methods do not in themselves increase the countries' productivity, that is, the total production which supports the whole population, active and dependent. The production that a country has available to support its inhabitants comes from its natural resources and their increase in value through processing, from its employable population, and from its level of productivity. There must, therefore, be a harmonious equilibrium among these three elements. Social security has the role of sharing the riches among all citizens.

Social assistance, unemployment insurance, old-age pensions, family allowances, medical insurance, and so on are only possible if the state has sufficient resources available. Let us recall that with the aging of certain populations, state-run, comprehensive pensions eat up a good part of the national revenue. "Already in 1972, spending on old-age and survivors' insurance represented between 8 and 10% of national revenue in the countries of the European Economic Community. It was practically twice as much as state-run, medical insurance which is already, itself, quite high.[11]

On the one hand, in spite of a strong tendency toward state take-over of all services offered to dependent populations, young and old, very few studies are produced on the duration of this dependence, and the comparative maintenance costs of children and the aged in relation to their respective needs and to the population structure. On the other hand, one may wonder what percentage of its salary the active population is ready to devote to the protection and security of its members. An investigation undertaken in ten industrialized countries shows that social contributions have attained a high level:

This development is due notably to the considerable extension of social insurances during the 1960s and 1970s. . . . According to a study by the OECD, the taxation an social burdens weighing on the economy have gone from an average of 29.8 percent in 1965 to 34.9 percent in 1975. An exaggerated increase in taxation and social con-

[11] *Ibid.*, p. 6.

tributions may encourage inflation in the instance that they are based on prices, or, in the opposite case, provoke a decrease in investment with all the negative consequences that may hold for employment and economic growth.[12]

Only economic growth can guarantee all the citizens of all countries a similar standard of living throughout their existence. This presents the problem of security in the future. As citizens become conscious of their rights, is it not possible that we shall head toward a society that will demand not job security, but the availability of resources and services, and income security throughout their lifetime, and in all situations, while obliging the state to take more and more reponsibility in the fields of production, consumption, and demographic reproduction? Faced with this latter responsibility, a large number of countries have already established family allowances. Some have the goal of encouraging the birth rate. The state also looks after setting up child care centers or nurseries. In many countries, it looks after health care and education. More and more pressure is being felt so that children may no longer be considered the exclusive reponsibility of the mother, the father, or other relations. Demographic reproduction contributes to assuring future economic production and the survival of the community. "The majority of countries are aware of this as they fix objectives as to the desirable optional size of their population and its evolution through time. Moreover, they generally have an immigration policy which, beyond serving humanitarian ends, is often used as a regulatory device for their population growth."[13] It is in this sense that the mother cannot be classified as unproductive during the period in which she rears her young children. She ought not to be penalized, either, in the job market simply because she temporarily devotes her energies to a task with a limited time period. A woman makes an economic contribution to the country through giving birth to new citizens for which the nation has a need, and through exercising her profession in the work force. Neither the one nor the other can be done without. In

---

[12] *Ibid.*, pp. 29–30.
[13] *The Economic Condition of Women in Quebec,* I, 10.

both cases she comes to terms with her personal, family, and civic responsibilities. These responsibilities are, moreover, increased whenever she is the head of a single-parent family.

To social security measures and legal services must be added psychological services which enable individuals to absorb changes that arise in society and the new family. These measures have the goal of making the negative effects that occur in societies less harsh, and reinforcing the positive effects in order to assure the optimal well-being of all citizens. In the same line of thought is seen, for example, the creation of advisory services for determining who will assume the care of children in case of divorce, separation, or even in the case of parents' mistreating or abandoning their children.

This list of sociopsychologial services concerning all population groups, according to age and condition, could thus be extended. After having satisfied the primary needs relating to survival and preservation of the species, the individual seeks satisfaction of more refined, secondary needs. He becomes conscious of his own personal value: the individual seeks, first of all, to give a meaning to what he does. A reflection by the sociologist Marc A. Lessard is well-applied to our changing societies:

It may be said that there is never a social or cultural vacuum, there are only cultures and societies that are, for a time, impossible to interpret or to describe. Such situations always come about in periods of rapid mutation, when the new has not yet been explicitly lived.[14]

Up till now, countries with a need for manpower have favored adult immigration. According to the needs of the country, one promoted the arrival of either nonqualified manpower for manual work, or more highly qualified manpower according to the special needs of the job market. Whether this policy equally suited the needs of the country of emigration was not always a particular concern. With the development of an awareness of the necessity for a good balance in the demographic pyramid, and of the wealth which the human capital is for each nation, a new phenomenon has been developing dur-

[14] Lessard, *op. cit.*

ing the last fifteen or twenty years: the immigration of children by means of international adoption. In Quebec, from 1975 to 1978, 289 children were adopted from such very different countries as Bangledesh, Korea, Haiti, Honduras, the Philippines, Guatemala, and Vietnam. While keeping in mind that there are very few international agreements on this subject, and without entering into the ethical problems presented by these adoptions for the individuals and the countries concerned, the fact of this new sharing of wealth cannot be denied; and it can only be hoped that it is carried out with respect for human rights and with regard to the needs of the countries of emigration and immigration.

Finally, have the societies with a markedly aging population asked themselves what this effect will have on the over-all behavior of their citizens, and on their reactions to the political system? In our society, citizens influence the political system by their vote, which they can exercise from the age of eighteen. It is known that, by nature, the older person is more conservative, seeks economic and political security, and adapts less well to change. It should, then, be possible to foresee political and cultural mutations of a less pronounced nature in the countries considered old, than in the young countries.

The René Sand Award

PRESENTATION TO THE UNITED NATIONS CHILDREN'S
FUND

LUCIEN MEHL

PRESIDENT, INTERNATIONAL COUNCIL ON SOCIAL WELFARE

IT GIVES me great pleasure on behalf of the International Council on Social Welfare to present to the United Nations Children's Fund the René Sand Award. Since the death of René Sand, the founder of the ICSW, an award bearing his name has been bestowed at each conference to an individual who has made an outstanding contribution to international social welfare or related fields and is recognized and esteemed internationally. It is the highest award the ICSW can give. Selected after consultation with all our national committees, our international member organizations, and our International Advisory Board, UNICEF is the first *organization* chosen for the award. I believe that there is no organization better suited to be the first such recipient of the award.

Created in December, 1946, the Fund's resources in its first several years were largely devoted to meeting the postwar emergency needs of children in Europe for food, drugs, and clothing. In the 1950s the main emphasis of UNICEF shifted to programs of long-range benefit to children of developing countries. Today it is cooperating with over one hundred developing countries through help for the planning and design of services benefiting children as part of national development plans; through the provision of supplies, equipment, and other aid for developing and extending these services; and through the provision of funds to strengthen the training of nationl personnel.

Its advocacy role in helping raise the level of consciousness of children's needs and practical ways in which they can be met, the flexibility of its aid which reflects the diversity of situations in the countries with which it cooperates, and its ability to make quick and effective responses to changing situations, have earned the Fund a preeminent position among operating agencies in the social welfare field. Awarded the Nobel Peace Prize in 1965, the work of UNICEF, which transcends political considerations, constitutes a recognition that the well-being of today's children is the concern of people everywhere and is inseparably linked with the peace of tomorrow's world.

The René Sand Award to UNICEF comes at the eve of the International Year of the Child, proclaimed by the United Nations for 1979. Its purpose is to encourage each country to review the situation of its children and its policies and programs for the promotion of children's well-being, and to undertake specific practical measures—with achievable goals—to benefit children both in the short and the long term. In this, nongovernmental organizations, such as ICSW national committees, can play an important role at national and local levels. On the international level the ICSW intends to use the opportunities afforded by the Year to further the close relationship which has existed between the ICSW and UNICEF for such a long time.

I now take great pleasure in calling upon Dr. Charles A. Egger, Deputy Executive Director of UNICEF, to receive the award on behalf of UNICEF.

CHARLES A. EGGER
DEPUTY EXECUTIVE DIRECTOR,
UNITED NATIONS CHILDREN'S FUND

ALL OF us in UNICEF are profoundly touched by the great honor to our organization in being selected to receive the René Sand Award. This recognition is even more meaningful because it coincides with the celebration by the International Council on Social Welfare of a half century of efforts to improve human well-being through social welfare and is presented at a conference concerned with analyzing changing conditions and perspectives and looking ahead to the social, economic, and political action required to achieve progress in human well-being. Like the ICSW, UNICEF is engaged in a continuing search for more effective ways to contribute to international cooperation in the social field, concentrating its efforts on cooperation with developing countries in their efforts to give their children a decent start in life and to realize their full potential both as individuals and as members of society. We are keenly aware that we must learn from our failures as well as our successes and from the experience of many others. Conferences such as this one provide a valuable source of such experience.

We regard the award as a symbol of the high hopes of the world for the coming generations and for an increased commitment to do everything we can to lay the basis for the fulfillment of those hopes. This includes working for a world in which nations will be able to divert resources which now go to armaments, to the entitlements of children under the Declaration of the Rights of the Child. This is equally justified by humanitarian principles and the pragmatic necessities for sustained development.

Receiving the René Sand Award at this particular conference of the ICSW gives us a very special pleasure because of the long and intimate association between UNICEF and the chairman of your International Program Committee, Zena Harman. Mrs. Harman made outstanding contributions to the policies of UNICEF during the many years she represented her government on the UNICEF executive board. She was chairman of the executive board at the time UNICEF was awarded the Nobel Peace Prize in 1965. Currently she is chairman of the Israeli National Committee for UNICEF and is a key person in the organization of the Israeli National Commission for the International Year of the Child.

In a paper by UNICEF available to participants at this conference we discuss some major areas that we believe are of mutual concern to our two organizations, with emphasis on the well-being of children in developing countries. I intend only briefly to highlight the main ones. Before doing so, however, I should like to remind you of the setting in which the efforts of UNICEF take place—the immense unmet needs of children in the developing countries with which UNICEF cooperates. In these countries, on an average:

1. The infant mortality rate is four times that in the industrialized countries, and the child mortality rate is forty to sixty times higher.

2. Malnutrition affects one quarter of all children.

3. Less than one half the children in primary school age attend school.

4. Less than 20 percent of rural children have access to adequate health facilities.

Many people—government officials, economists, and others—believe that the needs of children in the developing world are so vast that there is little point in trying to address them seriously until some of the urgent problems of economic development are resolved. UNICEF, and a growing number of other voices, does not share this view. They have been pointing out, for example, that the move toward a new international economic order, in addition to its main emphasis on equity among countries in international financial and economic matters, also requires equity within countries and the promotion of self-reliance. The care, protection, and preparation of children are preconditions for achieving these goals, as well as being absolutely essential for sustained economic progress.

It is important that decision-makers recognize the vital link between programs for children, on the one hand, and economic and social progress, on the other, and understand that such programs are complementary to the goals of the new international order. It is equally valid that those concerned with programs for children recognize that the needs of children cannot be effectively tackled in isolation from the family and community of which they are part, nor can they be compartmentalized. They need to be met on a holistic basis through intersectoral, mutually supportive services covering all the essential needs of children.

A program approach called "basic services for children," now being encouraged by UNICEF and other organizations, has this emphasis. It has become clear that in many developing countries it is not possible to extend the present pattern of services sufficiently in the foreseeable future to reach the very large numbers of children now poorly or not at all served. In order to bridge this gap, and help raise the quality of life of the lower-income groups and contribute to building up national capacity and self-reliance, efforts are required not only from the senior governmental levels down, but also through mobilizing the interest and involvement of people at the community level. An essential aspect of the basic services approach is that the people of the community are involved from the outset in identifying their needs, deciding on priorities, choosing from among themselves resident community workers and managing their services. An essential element in the link between the community workers and district and subdivisional facilities which provide advice, supervision, training, referral services, and administrative and logistical support.

Acceptance by governments of the basic services concept,

with its greater decentralization and popular participation as an integral part of their national development strategy, is essential for its growth on a substantial scale as is, also, the reorientation of government extension services to support this approach. Nongovernmental organizations can be dynamic agents in this process, providing important links between the community and the government. This should be especially true of ICSW national affiliates which serve as coordinating bodies of multidisciplinary social agencies and whose member agencies can reach down into the provinces and localities.

We feel that it is important in terms of human rights that we do not justify greater investment in the child solely on grounds of social utility. We need to give greater recognition to the intrinsic value of childhood in its own rights, to the great importance of nurturing the imagination and the spirit of children, providing them with the opportunities needed to realize their full potential.

We are happy to see the increased stress at the 1978 conference on the developmental function of social welfare, an emphasis with which UNICEF is completely in accord, especially in developing countries. While full recognition must be given to the continuing importance of serving groups in special need in all countries, the very concept of vulnerable groups takes on a much broader meaning in developing countries, where it refers to large proportions of the population. In policy and practice, therefore, welfare—including child welfare—has to be seen increasingly as dealing with the well-being of large segments of populations, particularly those who live in poverty-stricken areas.

I wish to add a word of sincere appreciation regarding the secretary-generals of the ICSW. We have valued very highly indeed the close association we have had over the years with your present secretary-general, Kate Katzki. This was also the case with her late predecessor, Ruth Williams. They have provided us with advice, have given us the benefit of their experience, and have worked with us in practical approaches to promote the basic values which our two organizations jointly share, including strengthening our relationships with the international nongovernmental community as a whole. We look forward to building upon this solid foundation as we work on our mutual concerns with your new secretary-general, Ingrid Gelinek.

The International Year of the Child in 1979 provides a unique opportunity for improving commitments to the child, bringing together in each country the government ministries, national organizations, community groups, and individuals interested in education, advocacy, and action to benefit the child. We believe that the ICSW national affiliates can play a key role in this heightening of awareness of the needs of children and ways of meeting them through ideas, expertise, and effort. This contribution toward combining the humanistic with the development aspects of social welfare could well be seen as a most fitting tribute to the vision of René Sand.

The UNICEF Experience from Programs for Children—and Needs for the Future[1]

THE GREAT honor which the United Nations Children's Fund feels—as an organization, as a member of the United Nations family, and as a global community of concerned individuals—in receiving the 1978 René Sand Award is a humbling but invigorating experience. That any organization should be so recognized while the needs of the world's children are still so grossly underserved can only increase the motivation of us all in trying to meet those needs.

It would be a less than human reaction, however, not to acknowledge a genuine pride in this recognition of UNICEF's work. But such an emotion can only be fleeting in the face of the magnitude and extent of the problems which still remain to be solved if the lives of millions upon millions of children are ever to be freed from the deadly effects of poverty, of injustice, of ill-health, of ignorance, and, perhaps worst of all, of our inadequate concern for fellow human beings.

It is not empty rhetoric to remind ourselves that, even as we discuss their welfare, so many of the world's children continue to suffer, and die, in conditions which we know in our hearts should not prevail. If we accept the idea of a global community, then we should automatically accept global responsibilities. The world has the resources, human, physical, and intellectual, to eradicate the blight which threatens the light of life among a majority of the world's children. What we often lack in considerable measure is the will to effect necessary changes and to learn from others.

We think that the memory of René Sand would best be served if, in his honor, we attempted to share in a modest way some of the experiences of three decades of cooperation by

[1] Prepared by the United Nations Children's Fund on the occasion of receiving the René Sand Award from the International Council on Social Welfare.

UNICEF with countries in programs to improve the situation of their children. Such an exercise is particularly appropriate in this the fiftieth anniversary year of the International Council on Social Welfare, and particularly so given the theme of the XIXth ICSW International Conference and its emphasis on human well-being, on challenges for the 1980s, and on social, economic, and political action.

This opportunity to share experiences with such a distinguished international audience is also especially welcome as UNICEF itself is currently deeply involved with a special year in its own history—the International Year of the Child, which begins officially in January, 1979—during which time all countries are being encouraged to prepare and commit themselves to major, long-term improvements in the well-being of their children.

THE EMERGING NEEDS OF CHILDREN'S WELFARE

The need for modesty in an exercise such as this is paramount: what has been learned is still far outweighed by what we have yet to learn. The very creation of UNICEF, however, in late 1946 following the devastations of World War II, was an indication that humankind did possess the will and the capacity to progress on an international scale. For the first time in human history there was international recognition that children—and the state of childhood—were both valuable and vulnerable in a rapidly changing world, and that specific efforts were needed to guarantee their welfare, to help countries care for a category of human beings almost universally recognized as "special." Thus, the founding of UNICEF reflected the conception of the need for human values to predominate. It is only an acknowledgment of human imperfection, however, to recognize that this need still must be restated.

THE NEED FOR HUMAN VALUES

If there is one outstanding lesson from the last three decades it is that social and economic development can never fully succeed unless human beings are recognized as both the ends and the means of that development.

It is therefore encouraging to see that there is increasing acceptance that economic development needs a more human focus, based on a recognition that mankind does not survive by economics alone, and that economics alone can solve only part of the problems of the human condition. While there have been notable economic advances over the last three decades, we have also seen that these advances benefited only a minority of the world's peoples and that, much worse, the condition of the majority of people improved little, if at all. And for the world's poorest people—many millions of them children—their lives were blighted, indeed ended, by poverty while the aggregate levels of world prosperity reached new heights.

This changing focus of development is inherent in the international community's recent acknowledgment of the need for a new international economic order with its emphases on economic redistribution as well as economic growth, on the need for social justice at all levels—international, national, and local—and on the idea that interdependence rather than competition is a better strategy for human survival. Above all, the new wave of development thinking recognizes that human values should be paramount, and that the most tragic waste of resources is the waste of human resources.

In this context, the evolution of the development aspects of welfare and their contribution to self-reliance can play an important role. The old idea of welfare as a luxury to be afforded only when certain levels of material prosperity have been achieved is replaced by a recognition that adequate standards of well-being are not only a precondition and continuing requirement of societies but also a basic human right. At their most positive, the new ideas of welfare set their sights on realizing the full human potential—through human involvement, education, individual and community participation in social and economic development—for the common good.

In the field of children's welfare, it is also possible to see a related emerging concern for meeting the full human range of children's needs: the utilitarian concept of children (as future members of the labor force, as economic assets, and so on) is being succeeded by a richer concept of children which emphasizes humanistic as well as national development objectives. This new concept regards children not only as human beings with rights to a full adult life but also with rights to develop the particular human potentialities available to all of us in the years of childhood.

Thus, the need for activities which improve human well-being can be seen as emerging from a position in which welfare is often a secondary priority, into being at least an equal partner with economic and political factors in development, and perhaps leading to a future where it will be a recognized human right. For those of us concerned with human well-being this can only be an encouraging trend, and one which deserves the highest consideration. Philosophically, the causes of this trend may lead to some cautious optimism that human values are now being accorded higher priority. But in the everyday world we must also acknowledge that such values can be clouded by other more pragmatic considerations encountered in socioeconomic-political processes. It is, therefore, necessary to consider strategy.

THE NEED FOR STRATEGY

The evolution of UNICEF's outlook on a strategy for programs benefiting children has been based on experience in many countries in many years, and has involved countless organizations and individuals. It can be seen, therefore, as an international, interdisciplinary endeavor. It represents a consensus which has emerged on general guidelines, within which there can be considerable differences of national emphasis and priorities.

Very broadly, this strategy for UNICEF, in its cooperation with efforts of countries to improve the situation of their children, has evolved through four stages. The first was the concentration on meeting emerging postwar needs of children, mainly in Europe. The second, which took place throughout the 1950s, shifted attention to the longer-term needs of children in developing countries. The third stage was the change from a series of single projects in a country in sectoral fields (health, nutrition, education, social welfare) to emphasizing the delivery of services at the community level so that they complement and reinforce each other, and would fit more logically and effectively into over-all national development efforts. The fourth stage, which recognized that the "reach" of programs needed dramatic improvement, has been the development of a "basic services" approach in which there is a concentration on the mobilization of the interest and the involvement of people at the community level.

Related to this has been the need to improve the organizational means of meeting children's needs; the need to recognize the linkages between various services to children; and the need for innovative approaches and "starter" activities which help prepare a country's base for expanding services for children. This has required the development of a comprehensive view of children, both in terms of their vulnerability and their potential as individuals and as future participants in social and economic change.

It is essential to recognize that the problems of children cannot be solved in isolation from services that benefit their family and community. The availability of water, food, and health services, for example, interact on the well-being of children, and they are all affected by education and the integration of women in the process of development. The latter, in turn, can improve nutrition, which because of its impact on health care reduces the load on health services.

This program perception requires flexibility and a high awareness of a broad front for action. To encourage this, UNICEF follows a number of guidelines in its cooperation with developing countries relating to a "country approach" to programming, the building of national capacities, advocacy on behalf of children, and the application of a basic services approach.

A "COUNTRY APPROACH" TO PROGRAMMING

In no country can the indirect consequences of economic development alone be relied on for meeting children's needs. Some of these consequences may even be unfavorable unless precautions are taken. Specific services and activities that benefit children are required. Experience has shown that these services are most effective when they are part of a systematic approach toward improving the situation of children within the framework of a national policy for children, which in turn forms part of the country's development effort. So far as UNICEF is concerned, there is no centrally decided standard pattern of cooperation to help further this approach. UNICEF is ready to cooperate with each developing country regarding the priority problems of the country's children about which action is possible.

THE BUILDING OF NATIONAL CAPACITY

The success of a longer-term effort to meet children's continuing needs is now recognized as being critically dependent on improving national capacities of developing countries to be self-reliant in the whole range of child-related services. This includes:

1. Strengthening the organizational capacity of ministries and governmental units and the capacities of their personnel
2. Orientation and training of staff in planning and delivering services
3. The strengthening and greater use of national technical institutions and resources
4. Promoting appropriate simple technology that helps improve the nutrition, health, and well-being of children and their families
5. Increasing the local production of supplies and equipment for services that benefit children
6. Encouraging local production and preservation of nutritious foods
7. Improving local supply logistics and delivery management
8. Strengthening national evaluative activity and procedures
9. Facilitating the exchange of relevant experience between developing countries.

Of key importance is an emphasis on the training of those involved in the delivery of services, ranging from volunteer village-level workers to professional staff involved in planning, directing, and supervising services. Increasing attention is now being directed to the content of the training, including its relevance to local needs, to its imparting of attitudes as well as skills, to the training of community leaders, and to developing managerial skills in middle-level staff.

ADVOCACY ON BEHALF OF CHILDREN

Advances in services to children have not prevented many millions of children from suffering from what has been called in recent years the "quiet emergency." There is considerable need to raise the level of consciousness of children's needs, both at local and national levels and throughout the international community. Such advocacy is intended both to reflect and to strengthen demands for economic and social justice for the impoverished majority of the world's people.

As part of its advocacy role UNICEF attempts to focus attention on the critical needs of children and the opportunities to meet them, and tries to secure a larger priority in national and international development efforts for services that benefit children. This includes the greater deployment of resources for these services, both by the developing countries themselves and by outside aid through the UN system, bilateral aid, and nongovernmental services. In the countries with which it cooperates on programs, UNICEF seeks to promote adequate provision for children in national development plans, or development plans for particular areas or zones within a country.

In addition to emphasizing the importance of policies and programs to benefit the majority of children in a country, it is necessary for advocacy to focus attention on the needs of those who are often especially difficult to "reach" through over-all programs, such as children in underserved rural and urban areas or in certain ethnic or geographic groups. Advocacy should include a concern not only with the physical needs of children but also with their intellectual and emotional needs and their preparation to function in society. Particular attention should be given to the needs of young children because they are the most vulnerable, with a recognition that progress at that stage in a child's life can be undone by neglect at another stage.

THE BASIC SERVICES APPROACH

In partnership with other agencies of the UN system, and on the basis of local experiences in many developing countries, UNICEF is now trying to accelerate the extension of services for children through the basic services approach.

It is clear that in many countries it is not possible by extending the present pattern of services to reach, in the foreseeable future, the very large number of children now poorly or not at all served. In order to bridge this gap, the basic services approach provides for:

1. Simple services at the level of villages and urban communities

These services would be in the fields of maternal and child health, safe water supply, better nutrition, local food production, responsible parenthood, literacy, elementary education, and the advancement of women. It is not essential that all these services be started simultaneously in a given area, but it is important that all be established as soon as possible in order to gain the advantages of their mutually supporting and reinforcing nature.

2. A main emphasis on involvement and active participation of the people of the communities

This emphasis would be maintained especially through the use of responsible volunteers or part-time workers who can be trained for specific duties.

3. The orientation of the relevant national and district governmental structure to direct and support this approach.

This would be accomplished by using, for example, many more paraprofessional workers as part of the support system for the community workers, allowing the professional workers to devote more time to direction, supervision, training, and related activities.

Within the basic services concept, the development of community-based, self-help primary health care systems is currently the focus of much attention. Primary health care involves an extensive use of community workers to carry out front-line curative, preventive, and promotive tasks. Community involvement in planning, supporting, staffing, and managing the community's health services is an essential element. Primary health care workers are selected by the community and trained to diagnose and treat normal ailments by using simplified medical technology. The complex cases are referred to health centers and hospitals. Such an emphasis is in stark contrast to today's reality in developing countries where only about 20 percent of the population have access to health services, and where, moreover, such services are concentrated in urban areas and absorb four fifths of all public sector expenditures on health.

The urban/hospital approach to health care has been largely influenced by the adoption of Western-style health policies in situations where they are not suitable or relevant. The development of primary health care systems, as part of a basic services approach, thus offers a vital opportunity to effect the drastic changes necessary in health policy if even minimal improvements in health services are to reach the vast majority of people at present totally unserviced.

The increasing dissatisfaction now being expressed in even the richest countries about health care systems which concentrate on the needs of urban and high-income groups also points to a significance for primary health care which is in no way restricted to developing countries.

It is hoped that an international conference on primary health care held in Alma Ata, USSR, in September, 1978, jointly sponsored by the World Health Organization and UNICEF, will lead to stronger governmental and international commitments for primary health care.

The policy guidelines which have emerged during the evolution of the basic services strategy for chilren are, of course, applicable to a wide range of developmental activity. Mention must be made, however, of certain pragmatic advantages which often emerge from programs focused specifically on children's needs. These include the value of children's programs as a focus for multisectoral action, the motivational effects of considering children as today's investment in a better tomorrow, and the essentially apolitical "constituency" of children which is often insulated from the political upheavals which can severely affect more sectoral and "adult" developmental activity.

It would be easy to overstate such advantages, and the present situation of children around the world quickly belies them. But as we turn to the future we must acknowledge that, in the struggle to secure scarce resources and in mobilizing popular participation, a mandate for children can be a valuable asset.

A LOOK TO THE FUTURE

The dark shows from our imperfect past can, fortunately, be lightened by our hopes for the future—if not our own future, then our children's. But we live in a world where the future of millions of children threatens to be as dark as the past unless we can mobilize our resources and ourselves to improve their future. Experience cautions against excessive optimism, and it is with due temerity that we suggest three possible areas of activity which may yield pragmatic benefit to the world's children: (1) improvements in our concept of children and of childhood; (2) a review of the role of children's welfare services; and (3) improvements in our commitments to children.

TOWARD A BETTER CONCEPT OF CHILDREN

Childhood as a social issue has only emerged in the last century. Even within the period of recorded human history this is a very brief span of time in which to acquire a sufficient body of knowledge about children—and the literature of childhood bears witness to our ignorance. In recent years, however, childhood has attracted an increasing volume of scholarly attention, the results of which are both invaluable additions to our knowledge and an indication of how much remains to be done.

We must also recognize that there can never be a single, universal conception of the child; this would be a denial of the value we place on human and cultural diversity. Our views of childhood will always be conditioned by the societies in which we live, by religion, by socioeconomical class, and by rural-urban differences. Nevertheless, the emerging historical studies of childhood demonstrate very real value in understanding how different socieites and groups view their children. The purpose of such study is to understand diversity, not to further universality.

Such a view was presented at the ICSW conference in Helsinki in 1968 by Herman Stein, a long-time consultant to UNICEF. Having pointed out that the UN Declaration of the Rights of the Child could not have been promulgated in any other century than this one, he stated that even the conception inherent in the Declaration was still far from universally accepted:

> It [the Declaration] affirms that the child must be viewed as an individual, that the responsibility of the family is superordinate to that of the state, and that the state has responsibility not only for protecting the child physically but for making sure that his imagination and spirit are nurtured. These are not universally held views, nor have they been so in the course of history.[1]

Various studies have suggested differing conceptions of the child—as a miniature adult, as an economic asset, as a future public servant, as a soul to be saved, as an agent of family continuity—and it is not difficult to illustrate such conceptions with examples from our own experience. The contemporary conception of the child, as reflected in the Declaration of the Rights of the Child, is more composite, accepting parts of early conceptions, rejecting others. "The best interests of the child shall be the paramount consideration" and "the child . . . needs love and understanding," says the Dec-

[1] Herman D. Stein, "Conceptions of the Child," in *Social Welfare and Human Rights* (New York: Columbia University Press, 1969), p. 231.

laration, which also makes repeated reference to the paramount responsibility of parents and the need for protection against employment before minimum age. The child is seen as having an identity partly unrelated to the family or state although with obligations to both. The idea of the child as a servant of the state, which dates from ancient Greece, is not entirely dropped in the contemporary view, but has been modified by seeing the child as a potential agent of change, with the state responsible for creative development.

There is keen interest in studies of the relationship between conceptions of the child and national development. The general relationship—that investments in children, social and psychological as well as economic, are extremely important to national development—is increasingly recognized. But there is still a great need for knowledge about the requirements of children beyond those of physical welfare.

Stein concludes:

There is reason to believe that the capacity for innovation, experimentation, the acquisition of new knowledge, and invention, are necessary to development. To develop these capacities requires that children be exposed to an atmophere where their curiosity is stimulated. their right to ask questions insured, where they have ample opportunity to play that gives free expression to imagination as well as to physical skills, and where their health is protected. If these conditions do not exist, economic and social development is retarded.

It is important, however, that we do not exclusively emphasize these grounds of social utility in order to justify greater investment in the child, particularly the young child, and so fall into a variant of the conception of the child as a servant of society. We should pay heed to enhancing the joys and wonders of childhood as objectives in their own right.[2]

Further studies over the coming years can be of the greatest value not only for UNICEF's own work but for an improved universal understanding of the value of children and the state of childhood.

[2] *Ibid.,* p. 236.

REVIEWING THE ROLE OF CHILD WELFARE

Many if not most of the components of today's welfare services for children have their origins in the social movements in the late nineteenth and twentieth centuries when childhood emerged as a social issue, an issue which was related to changing conceptions of the child, and the influence of urbanization and industrialization. During this period many child advocacy movements led to creation of new institutions and professions, which today constitute the fields of child welfare, such as early childhood education, child development, child psychology, pediatrics, public health, and social welfare—all of which are of vital concern to both UNICEF and the ICSW.

At the same time, many of the reform movements concentrated on remedial work for specific disadvantaged groups of children (the handicapped, neglected, impoverished). One of the results of this was to have child welfare generally regarded as a marginal operation for which financial backing by governments need not have a high priority.

This has relevance to our understanding of the modern role of welfare services in all societies, but especially in developing countries. The slow emergence of welfare services as a human right is welcome, but the dangers remain of seeing welfare as a need of the minority rather than the majority of developing countries. Moreover, in the transfer of welfare models and expertise from more developed to developing societies usually insufficient attention was given to different values, priorities, and needs in the "importing" countries. The transfer of models, even with the best will and understanding as, for example, in the health field, can create future problems. The trend now in a number of countries is to ascertain their own most effective approaches. This generally requires some undoing of old concepts and patterns of operation as well as the building of new ones along developmental lines appropriate to national situations and goals. In this process, which UNICEF is trying to encourage, there is a growing interest among developing countries to learn from each other's experience.

We must face the evidence that the "reach" of our services is far from adequate, in part due to the legacy of the past. The development of the basic services concept—with its emphasis on meeting the basic needs of the majority through community participation and the use of relevant and available technology and expertise—is an attempt to develop a better strategy for development and human well-being. The use of a basic services approach in the field of health services is resulting in encouraging developments in primary health care. But we are also conscious of the need to undertake a similar reassessment and review in the field of social welfare services and training.

Such a review is of the greatest importance, given the importance of community participation and involvement in present developmental strategies. In its early years UNICEF was closely involved with much work in the field of community development in which multipurpose governmental workers were sent into communities. Drawing upon the weaknesses as well as the strengths of this experience, the community participation aspect of the basic services approach has taken on some new dimensions: primary health workers, for instance, are not civil servants but are chosen and employed by the community in which they serve; the community itself determines its own priorities for action; the government provides support rather than direction. Nongovernmental organizations which have a long history of active involvement in the promotion of human well-being can work as dynamic agents in the process, providing important links between the community and the government. It is within such contexts as these that a comprehensive review of existing social welfare services and organizations is required.

IMPROVING THE COMMITMENT TO CHILDREN

Having pointed to some of the problematic legacies of the early child advocacy movements it would be less than fair not to point to their strengths, particularly their resolve in affecting the sociopolitical structures of their day to achieve lasting benefits for children. Ruby Takanishi makes this point, which is particularly relevant at this time:

People in the child-helping professions . . . owe the very existence of their roles to the political activists of the late nineteenth and early twentieth centuries. These individuals carried out "scientific investigations" . . . gathering large amounts of data as a basis for lobbying and legislation. Once the programs were funded, they actually brought them to life. Throughout the entire process, they grasped what we have lost—an understanding of the power of political action for the promotion of children's rights.

We are beginning to rediscover our historical roots which could once again move us to integrate our scientific activity with advocacy and social action.[3]

Similarly, over a somewhat shorter time span, covering the last three decades of concerted international development assistance, there is growing acknowledgment that the necessary improvements in the majority of people's lives depend on our will, especially our political will, to apply the necessary material and human resources to the solution of these problems. As a result of the impetus of the International Year of the Child, which will involve a world-wide series of national reappraisals of policies on children, it is hoped that these resources will be substantially increased.

INTERNATIONAL YEAR OF THE CHILD

The main objective of the International Year of the Child (IYC) is to have all countries prepare and commit themselves to long-term measures to improve the situation of their children. In many countries the IYC is being seen as an opportunity to identify and analyze in depth the complex problems which affect so many of their young generation, and to institute concrete action programs. The IYC provides a unique opportunity for advocacy on behalf of children, especially to heighten the awareness of their special needs among decision-makers and the public.

[3] Ruby Takanishi, "Childhood as a Social Issue: Historical Roots of Contemporary Child Advocacy Movements," *Journal of Social Issues*, XXXIV, No. 2 (1978), 21.

The need for national action has been emphasized by a decision not to have a major global conference in connection with the IYC, but to encourage the formation of broadly representative national IYC commissions, or some other central national point, for planning and coordination which will bring together government ministries, national organizations, community groups, and individuals interested in the objectives of the IYC.

In the industrialized countries, it is hoped that, in addition to setting general goals and specific targets for achievement over an appropriate period of time for the children of their own country, IYC national commissions will also generate enhanced awareness of the needs of children in developing countries and increased support for programs to assist those children. As part of its input, UNICEF is helping developing countries to defray the costs for inventories and reviews of existing policies, legislation, and services that affect children; for identifying opportunities to improve services, especially in the context of a basic services approach; for setting priorities and operational objectives and for preparing national programs; and for the mobilization of popular support.

Nongovernmental organizations have been in the forefront of planning for the IYC, and their role in its success is crucial. Many international nongovernmental organizations (NGOs) are in a position to inform, guide, and, to some degree, coordinate the activities of their national affiliates. For organizations specifically dealing with children's needs, the IYC is resulting in the expansion of existing programs, and some new activities. Other NGOs, not directly providing services for children, will be featuring the IYC theme at their meetings and conferences, arranging symposia on children's problems, sponsoring or supporting legislation on children's affairs, and adopting projects for support by their members.

A committee of NGO's has been established and is very active in the preparations for the IYC. Membership is open to any international NGO interested in the welfare of children or any NGO with programs international in character. The committee's aims are to help the exchange of information, to help communication with the IYC secretariat, and to encourage the development of NGOs related to children's needs in both developed and developing countries. Over one hundred organizations are now members of the committee. They represent people from all walks of life, from every geographic region, from different ideological, cultural, and religious persuasions, who are concerned with the wide variety of subjects which touch the lives of children throughout the world. The ICSW is a member of the coordinating group for the committee, and the secretary-general of the ICSW has played a leading role in the organization of the committee and the development of its policies.

On the national level, NGOs, such as the national affiliates of the ICSW, can encourage the estabishment of a national IYC commission and participate in its activities. Because of the expertise and experience it commands, the ICSW national affiliate in many cases can provide cooperation, and in some instances leadership, to the IYC national commission, particularly in the coordination and planning of social welfare activities.

In addition, national NGOs and their affiliates at regional, provincial, and local levels can reach down to the grass roots in eliciting citizen support at the community level for causes that benefit children. In some places they have played an important role in involving local participation and eliciting local resources, as well as in focusing attention on neglected problems. Through innovative projects and experimentation, many of them are in a position to demonstrate what might later be undertaken on a broader scale. This is especially true of the ICSW national affiliates which serve as coordinating bodies of multidisciplinary social agencies and whose member agencies can reach down into the provinces and localities. We are pleased to note that the ICSW has asked each of its national committees as part of its IYC effort to choose a specific aspect of the well-being of the child and to search for new approaches or ways to deal with tht aspect.

The activities of the IYC are not conceived of as an end in themselves. A number of governments, as a result of their own aspirations, but stimulated by the IYC, will undoubtedly wish to set targets in fairly specific terms toward meeting the needs of their children as soon as possible. ICSW national committees could play an important role in this process, and in the education, advocacy, and action required to reach the targets. It is conceivable that national IYC commissions might, in a number of countries, serve as a start for permanent national bodies concerned with children. ICSW national committees could make important contributions toward such a development.

It is, with these goals in mind—goals with which we feel sure René Sand would fully concur—that we invite the cooperation and involvement of the ICSW with UNICEF in work for children in the years ahead.

With increased and imaginative efforts, and with investments well within current capacities, it is possible to see to it that millions of children in the developing world, as well as in the industrialized, have a decent start in life. The quality of the future of children yet unborn represents, after all, the future of the world.

Remarks by the Outgoing Secretary-General

KATE KATZKI

IT WILL not come to you as a surprise that as the retiring secretary-general of the ICSW I have given some thought to the past, present, and, especially, the future of our organization.

Many among you have witnessed the growth of our organization, not only in the number of our committees and member organizations, but also in the scope of our world-wide program. We have gained global recognition as the international nongovernmental agency most directly concerned with social welfare. We have increasingly assumed leadership in our field; we are consulted, respected, and appreciated. One of the main reasons for the solid reputation which we enjoy is the fact that we are a representative group of agencies and individuals functioning as a unified body.

During this, our fiftieth anniversary celebration, all of us are thinking of the ICSW and its past. I want to focus our reflections for some moments, then, on our future.

In recent years, it has become rather popular to try to predict the future. New skills are being developed to enable us to foresee development more and more accurately and to prepare plans and proposals for their realization in the next decade and longer. I do not pretend that I can give a clear picture of what will be the future for the ICSW. However, I shall try to express some of my thoughts and some of my hopes for our council.

The future of the ICSW is closely related to the future of the world, to socioeconomic development, the political situation, and to the attainment of peace. A world where human inequalities are as prevalent as they are today, where populations are threatened by war, where extreme poverty destroys a large number of people, where provisions for health and decent living are nonexistent or insufficient—such a world makes our work all the more essential, even while rendering our goals more difficult to achieve.

There is, indeed, a great deal of uncertainty ahead of us. But we share a strong will to survive; a will to help others to survive. We are an agency that advocates the betterment of the human condition, the improvement of the quality of life, and which wants to assist in enabling those who live in misery to attain a dignified level of well-being.

Will we survive and will that urge which strengthens our will to act also survive? I believe it will. I believe that the ICSW will be the gathering ground for those who care and who are ready to act. The ICSW should be the body that expresses, if I may say so, the social conscience of the world.

Social action is not necessarily positive action. It can be negative, even destructive. We must be sure that our action leads toward the improvement of welfare conditions. We may be well-meaning but ineffective.

We must define basic principles and goals, and be guided by them. Our present resources are, and will be, limited for quite some time. They will restrict our action, our programs. We must carefully weigh what is most important and, accordingly, establish priorities. However, do not let us be too rigid about our priorities. The world changes too rapidly for us to be bound and restricted by a framework which we may have set for ourselves. Our principles, our priorities, our framework should help us to march ahead; they should not be a handicap for our action.

In order to make an effective impact and to be of real value in the field of social welfare, I believe that we must strengthen the ICSW. We must develop a program which is broad enough to be acceptable to our national committees and member agencies. We must, at the same time, recognize that we have among us a great variety of economic, cultural, and political concepts and realities. We must recognize that one concept may not be applicable in all regions. What is a grave problem in one country may be unknown somewhere else. But in all countries it is important to study certain fundamental situations, to get to know why they exist and, wherever possible, to learn whether something has been done about them somewhere else and what was the result. The ICSW could be enormously useful as a clearinghouse for innovative projects. It could make known what has been and is being done in social welfare in various parts of the world. National committees could be of great value in providing information on innovative activities by government and the private sector, by trained persons, and by untrained individuals.

We have close to eighty national committees, many of them very active. We have others that are less active but which may be doing interesting work we know nothing about. We must try to stimulate our members to keep us informed of current activities and plans. So far, we have not done enough in this respect. When we asked for reports, the response has often been sketchy. Perhaps we can find ways to change that.

I believe it is an urgent need that national committees be strengthened where strengthening is required. The ICSW has a role to play in helping a country set up an over-all body which is equipped to guide and advise its member agencies in regard to their programs or to develop an integrated program which is meaningful and useful for the people who should be served by the organizations.

We must help our committees to acquire the knowledge of how to interest the broad population in the social issues of their country, their region, their town or village, and of how to activate them. We must find the means to help with instituting programs in the field of social welfare which are acceptable to them, and we must help in finding the people to carry out the programs without imposing our own values and standards on others.

This work will be the work of many professions. It will involve the welfare workers, and the health people, educators, and many more. It must concern the environmentalists, the legal profession, and the vast field of those who are not trained as "professionals," indeed, who are not trained at all.

People with various backgrounds will have to work together for social development and will have to learn from each other.

Social development is a process which must be shared by all and in which all must participate. Regions will need to recognize what is specific and unique in their geographic area. But I want to express a word of warning: regionalization can lead to isolation, to splintering an organization which will be healthy and strong only so long as it carries on its program undivided and united in spirit and in action.

The ICSW must become the natural meeting ground for people in the helping professions the world over. It should provide the means for exchanging views; the challenge for planning and experimenting on pilot projects and studying the results; the impetus for social change and the inspiration for bettering the human condition everywhere.

I believe wholeheartedly that these goals are realistic for an organization which has already completed a half century of service in the field of social welfare. May the next fifty years lead the ICSW to even greater achievements, toward the elimination of poverty and inequalities, toward better health and welfare, toward a dignified life in peace for all peoples of the world.

Remarks by the Incoming Secretary-General

INGRID GELINEK

I WANT to express my gratitude for the kind and encouraging words of welcome and all the warm wishes for my future activities. I am pleased and thankful, as one always is when one receives an undeserved gift.

I do wish to take this opportunity to express my commitment to find ways and means for international understanding. I believe it is of utmost importance that we accept and appreciate the differences, the variations in the cultures of this world, and that we find meaningful and stable bridges for mutual comprehension, for mutual help, for effective action in the field of social welfare. I will do everything within my power to further the goals and to protect the underlying values of the ICSW.

I feel that my commitment to international organizations and to social welfare concepts allows me to be critical of these institutions. I resent all the numerous critics of international work and social welfare endeavors who do nothing to improve the shortcomings. Because, indeed, we are confronted with weakness. International organizations in general, but particularly in the social welfare field, have become sterile, bureaucratic, self-serving, ivory tower organizations—far removed from the people they are supposed to serve. We all have a tendency to cover this sad fact by talking about brotherhood and our family. Every social worker knows that nowhere are hate, misunderstanding, and contempt so deep and disruptive as in a tightly knit family, removed from reality.

Effective social development agencies have to be supported by a community, financially, morally. But is there really a world community at present which would support international welfare operations wholeheartedly? "World community" is an idealistic concept; the reality, however, is quite different.

So, international welfare organizations are faced with a double challenge: our base of support is weak, and it must be our task to strengthen this base. Secondly, and in spite of the weak base, we have to design need-oriented programs and develop effective actions to contribute to improving the quality of life of all people.

Faced with this grave situation it is sometimes more than frustrating that we all have a tendency to congratulate ourselves on being here, on being active, and only rarely mentioned is the purpose for which we are here, why we are supposed to be such exceptional people. Maybe we should mention more often the problems in our so-called "family," maybe we should try to work out the difficulties among us, maybe we should venture more into the realities surrounding us at any moment, maybe we should, however painful the process may be, review our honesty in communication patterns.

The Canadian report prepared for this conference contains essays on how people see their situation and what they think. It states:

Dialogue among representatives of nation states is not an effective mode for discussions of human well-being. The way in which nation-states are related—mutually exclusive territories—is not the way in which human beings are related. We have a deep interrelatedness in many ways and we may need forms for discussion which reflect that, which simply take that for granted and don't have to negotiate toward it. Maybe Jerusalem can provide such forums. Maybe we should simply be talking together about a "new order."

I feel that Jerusalem did provide such a forum, and we all should be thankful for it. It seems to me that the foundations of the bridges I mentioned earlier have been laid. I wish to invite your constructive criticism, your active participation in our search to build these bridges, to stabilize our base, to act close to the people. I for one will try and I earnestly request your help and support.

Summary and Review of the XIXth International Conference on Social Welfare

DAVID H. F. SCOTT

AUSTRALIA

WE HAVE enjoyed several Israeli musical performances during our conference, so it may be appropriate to describe the role of the rapporteur as similar to that of a music critic. Our performance began with the score provided by R. A. B. Leaper. This was the background paper, built around the regional contributions to the theme of the conference. Our choreographer, Zena Harman, gave us an innovative structure and pattern of movement that would allow everybody to participate. Table and focus leaders have been our conductors, drawing out the shy or timid players and restraining the stronger solo performances.

Section rapporteurs have brought the themes and variations together—and it now remains to see what we make of this unfinished symphony. The rapporteur's task is to identify the way we have responded to the theme—"Human Well-being—Challenges for the 80s"—to comment on the structure, and suggest some of the tunes that we should take home and share with others.

ORGANIZATION

First, let us look at the structure, which was radically different from that of any previous ICSW conference. I have not heard any criticisms of the purpose, which was to increase opportunities for participation, but then everyone is in favor of participation. More important, I think that most people believe the organization has worked well in practice.

There were minor difficulties on the first day which gave us an opportunity for some good-natured grumbling, but generally people fitted into the design easily. Belonging to a table group and then to an identifiable miniconference of 200 people and finally to the whole group of 1,500 has enabled everyone to be involved. Some people have moved around, but not in sufficient numbers to disrupt the organization.

Attendance in discussions has been maintained better than most would have expected.

It has, as always, been difficult for some national groups, particularly those from Latin America and Japan, to participate in discussions. We must continue to work at the improvement and extension of translation facilities.

The suggestions for organizational improvement include: reducing the number of discussion sessions and/or having a break in the middle of the week; larger groups at each table; one or two morning plenary sessions for all participants; and fewer section speakers.

Some people have commented that they approve the design, but they feel it has restricted learning opportunities. If this means that they miss the more expert reports that have been produced by commissions in the past, it might be worth considering having a working party of people with particular expertise to meet together during the week to examine and report on an aspect of the theme, which leads itself to regional or intentional consideration by a think tank of key people. We need help to clarify the increasingly complex changes, problems, and opportunities which we analyze and identify more readily than we find possible solutions.

In this report, and in reading the published proceedings, we must remember that the African region received little consideration and that there are only a few participants from that continent. Approximately 1,200 of the 1,500 participants came from Latin America, North America, Israel, and Europe. As a consequence, most of the issues were discussed from Western viewpoints.

One suggestion was that there should be special sections at future conferences, concentrating on issues of particular relevance to developing countries. People from other countries could, of course, also attend.

We should also remember that we are almost entirely cut off from the theories, problems, and progress of the socialist countries which in some areas surely can provide alternatives in ideology and organization, and critiques that would be helpful to us.

The source material for this report is considerable in its volume, scope, and quality. It began with the ICSW's 50th Anniversary Publication. I am sure that not many of you will have had time to read it, but I urge you to do so, especially the introductory review and discussion of the contents by our president, Lucien Mehl, which is a model of rapporteurage. Other sources include R. A. B. Leaper's background paper, and twenty-four other papers. Then there are the table, focus, and section reports from the sixteen hours of meetings by sixty discussion groups.

As I am the only person who has had access to all this material, no one is in a position to challenge my inclusions or exclusions unless he/she is prepared to read all the resource material—a good example of power over information! I have had to be selective and have tried to avoid repeating too many obvious, agreed-upon propositions in order to focus on new and relevant areas of consensus or disagreement.

I cannot quote reference sources, but please remember that my skimming will be supplemented by the conference report. Nor is it possible to keep to the many divisions and subdivisions of focus and subject matter that we used in our meetings.

PHYSIOLOGICAL AND MATERIAL NEEDS

The need for global responsibility to ensure that food, water, and housing standards are improved and the need for comprehensive and integrated mutual assistance programs were restated, as they have been for years, but there were few suggestions as to how these admirable objectives were to be achieved. Variations in desirable standards in the supply of housing, food, and water, and in the availability of resources, are so great that they defy summary in a brief report, but you will find some of them in the conference proceedings.

In attitudes toward health needs and services, there is an interesting convergence of new approaches in developed and developing countries. Developed countries are confronted with evidence that professionally controlled open-ended health schemes create a self-generating and insatiable demand, particularly, some say, if fee for service is the basis of payment. As the political limits of the provision of funding become apparent, there is a political reaction or even explosion. The victims are the most vulnerable sections of the community.

The developing countries, which at first accepted the Western health systems imposed on them, are discovering that only a minority of the population can benefit from these expensive services and that coverage is largely confined to urban areas at the expense of the more highly populated rural sectors.

UNICEF is convinced that there is now a noticeable shift to acceptance of simple, effective measures which involve the community as a participating constituency rather than a passive, mystified, and demanding clientele. In this, as in several other areas of social development, when the old models become too expensive, the West is beginning to look at the simpler and less costly methods followed in developing countries. Sometimes we even recognize that they have intrinsic values quite apart from their economy. They involve more participatory processes which we all espouse but are slow to implement, especially when we have an interest in more institutionalized services.

From the group discussion it seems that more people are recognizing that simplicity, relevance to local culture, and the use of appropriate, but not necessarily the most advanced, technology are the most effective means for improving the supply and distribution of housing, food, water, health, and education services.

ECONOMIC AND SECURITY NEEDS

With the possible exception of Israel and Japan, unemployment is the dominant issue for the developed world as it has been for many years in the developing countries. It is a complex and emotional issue. Its causes seem various, but one predominates. It is the advent on a large scale of the long-promised, much-worked-for day when machines can replace human labor in the production of goods and services. It is called "structural" unemployment as distinct from frictional and seasonal unemployment.

Our victory over traditional work occurs at a time when we are faced with an increase from 1.6 billion to 2.5 billion in the world's work force in the next twenty years. About 85 percent of the enlarged labor force will be in the Third World.

Chronic unemployment has pervasive effects, not only on the unemployed and their dependents but also on those who are employed. For the former it means low living standards, loss of status and security, and an increased vulnerability to physical and mental illness, crime, delinquency, and dependency.

Those who are in employment in a period of increasing unemployment become aggressively defensive about keeping their jobs and maintaining their incomes. The unemployed are a reproach and a threat. The employed resent having to maintain the unemployed, and even if it is obvious beyond argument that there are no convenient jobs, they will insist that the unemployed are work-shy.

The economic and in some cases social benefits that could derive from some technology are not shared by the community or by the victims of displacement. They are appropriated by the people who make the technological instruments, those who own them, and the skilled and highly paid workers who operate them.

The utopias of the past all assumed that the benefits would be shared. The "fortunate" few for whom there was no work would be entitled to a standard of living generated by a surplus created by the machines and the men and women who worked them. This living standard could, and would, be high enough to permit a useful creative existence for all. The machines and the productive capacity exists, but the sharing ideal has not eventuated.

These manifestations of the problems and the creative possibilities that arise out of unemployment are the fundamental challenge of the 1980s, according to most groups.

The papers and the discussions explored ways of relieving unemployment by job sharing, and thus reduction of the hours, weeks, or years spent at work. Improvement will also call for a new definition of work and less distinction between work for which the money paid has a direct relationship and work done for the community by those who receive their income from public or other private sources. Provision of work rather than increase in production should be the primary aim of policy. Social impact statements on the effects of new advances in technology should be made mandatory as environmental impact statements are now required in many countries before potentially destructive physical development is allowed to take place. The need for more labor-intensive production using appropriate technologies should be considered.

For those who cannot find renumerative work there are many different arrangements. For most of the world's unemployed, there is no social security. They are supported in some way by family or local community. An enormous step was taken recently in West Bengal when a monthly payment of $10 was introduced for people with no other source of income who have been unemployed for five years.

Groups concentrated on unemployment income-security schemes of various types. Their objectives, cost, and management are lively political issues in most developed countries and of interest to developing countries that are hoping for, or are about to introduce, similar provisions. Should they be funded by revenue, be contributory, means-tested, or taxed? The central dilemma that seemed to come out of the discussion was, on the one hand, a desire to have a universal scheme and on the other, a wish to concentrate resources where need was greatest.

The debate as to whether income security and welfare should be provided on a universal or a selective basis is not worked through sufficiently. It is vital that it should be, when funding is under threat and economic growth can no longer be relied on to provide employment and at least some spin-off that will help poorer people.

It seems that universal policies can only work if people are prepared to accept low differentials in incomes and a moderate to high rate of distribution or transfers. If they are not, and they are clearly not prepared to in most developed countries, then the poor suffer. The cost of even indexing, let alone increasing, the real rate of income levels is so high that it becomes politically impossible to maintain. The universal rate is held down, and supplementary benefits schemes are introduced which require the poor to submit to a strict and often humiliating means test to establish eligibility for a meager supplementary benefit.

A means test to exclude some at the top, or a taxation provision that retrieves income-security payments on a progressive basis, is preferable to a universal scheme which cannot maintain adequate levels for all and requires a second supplementary assistance provision.

There is considerable interest in various forms of a guaranteed minimum income which eliminates the categorization of disabilities and could simplify and reduce administrative costs of income security. Some groups warned that subsidized services could be reduced, in the belief that people with guaranteed incomes could meet their needs on the open market, but felt no scheme was likely to be generous enough to make this possible. A trade-off between the guaranteed minimum income and services must be watched carefully. The jobs and income debate is moving into a critical area. Twenty-five years ago Gunnar Myrdal predicted that people in the egalitarian welfare states of the West would become more inward-looking as their material status improved. This seems to be coming true, not only in aiding and trading relations with the developing world, but in attitudes toward the poor and disadvantaged within their own countries. Encouragingly, almost all groups concerned themselves with these dilemmas.

FAMILIES

The implications of the shift from extended families to nuclear which is occurring in most countries is discussed at many conferences. However, a new family unit is emerging, and it demands urgent attention. Large numbers of children now grow up in single-parent families. Most are in Western societies, but as old ties of religion and culture weaken and individualism and personal freedom increase, the single-parent family is likely to become more common in other countries.

The needs of the families with widowed, divorced, separated, or single mothers are increasingly, if reluctantly, being recognized in granting eligibility for income and other welfare services. The reluctance arises from the cost of supporting another large and growing claimant group, and from a belief that recognition and support will encourage the formation of more single-parent households. Just as it has been shown that unemployment pensions or insurance do not generally reduce the incentive to work, it is unlikely that income provisions will encourage single parenthood, although that could happen in poorer societies if social security payments are the alternative to absolute poverty.

One group urged clarification as to whether family policy was directed toward preserving the family or enhancing the feasibility of alternatives.

There was surprisingly little discussion of the role and status of women, probably because the issue is alive everywhere. What seems to be important is to ensure that women have choices open to them and that resources or policies should not be used to force women into one role or another.

One new role for women was noted in discussion on the need to encourage women to go into agricultural employment; it was reported that dairy cows cared for by women produce more milk than if they were looked after by men. It is not known whether this is a result of a gentle touch or feminine empathy.

DISPLACED PERSONS

This term is coming into general use, as one group pointed out, to encompass refugees, migrants, and guest workers. The motivation, the implications, and some specific current refugee situations were discussed. There seemed to be strong support for encouraging migrants to retain their own cultures in contrast to earlier assimilation policies. However, one report expressed the view that if migrants remained within their own cultural groupings they would have less chance of securing jobs and positions of influence in their new homeland.

Ethnic agencies were recognized as important informal support structures and as loci for services. More social workers of different ethnic origins are needed and should be helped to gain access to training.

Hopes that the refugee stream might diminish as national boundaries consolidated and racial tolerance improved have not been realized. Large numbers of people are still obliged to leave their homes, and some of the doors that were previously open to them are closing. Israel, of course, is an exception.

One group recommended that in view of the existence of 18 million refugees, the UN be urged to convene a meeting of voluntary agencies.

It is distasteful to dismiss the immense human suffering caused by the complex problems of displaced people in a few lines. They were not forgotten in discussion. More detailed consideration was given at the XVIIIth ICSW conference in Puerto Rico in the context of equality of opportunity and minority groups.

VOLUNTEERS

There is an increasing interest in volunteers and voluntarism. Voluntarism thrives under adversity and challenge, as the people of Israel well know. It may diminish with prosperity and security, as developed nations have discovered, and requires organized promotion when services become institutionalized and there is an expectation that public funds and public agencies, that is to say "they," will provide for "us."

But a new phase is emerging. Partly due to economic constraints, but also as a result of recognition of the intrinsic value of participation, developed countries are encouraging volunteering and providing training, promotion, and selection initiatives. It is unfortunate that we always have to go through such a tortuous rediscovery of simple propositions.

It is important to find the right mix between public service provisions—nongovernment agencies, professional and clerical staff, and volunteers. Voluntarism can be used to exploit people, save money, and restrict services to areas where voluntary resources are available. It should be encouraged in the context of comprehensive planning for which the community through the government accepts ultimate responsibility.

EDUCATION, CULTURE, VALUES, AND COMMUNICATION

Self-actualization, or becoming what a person has the potential to become, was the subject of one important paper which pointed out that many of the hindrances to meeting the higher basic needs for loving, sharing, and belonging are associated with mass society and that the mass media are among its questionable institutions.

We are also reminded that creativity is a welfare value because of the pleasure it brings.

Happiness, a word that has been dropped from our austere welfare vocabulary, as if it were too much to hope for, received considerable attention in Lucien Mehl's introductory paper. I mention this because it was the keynote address to our only plenary session, and many of us could not appreciate it because of translation difficulties. The paper discusses concepts, ambiguities, conflict, and harmonies which need clarification before moving to the debate of where, when, and how in social welfare.

Many groups emphasized that education should be for tomorrow. Education is now a conservative institution focused too much on the past or the present, which soon becomes out of date. An interesting new trend in education is becoming apparent. There has been some shift in emphasis and funding from university to technical education. Now attention is moving to adult education. This is very important. Adult education provides a medium for communication, participation, and the encouragement of critical faculties for those whose formal education ended years ago, and for the even larger number in the world who have never been to school beyond elementary levels.

One group stated that a man who works must have education for self-expression amd cultural activities. This is true, but how much more important it is for the man who does not work to have access to education for self-realization. The ideas of Ivan D. Illich and Paulo Freire are becoming more widely known, and several innovations in education in Western and developing countries can be read about in the final reports.

Education should be for life and not for jobs, was the view of several groups. The disabled and displaced should be educated within the normal system with special provisions being available rather than segregated.

Social work education should have a stronger policy and advocacy content. There is also a need to attract more men into social welfare since they can work more effectly with men.

RESEARCH

Everyone wants more research, but its purpose must be clear; otherwise research can become an end in itself—a diversion of resources and a distraction from policy development and service delivery.

Criticisms and cautions were expressed about placing too much reliance on research based on outcome of activity in areas where there are many variables, some of which are not measurable in an acceptable way. More emphasis should be placed on inputs to programs and to processes. An immense amount of research and factual data is available. High priority must be given to its diffusion and utilization. Better utilization, particularly by the public and policy-makers, will require simplification of research language.

The increase in the use of consumer and social surveys in many countries creates some resistance to surveys, and possible conflicts between personal privacy and the public interest.

The development and application of social indicators, which almost gained the status of a movement a few years ago, are now regarded more cautiously. Indicators are helpful as a guide, but variables are too great for social indicators to be relied on too precisely.

Critical evaluations of programs should also include some alternative possibilities in terms of efficiency, effectiveness, and equity. One Latin American group emphasized the need for research to assist in understanding the implications of the very considerable demographic changes taking place in that region. There is a need for more research under independent auspices in order to reduce political or professional influences.

POLITICAL ACTION

"Political action" was one of the challenges in the theme of our conference. At the beginning of the week the only people who seemed to raise the issue were public officials.

One suggested that social welfare personnel find counseling particularly congenial and prefer the theory that handicaps arise from individual incapacities rather than acknowledging that structural and societal influences are equally important, or possibly more important, causative influences. This speaker even hinted that social workers might see improved income security, or successful community development that reduces dependency, as a threat to their status and income—or, if you prefer, to their power.

Gradually during the week attention began to focus on the issue of political action. It happened spontaneously because there was no special focus in the program on this as a topic of discussion.

Labor movements once led reforms, but today the interests of the workers not only do not coincide but, increasingly, they conflict with those of people outside the work system because of unemployment, disability, or age. Fewer workers have to pay more taxes to maintain more people who cannot work. In some countries every 100 workers now have to support 30 other people as well as themselves and their families.

Although many groups said that social welfare should become more influential, there was uncertainty or confusion as to the appropriate role. In one instance a strong plea for welfare to exert more influence was qualified by adding that it should not be political. One group emphasized that individual social workers and nongovernment agencies should not be penalized for working with, and being advocates for, disadvantaged groups.

Values, priorities, and processes are the key to the future, and if by default social welfare lets more selfish interests capture the high ground it cannot really be as concerned about people as it professes to be. The opportunity for participation in public debate and action for social change varies enormously, depending on the political system. The reports suggest that we must examine what is appropriate in different situations and develop theory, strategy, and techniques as has been done in safer areas of casework, community organization and development, research, social policy, and other areas of social welfare.

The role and function of nongovernment organizations, particularly in relation to community education, values, and action for change, suggests itself as a theme for the next conference.

INTERNATIONAL

The interest shown in the ICSW and discussion of its potential for promoting human well-being in the 1980s have been among the most encouraging aspects of the conference. Information exchange and research were listed as important functions. The ICSW could also help to influence the direction of relevant research carried out by other international and national organizations. It should help to identify the role of nongovernment agencies.

It was also suggested that the ICSW, given greater resources of money and staff, could be an effective force in asserting the primacy of human values with other international organizations and in supporting and giving legitimacy to the review and advocacy activities of national committees. In its operations the ICSW should demonstrate the values and processes that it wishes others to adopt. Kate Katzki's remarks at the René Sand award ceremony should be taken into account when looking at the future role the ICSW.

Objectives, policies, structure, and the potential of the ICSW should be the subject of special meetings at regional and ICSW conferences to generate support and understanding for an organization which comprises a unique international network of nongovernment agencies.

Multinational corporations and their influence on the life of societies far removed from their centers of power did not escape attention. Nor did recognition of a decline in development aid to developing countries.

JERUSALEM

This view of the conference would not be complete without some reference to the country and to the city in which we have worked together. International conferences are no less immune to the influences of environment and atmosphere than the activities we take part in during our day-to-day lives.

It would be easy to become immersed in the past in Jerusalem, and many of us have been moved and deeply involved in discovering the visible threads that link us to many of our cultural and religious sources. On the other hand, Jerusalem and Israel are nothing if not highly dynamic, and this quality has helped us to keep our feet on the ground and focus our attention on the present and future but with a regard for the past. It has been a good place to meet together.

There cannot be any conclusions, only a comment on the thrust of the conference discussions.

People seem to feel that in the West and in the Third World, the newly acknowledged Fourth World, and perhaps also in the Second World, an era is drawing to a close.

The West is realizing that limitless expectations can no longer be sustained by economic growth or well-being built on existing values and structures. There is, in the West, no scarcity of resources to meet modest but adequate living standards, but the political limits of redistribution of opportunities and resources seem to have been reached. On the other hand, it would be foolish and hypocritical to deny the benefits that have been achieved in the past fifty years and to pretend that we do not enjoy them.

An urgent reappraisal is needed, particularly of the impact of technology on society. Human well-being in the 1980s and beyond will depend on this. There are hopeful signs of adjustment. More people are prepared to say "enough is enough." Others are experimenting with simpler alternative social arrangements. Against this, the locus of power and influence becomes increasingly difficult to locate in highly complex industrialized societies.

In the developing world, there is a more critical attitude toward the values of the industrialized world, but there is still a momentum to catch up economically. There too the locus of power and influence is difficult to identify and is often beyond national boundaries.

Strategies such as community development, structures such as kibbutzim and cooperatives, basic education, appropriate technology, the surviving extended family system, and local-level forms of organization suggest that the developed countries can, with profit, look to the Third World for models which are derived from more natural and simpler responses to basic human needs. The problem, as one speaker said, is that we have interrupted too many of the natural rhythms of individual and community life, replaced them with expensive costly structures, and established a want-creating society.

There seems to be considerable verbal agreement about these propositions but not much evidence in practice of personal or organizational commitment to change. Commitment and greater knowledge of the processes required to change some things and preserve others is the real challenge for social welfare for the 1980s.

Appendix

International Council on Social Welfare

EXECUTIVE COMMITTEE

Chujiro Kimura, *Japan*
Carlos Mancini, *Brazil*
Rudolf Pense, *Federal Republic of Germany*

Eugen Pusić, *Yugoslavia*
Charles I. Schottland, *United States*

ISRAEL ORGANIZING COMMITTEE

Patrons

Ministry of Labor and Social Affairs
Ministry of Health
Ministry of Education and Culture
Ministry of the Interior and Police
Ministry for Foreign Affairs
Ministry of Finance

Ministry of Construction and Housing
Ministry of Industry, Commerce and Tourism
Ministers Committee for Social Affairs
The National Insurance Institute

Local Organizing Committee

Moshe A. Kurtz, *Chairman*
Esther Aricha, Israel National Committee
Shimon Bergman, Israel National Committee
I. Brick, Ministry of Labor and Social Affairs
M. De Shalit, Treasurer
Zena Harman, International Program Chairman

J. Kadman, Association of Social Workers
Joe Neipris, Board of Social Work Education
Harold Trobe, American Joint Distribution Committee, Inc.
Arnulf Pins (*deceased 1978*)

Subcommittees

Israeli Workshop (Arad): I. Brick; Dani Gal
Host Committee: Chana Daskad, Chairman, Jerusalem

Local Committee of Voluntary Organizations
Agency Visits: Abraham Levin; Chaya Daskal

PROGRAM COMMITTEE

Chairman: Zena Harman, *Israel*
Ex Officio: Lucien Mehl, ICSW President, *France*
Reuben C. Baetz, Immediate Past President, *Canada*

Members

Jules Ahouzi, *Ivory Coast*
Geneviève d'Autheville, *France*
M.-C. Azizet Fall Ndiaye, *Gabon*
Annika Baude, *Sweden*
Martha Bulengo, *Tanzania*
Edna Chamberlain, *Australia*
Bernard J. Coughlin, *United States*
Felicidad R. Catala, *Puerto Rico*
Anna Maria Cavallone, *Italy*
Valy Lenoir-Degoumois, *Switzerland*
Rosalinde O. Forde, *Sierra Leone*
Sybil Francis, *Jamaica*
Ingrid Gelinek, *International Social Service*
Ralph Goldman, International Council on Jewish Social and Welfare Services
K. E. de Graft-Johnson, *Ghana*
Y. F. Hui, *Hong Kong*
Carlos Campos Jimenez, *Costa Rica*
Moshe A. Kurtz, *Israel*
Dorothy Lally, *United States*
Robert A. B. Leaper, C.B.E., *United Kingdom*
R. Bwembya Lukutati, *Zambia*
Pran N. Luthra, *India*
Salvador Martinez Manzanos, *Mexico*
Kokab Moarefi, *Iran*
Yuichi Nakamura, *Japan*

Maritza Navarro, *Panama*
J. K. Owens, *United Kingdom*
Rudolf Pense, *Federal Republic of Germany*
Norbert Prefontaine, *Canada*
Eugen Pusić, *Yugoslavia*
Mukunda Rao, *United Nations*
Sayom Ratnawichit, *Thailand*
David Scott, *Australia*
Teresita Silva, *International Federation of Social Workers*
Richard B. Splane, *Canada*
Herman Stein, *International Association of Schools of Social Work*
John Turner, *United States*
Jimmy Verjee, *Kenya*
Nicholas Zay, *Canada*

Kate Katzki, *Secretary-General*
Maria Augusta Albano, *Assistant Secretary-General, Latin America and Caribbean*
Sharad D. Gokhale, *Assistant Secretary-General, Asia and Western Pacific*
Dorcas Luseno, *Assistant Secretary-General, Africa*
Marie-Cécile Larcher, *Regional Administrative Director, Europe, the Middle East, and the Mediterranean*

SECTION CHAIRMEN AND RAPPORTEURS

Over-all Conference Rapporteur: David Scott, *Australia*
SECTION A *Chairman:* Charles I. Schottland, *United States*
    Rapporteur: Ian Yates, *Australia*
SECTION B *Chairman:* Y. F. Hui, *Hong Kong*
    Rapporteur: Shimon Spiro, *Israel*
SECTION C *Chairman:* Jim Murray, *Ireland*
    Rapporteur: Maritza Navarro, *Panama*
SECTION D *Chairman:* K. E. de Graft-Johnson, *Ghana*
    Rapporteur: Werner Boehm, *United States*

INTERNATIONAL STAFF

Secretary-General: Kate Katzki, United States
Region of Africa: Dorcas Luseno, Assistant Secretary-General, Kenya
Region of Asia and the Western Pacific: Sharad D. Gokhale, Assistant Secretary-General, India
Region of Latin America and the Caribbean: Maria Augusta Albano, Assistant Secretary-General, Brazil
Region of North America: Kate Katzki, United States
Region of Europe, the Middle East, and the Mediterranean: Marie-Cecile Larcher, Administrative Director, France
Representative at the United Nations, New York: Alden E. Bevier
Geneva Representative, ICSW: Antonia Kuenstler
Representative at the Food and Agriculture Organization, Emma Fasolo